Roberto Herr

THE VOYAGES OF THE Penelope

The three lives of a legendary wooden vessel in the South Atlantic and Tierra del Fuego

Translated from the Spanish by John A. T. Fowler

SÜD POL

Herrscher, Roberto
The Voyages of the Penelope : The three lives of a legendary wooden vessel in the South Atlantic and Tierra del Fuego. - 1a ed. - Ushuaia : Südpol, 2010.

320 p. ; 23x15 cm.

ISBN 978-987-24524-7-6

1. Relatos de Viajes. I. Título
CDD 910.4

First published in Spanish language by Tusquets Editores Argentina, 2007

(9410) Ushuaia, Tierra del Fuego, República Argentina
info@sudpol.com | www.sudpol.com

Diseño de tapa e interior: Magali Canale
maga@picaypunto.com.ar

Impreso en Argentina - Printed in Argentina

Primera edición: noviembre de 2010

ISBN: 978-987-24524-7-6

THE VOYAGES OF THE Penelope

For my wife Ifigenia
and my son José Pablo

*

For my mother Sonia,
my father Enrique
and my sister Carola

*

The author and the translator
would like to dedicate this English
language version of the book
to the memory of the
late Jane Cameron

INDEX

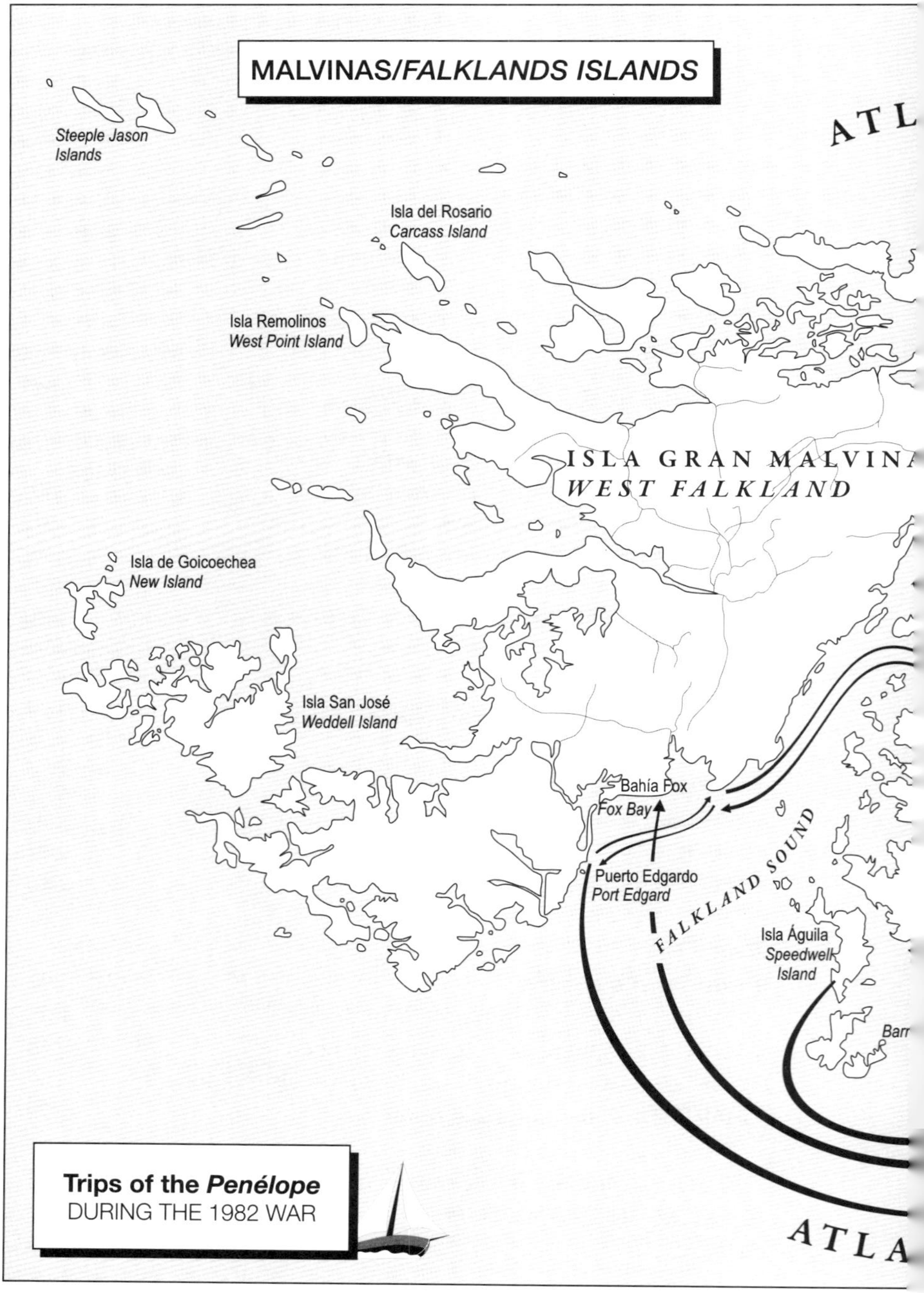
MALVINAS/FALKLANDS ISLANDS
Steeple Jason Islands
Isla del Rosario
Carcass Island
Isla Remolinos
West Point Island
ISLA GRAN MALVINA
WEST FALKLAND
Isla de Goicoechea
New Island
Isla San José
Weddell Island
Bahía Fox
Fox Bay
Puerto Edgardo
Port Edgard
FALKLAND SOUND
Isla Águila
Speedwell Island
Trips of the Penélope
DURING THE 1982 WAR

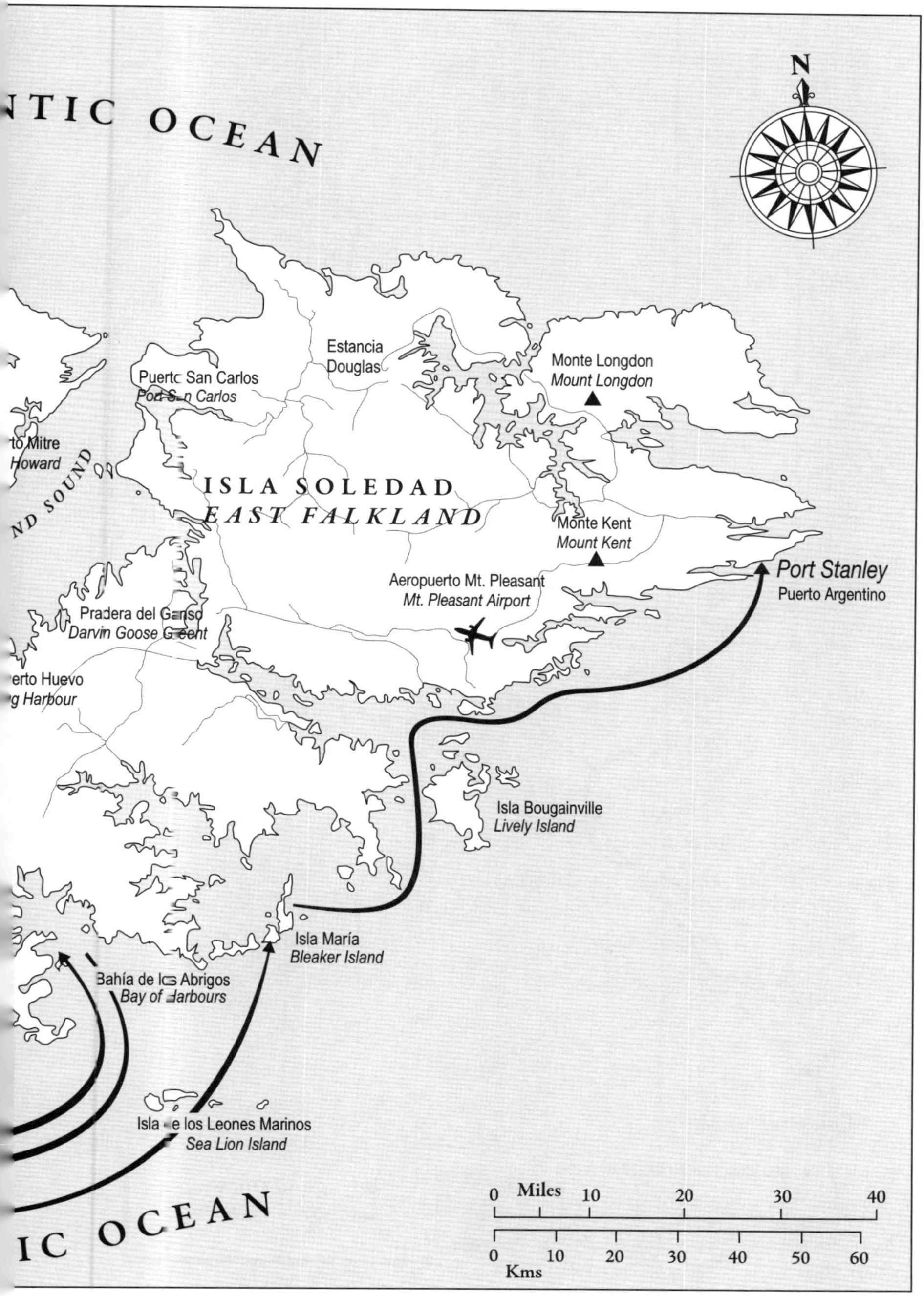

N
NTIC OCEAN
ND SOUND
Puerto San Carlos
Port San Carlos
Estancia
Douglas
Monte Longdon
Mount Longdon
to Mitre
Howard
ISLA SOLEDAD
EAST FALKLAND
Monte Kent
Mount Kent
Aeropuerto Mt. Pleasant
Mt. Pleasant Airport
Port Stanley
Puerto Argentino
Pradera del Ganso
Darvin Goose Green
erto Huevo
g Harbour
Isla Bougainville
Lively Island
Isla María
Bleaker Island
Bahía de los Abrigos
Bay of Harbours
Isla de los Leones Marinos
Sea Lion Island
IC OCEAN
0 Miles 10 20 30 40
0 10 20 30 40 50 60
Kms

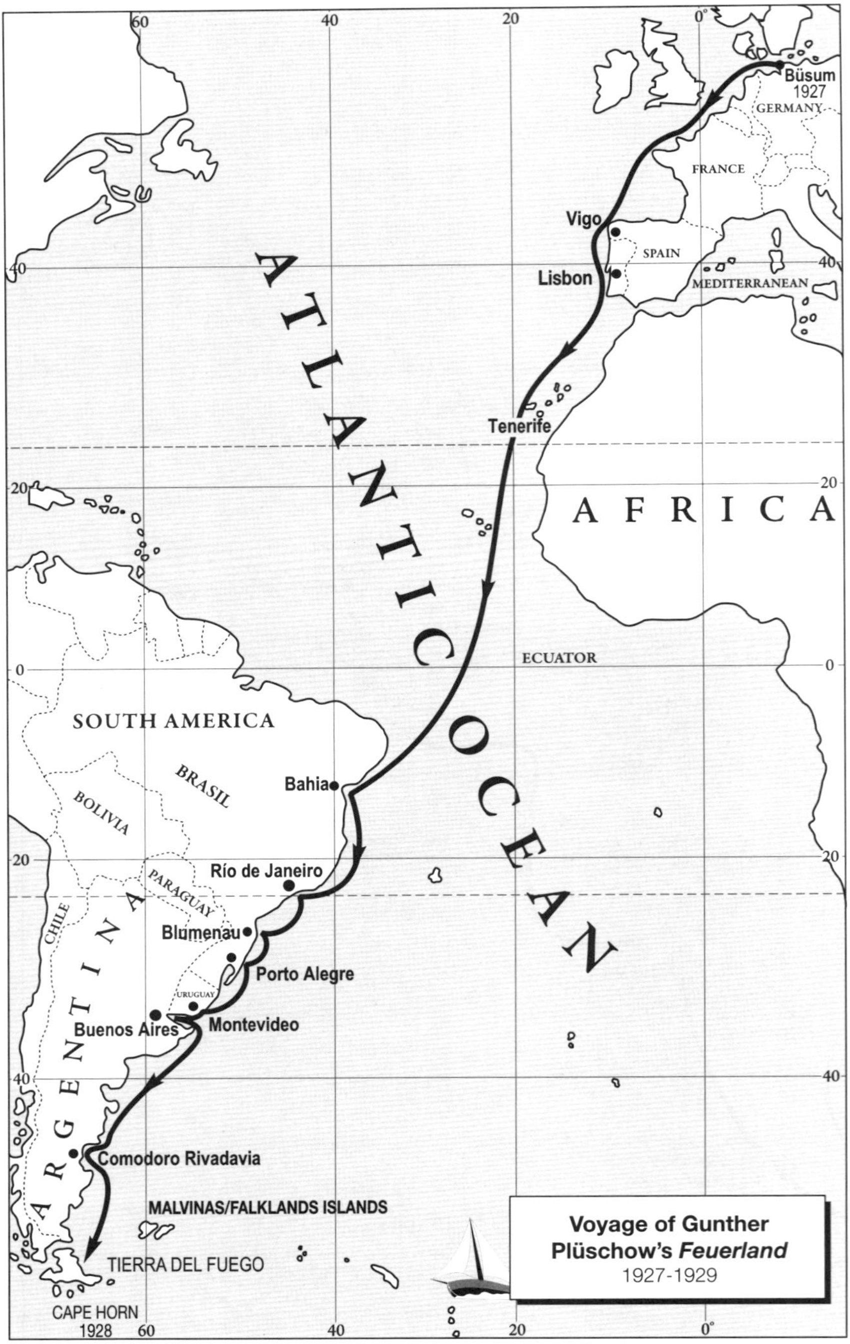

Büsum
1927
GERMANY
FRANCE
Vigo
SPAIN
Lisbon
MEDITERRANEAN
ATLANTIC OCEAN
Tenerife
AFRICA
ECUATOR
SOUTH AMERICA
BRASIL
BOLIVIA
Bahia
Río de Janeiro
PARAGUAY
CHILE
ARGENTINA
Blumenau
Porto Alegre
URUGUAY
Buenos Aires
Montevideo
Comodoro Rivadavia
MALVINAS/FALKLANDS ISLANDS
TIERRA DEL FUEGO
CAPE HORN
1928
60
40
20
0°
Voyage of Gunther
Plüschow's *Feuerland*
1927-1929

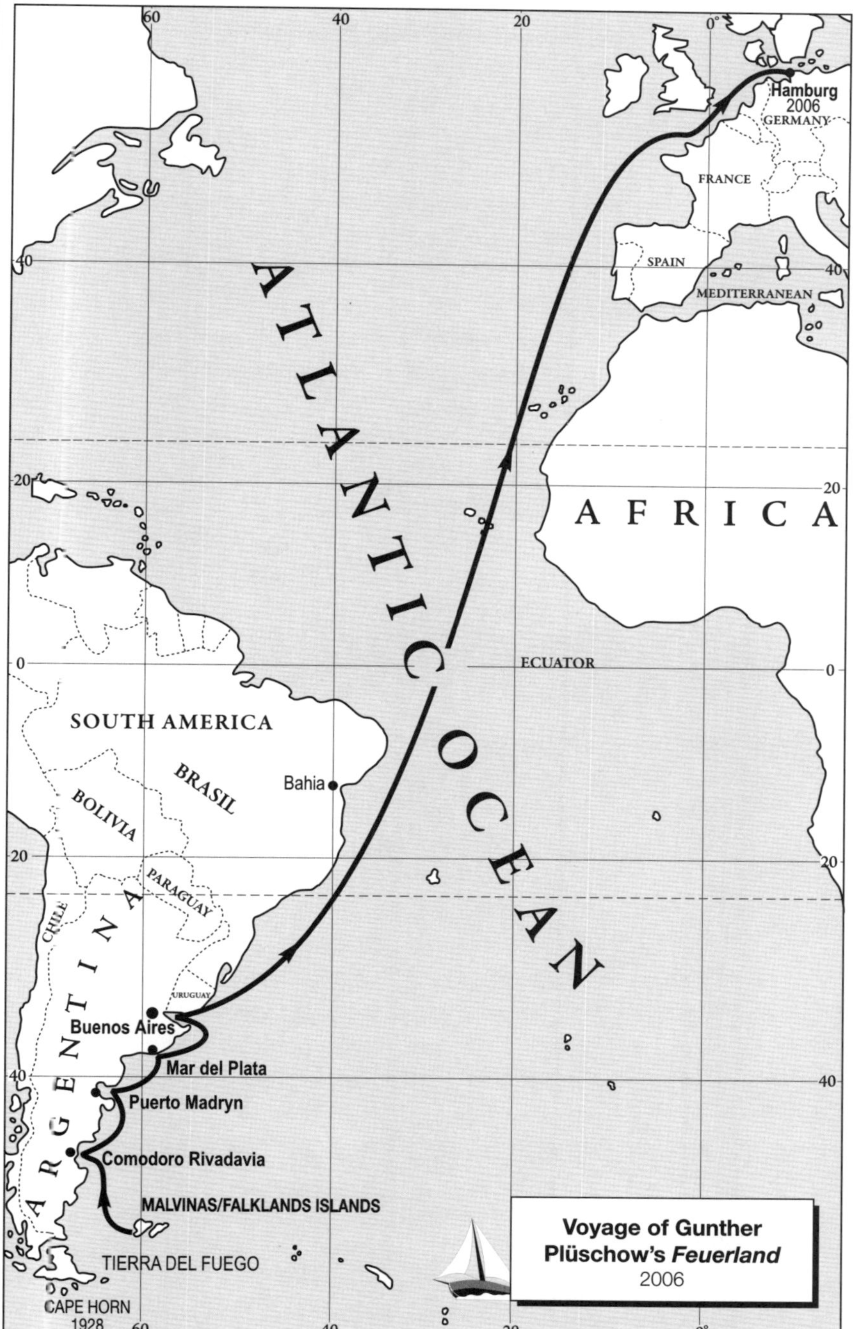

60
40
20
0°
Hamburg
2006
GERMANY
FRANCE
SPAIN
MEDITERRANEAN
40
ATLANTIC OCEAN
20
AFRICA
ECUATOR
0
SOUTH AMERICA
BRASIL
BOLIVIA
Bahia
PARAGUAY
CHILE
ARGENTINA
URUGUAY
Buenos Aires
Mar del Plata
Puerto Madryn
Comodoro Rivadavia
MALVINAS/FALKLANDS ISLANDS
TIERRA DEL FUEGO
CAPE HORN
1928
Voyage of Gunther
Plüschow's *Feuerland*
2006

INTRODUCTION

From sea level

My 'schooner' is here at last.

It's the first of July, 2006. I am in Barcelona, where I have just received the email that I have been expecting for so long. The *Penélope* is coming home to Germany and I am going to see her again and perhaps begin to find an ending to the many stories that shroud this little old boat like fog. It's not very big, but capable all the same of arousing the passions and dreams of a handful of fanatics and survivors.

One of the fanatics is Bernd Buchner; he is the one who has just sent me the email. Bernd is a German sailor, who looks like a history professor from a distance, but up close resembles a young version of an old sea dog. Some months ago Bernd bought the aged ketch *Penélope* in the Falklands/Malvinas Islands and gave her back her original name: *Feuerland* (Tierra del Fuego in German). In his email Bernd informed me that the little vessel would arrive in Hamburg on July 8th, after a 22 day crossing from Buenos Aires, dismasted and swallowed up between containers in the hold of an enormous German cargo ship: *Monte Cervantes.*

He also told me that four days later he was going to give a press conference for the German media. For them the return of this 16m long vessel is news. In 1927 the legendary German explorer, Gunther Plüschow, First World War hero and pioneer of Patagonian aviation had ordered the construction of the *Feuerland* in the little port of Büsum, just an hour away from Hamburg. Now Bernd was bringing it back home, almost eighty years after its departure. Fans of both Plüschow and of the German nautical tradition would come to receive her. On the day of her arrival, one Hamburg newspaper carried the headline 'A LEGEND RETURNS.'

When I began this search I had hardly heard of Plüschow and in fact the story of his relationship with the ketch *Penélope* is a relatively short one. Obsessed with the possibility of travelling through virgin territory in Patagonia, the explorer ordered the vessel built, took it to the uttermost part of the earth and barely a year and a half later, sold it to a wool merchant, who changed the name to that of his daughter, Penélope, and took it to the Islands in 1929. The story of Plüschow, which ended tragically in 1931, when he crashed his seaplane *Silberkondor* into Lake Argentino, has been the subject of books and films and continues to inspire admiration. Meanwhile the vessel that he constructed for his adventures sailed round the Islands as *Penelope* (without the acute accent), for 78 years until April this year, when Buchner found her, bought her, renamed her and then took her from the Islands to start to live his own dream.

When I arrived in Hamburg I observed the *Feuerland* fanatics from a distance with some apprehension. Neither did I know any of those who for 78 years had worked the vessel with the name, *Auxiliary Ketch Penelope*. I belong to a third group; I am a survivor of the *Penélope*, from those few but intense days between May and June 1982, when the vessel was the oldest, smallest and strangest component of the Argentine Navy in the South Atlantic War. I belonged to the crew of the Argentine Republic Navy's *(ARA) Penélope*.

Because of this, the moment I received Buchner's email I immediately bought a ticket to Hamburg and now, on this Tuesday July 11th, I'm flying there. I am totally unable to get out of my head the thought that I am going to see the 'schooner' again, from which 24 years ago I strained my eyes looking for survivors of a shipwreck, where I climbed up ropes onto a drifting and battered cargo ship, where I shared fears and dreams with other young men of my generation, where I nearly died and where my life changed.

Now I am in Hamburg already. In Stendamm, the street where my hotel is, heavily made up yet disdainful whores, sellers of stolen junk in their eternal Sunday suits and ruddy cheeked tourists, pass each other by in silence.

These are my surroundings as I emerge from the Metro: half the businesses are sex shops and the other half gaudy 'everything one euro' stores, where three-coloured shoes jostle with fake watches, Taiwanese china and a load of relics from the recent football world cup. In these shop windows for the first time I see the German flags: big, small, and in miniature, which will accompany me the whole trip. German flags hang from balconies, cars carry two or three little flags and half the passers by cover their heads with handkerchiefs or caps of black, red and gold. The other half cover their un-sportsmanlike bellies with tee shirts of the national football team. "It's the return of unashamed patriotism" Bernd Buchner will tell me next day.

This is the day of the press conference and I am in search of my past. From the station in Hamburg's old snobby district of Altona, I walk towards the wide River Elbe, the tongue which opens from the North Sea and leads to Germany's main port. Everything is so calm and bourgeois that it seems as if violence, hunger and injustice in the world might have ceased to exist. Crossing a park I come to the door of Altona's town hall, a precious little white palace of tall windows and powerful columns. The statue of a general on horseback, with plumed helmet, medals and sword held aloft, rears up in front of the door.

I cross the street towards the floral park where the children run and am met by another sculpture, which seems out of key in these surroundings. As if confronting the conventional statue of the warrior, there is an abstract and unsettling black-painted rectangular block. It is the monument created by a North American sculptor to Altona's Jews: the absent and disappeared ones. I don't know if it was intentional, but from his elevated position on his horse, the 19th Century general is now obliged for ever to rest his petrified gaze on the black block.

It's a warm summer morning and the citizens of Hamburg are jogging, cycling or walking their fat and panting dogs along the narrow dirt track, which runs along the Elbe. Passenger boats go up and down the river with tourists. I walk in the shade of the trees, just one more tourist with cap and knapsack. I carry a good digital camera, a recorder with a 77 hour capacity, a black notebook and three pens. Above all I am bursting with questions. The simplest have to do with the boat, with Gunther Plüschow and with Bernd Buchner's crossing; these are the kind of questions that I have been asking for the last twenty years since I became a journalist.

The most difficult questions have to do with why I am here, almost on the frontier between Denmark and Germany, in this well-maintained and peaceful garden of people and in the port where seventy years ago the German Jewish boy in short pants, who was my father, took ship for Buenos Aires, fleeing from the Nazis.

What am I searching for? It's not my family's roots nor anything to do with the Jews and the long history of persecution and war, which carries on in today's newspapers and seems to have no end in sight. This morning, when I switched on CNN in my hotel room, the Israeli air attacks on neighbourhoods of hovels in Lebanon appeared along with Hezbolah bombs falling on the residential suburbs of Israel. But, as horrible as it may sound, this dreadful war of today is not my war. I am walking through these streets, which are so peaceful that they appear dead, in order to meet up with an old sailing boat in which I spent the most intense days and nights of my war, in the Islands.

As a nineteen-year old conscript I was the only civilian of the seven-man crew of the *Penélope*. For one month, the Argentine Navy requisitioned the *Penélope* from its owner the Falkland Islands Company and from its captain, the old sea dog Finlay Ferguson. During these four weeks I lived through the greatest dangers and most vivid emotions of my life up till that point. The last time I saw the 'schooner' it was painted black and moving gently in the waters of Stanley harbour, bumping lightly against the old tyres hanging between it and the jetty.

It was June 20th, 1982, one week after the surrender and I was embarking on the transport vessel *Norland*, bound for Puerto Madryn. While I was in the line of prisoners, the British soldiers took my sacred relic from me: this was the piece of shrapnel, the size of an aubergine and weighing about a kilo, which had exploded a metre away from my head one infernal night on the *Penélope*. There she was now, bobbing up and down thoughtfully. This was my last picture of the Islands before entering the belly of the *Norland* and beginning the first three days of the journey home. And I say the first three days, because sometimes – less each time, but always unexpectedly – I am still attacked by the feeling that I never returned; that a part of me remains there, in the war, in the peat, in the wind, in the Islands and on the rough wooden planks of the *Penélope's* deck.

The ten minutes walk from Altona station seems to have become an eternity. I feel as though I left the statue of the general gazing at the black block about half an hour ago. I pass by house after house of prosperous tranquillity and manicured lawns and leave behind parks where kids throw frizbees and birds hop about the grass. I arrive sweating at the Ovelgönne jetty, where the only sound is the placid clacking together of a handful of old wooden sailing boats.

On the jetty, which is a floating pontoon where passenger boats moor, I spot a group of journalists with notebooks in hand, camera men, a few old guys in suits and ties and three people in blue tee-shirts saying 'Feuerland.' I ask for Buchner and they direct me to Carola Fiedler, his girlfriend and partner, who is at the head of the jetty absorbed in a telephone conversation. When she finishes talking I introduce myself and ask for Bernd. "He's there" she says, pointing to the middle of the river. I grab the hand rail, look carefully and I see it. Hardly visible in front of a great shed where they construct the biggest plane in the world from parts assembled throughout the whole of Europe, and manoeuvring between a passenger ferry and a tug, a little white dot is advancing, which bit by bit appears to be getting nearer, getting bigger, and getting mixed up with my memories, my dreams and with my worst nightmares. It is the *Penélope*.

Clumsily, like a photographic novice, I get the camera out of its case, hang it round my neck and begin to shoot. During the interminable time that it takes the sail boat without sails or masts to enter the inlet I hardly look. I am witnessing a unique moment. All around me German photographers and cameramen are also pointing and shooting, but they are seeing another boat, another story, another totally different homecoming.

When the vessel is finally moored, Buchner emerges from the small square wheelhouse where I stood watch so many times in Fox Bay and in the little islands to the south of the main East Island. I go closer to photograph details and to capture the moment as the captain prepares to answer the journalists' questions, when suddenly I realise that I am alongside the boat.

Stretching out an arm I can touch the rough surface of the gunwale, now stripped of black, red and green, bruised and wounded. I let the camera drop and stroke my 'schooner' with my fingertips.

Nobody looks at me, and around me a small army of strangers carry on with a dozen conversations in a language which I don't understand. They all seem far away, very far from the private and silent country where I try to connect with the ship of my memories.

Buchner shakes me out of my private world when he invites me to join the journalists' tour. I climb on deck to take part, as I have done so often, in a press conference with bored reporters, who an hour ago were interviewing a local politician and in the afternoon will be writing about the port's latest crime. My eyes flit from the bridge to the little staircase leading to the hold and from the rusty anchor to the long masts which lie on the deck. Do I remember these shapes and these colours or do I just want to believe that I remember them? Which of these details were in the dozens of photos that those who visited the boat in Buenos Aires two months ago sent me? Which in my deepest memories? Which in the distorted dreams of all these years? Am I reliving my frequently recurring dream of the first time that I felt the first sweet bobbling of the sea from *Penélope's* deck, or am I living it now?

Without looking for it, I find the answer comes from the most amusing person attending this reception party, who also has least to do with this entire story. Among so many fans of the *Feuerland*, admirers of Plüschow and accredited journalists, Christian Bauer is something of an oddity. Happy in his white Bermudas, sandals and straw hat, he decided to come to the presentation only when he read in the newspaper that the adventurer's mythical boat would be returning.

Like many lovers of the sea and discoveries in virgin lands, Christian had read Plüschow's books in adolescence and last

BERND BUCHNER and I posing on board the *Feuerland*, a few minutes after its arrival in Ovelgönne.

summer had been with his mother to Ushuaia where he had once again come across the tale of his epic exploits in the local museum. Accordingly he had got on his bicycle and pedalled the fifteen minutes, which separated him from Ovelgönne. When, in English, I give a brief account of my story to the press conference, Christian Bauer raises his head from his corner and, with a smile, wishes me "welcome" in good Spanish.

The conference takes place in a round wooden building in the middle of the jetty and lasts almost an hour. After taking us over the deck and the interior of the ketch, Buchner tells us some of the details of the voyage and the journalists ask him a lot of questions about what he intends to do now with the *Feuerland.* His plans are to repair her in Büsum, try to bring her back to how she was in Plüschow's time, and sail her. He also hopes to finish the book and the documentary about his adventure. The director of Ovelgönne's shipping museum says a few appropriate words before the guests break ranks to empty the trays of snacks and chat animatedly.

Outside, the *Penélope* is cooking in the summer sunshine and Christian Bauer has acquired a skiff to get him out to his own boat: an elegant shiny and black historic yacht by the name of *Rabe* (Raven in German). With the same friendly, sincere smile of earlier he invites me to get in. Seated in the boat we begin to go alongside *Penélope* and there, yes, approaching at water level and from down below, I am attacked for the first time by the true memory, the one I had been searching for and fearing at the same time: the memory of the fear, the intensity and the wildness of life in those days.

It is only for a second, but the scene which passes before my eyes leaves me paralysed. It was the night of the bombardment, May 26th, 1982. The ratings and I were taking turns with the night watches, which went from ten at night to first light at three in the morning and from then to broad daylight. Eduardo Rivero and I were on the first watch with the little boat some two hundred metres from the shore at Fox Bay. Rivero had gone to the toilet and I was the only one on watch. All of *Penélope* was mine: the sea and the night as well. These minutes before the attack were the calmest and most silent of the whole war. Only the constant wind could be heard, but this did not help; any fish poking up its head, any bird, any flash of light put all my nerves on edge. An attack was never going to come and yet it could come at any moment. And the cold and windy loneliness inclined me to thoughts about death, which took on more and more macabre forms as the night progressed.

I only remember that it was sudden, like a whiplash from the sky. Suddenly all the glass in the little windows of the bridge broke all around me. I was already outside on the deck, thrown onto my stomach between the drums of fuel that we carried there. The bombs were deafening, the shrapnel shrieking in fury, damaging the wood and perforating fuel drums. My companions emerged half-dressed and in flight. Soon we were throwing ourselves helter-skelter into the dinghy to pull to the shore. Bombs kept falling and one of the many forms of death imagined during these nights approached at the gallop. We hurled ourselves into the boat, shivering and stunned and I looked back at the *Penélope*, which was getting smaller and smaller.

I am sure that that image of the crusty red paintwork of the ketch's side, as seen from the dinghy, had not come to visit me in all these years. It returns to me precisely now, under the sun and

CHRISTIAN BAUER approaching the vessel with his wooden skiff. That is the moment I saw the same image of the night of the bombs, the night we almost died: May 26, 1982.

seagulls of Ovelgönne, from a rowing boat which swirls beneath 'my schooner' while Christian rows cheerfully in his straw hat, the newspaper photographers take my photo and the crowd disperses in cheerful knots of conversation. I use my camera to hide my tears, which are mixed with anguish and relief. I am at last alone, completely alone with my ship.

And with my fear.

And with my war.

FIRST PART

The crew of the ARA *Penélope*

CHAPTER 1

Ourselves again

To return is also, perhaps, to reduce our memories to powder and then to bury them at last.

Meeting the vessel again, in July of 2006, allowed me to reach inside myself and to strengthen and develop the memories of the war that had accompanied me for so many years. But now two months have passed and this Sunday, September 3rd, I am about to put my story on the table, to discuss it, to share it and perhaps to lose it. I am on my way to the barbecue where the seven members of the *Penélope's* crew are going to get together for the first time since the war.

For many years the war in the Islands was mine, my war. Like a diabolical toy, I stored in my trunk my memories of fear and cold and hatred and death flying straight at my chest from the nose cone of a Sea Harrier. The others had no place in my memories, and the military even less.

Over the years that passed since my return from the Islands, I went about selecting certain memories of the war which fitted with my way of seeing the world and how I present myself today. Although I didn't realise it, of course, with every story I repeated or discarded, I was making decisions. We all go around keeping the stories that confirm what we already think and letting those that don't fit fall into oblivion. Insofar as I was going around feeding my certainties with reading and argument and portraying myself as a leftist humanist, against all human rights violations and against the participation of the military and the militarisation of the politics of my country, I was sticking with the stories that subscribed to these theories. Who was going to take away my right to impose my own morality on the history of my war?

But I had not lived the worst moments of the war – those on the *Penélope* – alone. On the boat I was part of a group of men: an officer and a handful of naval NCOs, from whom I learned some vital things and whom I remember with affection and gratitude. They are Horacio González Llanos, Oscar Luna, Guillermo Ni Coló, Daniel Peralta, Carlos Contreras and Eduardo Rivero. I am heading for a barbecue with these men and their families.

I am at the point of meeting my old comrades, but when I share their memories, will my image of who I am be shattered into a thousand pieces? In this respect it is a good sign that González Llanos should have suggested meeting us in Puente Saavedra. Puente Saavedra is where the Navy's bus dropped me that had brought me from Ezeiza, which is where the plane left me that brought me from Chubut, which is where the British ferry left me that brought me as a prisoner from the Islands. Puente Saavedra is where I began to construct my post war life.

Sunday morning is gloomy with a leaden sky. Hordes of people rush about frantically, businesses overflow with cheap clothes, walls are on the point of collapse or demolition, some only held together by protest graffiti, painted on the cement or directly on the bricks. The buses which spew smoke through the four lanes of General Paz avenue, are heading for the Pan American Highway, to Liniers and to the whole east of Buenos Aires while more buses smoke underneath General Paz, entering and leaving the Federal Capital.

I approach Puente Saavedra with a rucksack that I carry with great care; it holds a dark cake full of dried and candied fruits. I brought it from the Islands a week ago and I want to share it with my comrades from the *Penélope.*

Celia Stewart, the lady who rented me a room in Stanley, an industrious widow, who spends day and night in her kitchen making sausage rolls, biscuits, cookies and cakes to sell, gave me one such typical cake of the Islands to try and it occurred to me to bring one, so that, after 24 years of remembering the war on our own we could all eat it together at our reunion.

The invitation came from Guillermo Ni Coló, who began work as a clerk in the National Congress when he came out of the Navy in 1983, then finished his secondary education, qualified as a lawyer and published his memories of the war in a book with the striking title *64 Days Dead.* We were lunching with Guillermo in the usual place, a café on the corner of Rodríguez Peña and Rivadavia, just a block away from the Congress building, when the idea of a barbecue with the whole crew re-appeared.

Guillermo had kept in contact with the captain of our little vessel, the then naval Lieutenant Horacio González Llanos. González Llanos retired from the Navy more than ten years ago and now works in the human resources department of a multinational car maker.

The Lieutenant in his turn had kept a thread of connection with the former petty officer, Oscar Luna. But out of all *Penélope's* old crew, the one who appeared to have maintained the most fluid contact with the others, particularly after he started work in the Circle of Officers of the Sea, was the former Able Seaman Eduardo Rivero. Rivero and his wife saw the Lunas quite frequently. Luna, Rivero, Ni Coló and González Llanos knew that Peralta and Contreras were still in the Navy and were petty officers attached to the Puerto Belgrano Naval Base, but no one had seen them again since the war.

Now, at last, the seven of us who almost jumped out of our skins in the aerial attack of May 26th, who were almost stranded on Bleaker Island and who arrived in Port Stanley almost out of fuel on June 2nd, when everybody had already given us up for lost, were going to meet.

* * *

But we'll go one step at a time. Let's go back to where I was in Puente Saavedra, manoeuvring between kids zigzagging home along the path and fatigued workmen waiting for buses. The operation was tricky, because I was carrying the rucksack with the cake from the Islands in my arms like a sleeping baby.

On General Paz Avenue, in the wide-open space where the buses stop, González Llanos's car is already waiting for me. 'Uncle' Luna at his side is dozing in the infernal heat of the sun filtering through the windscreen. After stowing the cake in the rear window, I get in beside Luna's wife, Susana.

We go past cultivated fields, bored cows and the tranquillity of the vast plain of the Pampa. Horacio passes me the road map and I study the quickest way to Saladillo. The 183 kms long route is well marked.

Susana, who recounts sad stories from old films and the shortcomings of the hospital where she works with equal emphasis, gets out to buy vegetables from a road side stall overflowing with greens and reds. Saladillo looks like a quiet little town of low brick houses with well-tended gardens.

We begin to leave the town along a tree-lined avenue, when Guillermo Ni Coló waves his arms at us from the gate of a bungalow surrounded by lawns. He still looks tall, with the solid build of a countryman. Even the grey hairs gathering at his temples seem to be the result of hard and useful work. Standing in the leafy entrance to his single-story colonial-style house, he is the image of a well-grounded man. Everything in his manner and his embrace speaks of cheerfulness, warmth and welcome.

In the porch of the house, smiling timidly, are María Inés, Guillermo's wife, who was his girlfriend for ever, even during the war days, and their three children, a little stunned by the effusions of these unknown people.

Guillermo leads us to the living-dining room, where the longest table is already prepared with plates, glasses and salads. A fireplace with a fire burning in the grate presides over the room and its brick walls complete the rustic and welcoming picture. Also dominating the room is a black and white photo of the *Penélope* taken in the Islands by the journalist Nick Tozer two or three years back and now framed and enlarged by Guillermo. The boat is tied up at a wooden jetty and while we draw nearer to the photo to discuss what changes might have been made to it, Contreras and Peralta appear from the kitchen door almost without being noticed.

I take a few seconds to adjust my memories and, like the effects of a medicine or drug which take hold little by little, previously submerged images begin to float up: Peralta's enthusiastic vitality, Contreras's sly but contagious humour, their 24 year-old versions wrapped in the green overalls which were all they ever wore. We hugged and studied each other, smiling. I had never seen them in civilian clothes and the truth is that they seemed very different from the idea of a naval chief petty officer that had stuck with me. Contreras sports a Van Dyck beard, almost as grey as my own and a ring in one ear. He came with his wife and one of his six children, who is already taller than him.

Peralta, enveloped in a mustard coloured track suit, appears much younger than all the rest with his usual elastic gait and his ready smile like a whiplash. He has five children, but came alone in the Contreras's car. They set off the previous day, and slept in

Azul (the Contrerases in the family home and Peralta in a little hotel). The NCOs' journey was a long one; they took turns in driving the 600 kilometres from Punta Alta (the town where most of those who work at Puerto Belgrano live) to Saladillo. Despite this they appear fresh and effusive with lots of things to say and ask. In fact, during these first few minutes we are all falling over ourselves to talk, when the door opens again and in come Eduardo Rivero, his wife Stella Maris, his son and his mother.

Eduardo greets everyone affectionately; everybody is introduced and the five kids sniff each other with the nervous formality customary among the children of friends, who have just met each other and are going to have to spend the day together whether they like it or not. We have all been there; the adults assume that the children will immediately begin to play together simply because they are the same age.

Suddenly, as if on someone's order, the seven of us separate ourselves from the rowdy group that picks up bottles and baskets and takes a guided tour of the house. We gather together in the middle of the living room, under the photo of the ketch. It occurs to me that we are like a family who don't see each other often, but maintain an inexplicable and indissoluble bond.

Guillermo brings out a photo of a group of ratings posing, half amused and half solemn. We pass around the photo, which seems to have been taken at the edge of the runway in Stanley and we begin to tell the story from the beginning. Little Contreras appears on the extreme left of the photo, wearing his habitual mischievous grin. At his side is Ni Coló, looking at the camera with this way he has of appearing serious and amused at the same time; then there is another rating and finally, completing the group, Peralta, half-mocking, with his arm crooked like a jug handle and his hand on his belt. Ni Coló, Peralta and Contreras take the photo and begin to imitate the attitudes of their former selves, as if to demonstrate to us and to themselves that they are the same, that we are still the same as we were then.

* * *

Just then the journalists arrive. They come in cars and trucks emblazoned with the logo of Saladillo's paper (*La Síntesis*) and those of the local radio and television channels. Guillermo Ni

Coló is well-known in his home town. In 2004 the Saladillo media covered the launch of Guillermo's book, then came back to interview him in May 2006, when the *Penélope* arrived in Buenos Aires en route to Hamburg. They couldn't fail to show up when its crew were meeting again.

We leave the house in a mob, somewhat under-dressed for the breeze and the drizzle that starts to fall and with our arms around each other we pose for the photographers and cameramen. The wives brandish their own cameras and the kids also point with their cell phones. It's a strange feeling that this intimate moment, which means something for the seven of us, something special and unique for each one, also has interest and meaning for Saladillo, a town which most of us are visiting for the very first time, and, like everything to do with the Islands, for Argentine society as a whole. Even before it is told our story already has a moral.

The journalists throw themselves upon their local personality, Guillermo Ni Coló. We continue catching up after the years of separation and with half an ear – out of professional habit – I pick out the occasional throwaway phrase from the local hero's

REMEMBERING TOGETHER in Saladillo. From left to right: Guillermo Ni Coló, Horacio González Llanos, Eduardo Rivero, Oscar Luna, Roberto Herrscher, Daniel Peralta and Carlos Contreras.

press conference. From the little that I manage to hear, Guillermo is describing us as 'brothers' and telling the reporters from his home town that he often dreamed of this meeting.

Following this, he tells them that I am a journalist, that I live in Spain and that I have just returned from the Malvinas. The colleagues hurl themselves on their new prey. They ask what this meeting means to me. A lot, I tell them. I had asked myself many times over the years what kind of life the men with whom I had passed the worst dangers of my own life might have had.

One of them asks me if, when I was there in the war, I had ever dreamed of a reunion like this. I laugh. I spend half my life telling my students not to ask this kind of question, but suddenly I'm attacked by the memory that it was indeed part of the future I had dreamed of during the nights of bombardment. I tell my Saladillo colleagues that I dreamed about surviving, about getting old and how I used to imagine myself as old as I am today, in my forties, with a belly and a white beard.

A young reporter asks me about my recent journey to the Islands and if I now see them differently from the first time, but I protest that this is not what this event is about. I want to bring in everyone, especially Peralta and Contreras, and I tell the reporters that none of the rest of us has had any contact with these two since the war.

The last question, for everyone in general is whether it seems to us that this reunion "helps with today's war, the post-war?"

We look at each other a little disconcertedly and an uncomfortable silence follows, which is interrupted by Ni Coló's cheerful and friendly shout that the journalists' time is up. The table is set and the reporters climb quickly into their trucks and cars with little time to put together an account of this historic reunion for the evening news programme and tomorrow's newspaper. But all during the barbecue and the following days when I interviewed my companions from the ketch, one by one, I kept thinking that the journalist from Saladillo was right essentially.

The post-war is another war and just as the little ship that sheltered us during that intense month keeps sailing and surviving, so the war in the Islands continues to be fought day by day in some solitary and inaccessible place inside us. It is from this place that I am now struggling to weave these seven distinct voices into one coherent story.

CHAPTER 2

Six sailors ashore on the Islands

The first of us to arrive in Malvinas, at dawn on the 2nd of April 1982, was Daniel Peralta.

At six in the morning he came up onto the deck of the *Almirante Irízar* to board a helicopter which dropped him at the side of the runway of the airport which was still called Port Stanley. It was dark, but was beginning to get lighter and before leaving the airport he saw a parked jeep, from which several marines were taking a stretcher. He now thinks it must have been the dead officer, Captain Pedro Giachino, or one of the wounded. Giachino, the only official martyr of the landing, fell at the crack of dawn, when at the head of a detachment of marines he attacked the residence of the colonial governor, Rex Hunt. Not one of the British defenders was even wounded in this action.

While they were still waiting at the airport, bullets began to fly about and his entire group crouched down expectantly. Daniel wondered whether he would be in combat. "We were under fire for a bit, and then an amphibious vehicle came to take us the few kilometres to the port." Daniel had hardly arrived before he was certain that the battle was over. He saw the Argentine flag flying on the flagstaff and the British one under some rocks at his feet. Without thinking the able seaman took the British flag and stuffed it in his bag.

The week before the taking of the archipelago, Peralta, a 22-year-old senior rating, had been about to embark on the cruiser *General Belgrano*, but at the last moment they transferred him to the *Almirante Irízar*. He says they gave him protective clothing and told him they were sailing south. In mid Atlantic a naval lieutenant called them together in the hold and told them they were going to land 'on the illegally occupied southern islands.' That night they toasted the success of the operation and also Daniel's birthday; that April 1st he became 23 years old.

Daniel was afraid that he might go into combat, but also enthusiastic. He knew that he was about to participate in something historic. He was born in Rosario de la Frontera in the northerly province of Salta and enrolled in the Navy's Engineering School (the notorious ESMA) in 1976. For him at this time, studying to be a naval NCO meant a way out, a future, and fulfilling the dream of getting to know the sea.

In the afternoon of April 2nd, Daniel was one of those charged with taking the already captured Royal Marines to the airport. "We arrived at two in the afternoon, but their lorry had been hit by bullets and was losing oil. Finally, at six o'clock the driver got it to go, but he wasn't used to its mechanical complexity or the fact that the steering wheel was on the right." Peralta says that they travelled the first hundred metres with the handbrake on, because the driver didn't know how to get it off.

The marines "behaved very well and didn't give us any problems during the long time that the operation lasted." comments the ex-NCO. "They seemed happy to be going home." When the lorry finally gained some speed Peralta had to hang on tight, perched as he was on the edge of its back board.

When he was sixteen and had started his studies at ESMA, Peralta went to live with an aunt and uncle in the Villa Crespo neighbourhood. In 1979 he passed out as a specialist in naval constructions. A little later he was destined to build a base on the island of Thule in the South Sandwich Islands, where he travelled aboard the vessel *Bahía Aguirre.* He will never forget his passage round Cape Horn. He considered himself fortunate and tried to enjoy to the full the wide horizons that the Navy opened up for him. In 1980 he moved to Puerto Belgrano and from there to construct shelters in Tierra del Fuego. "I didn't miss a thing; I always enjoyed the adventure."

The war found him working in a job involving little adventure, as a postal worker and librarian in an office in the Puerto Belgrano naval base.

The days that followed the landing and then the departure of the marines and other British administrators were peaceful ones in the Islands' capital. The senior rating became part of the staff of the Apostadero Naval Malvinas, which took care of port operations. "It unloaded ships, mounted watches. The watches were sometimes hard; the first ones we were under a fuel tank. We were on our knees looking out over the glassy surface of the water." A couple of weeks after his arrival the *Bahía Buen Suceso*, a cargo ship belonging to ELMA (Argentine Maritime Lines Company), came alongside the jetty. It was stuffed full of arms, supplies, food and clothing. Peralta slept aboard for the following days.

Because of his experience as a postal worker, he volunteered to pick up and deliver letters to the *Buen Suceso* and other outposts in the port from the only post office in the Islands. Besides personal letters, Peralta remembers the sacks and sacks full of letters "to one of my country's soldiers." He had to open letters from people of all ages and from all parts of the country.

Peralta remembers particularly the letters from a couple in Bahía Blanca, from some school kids who had written as a school exercise, and also from a girl in Mar del Plata, who without knowing who she was writing to, told all about her life and her worries and included photos of her summer holiday in Bariloche. Daniel was quick to answer her, telling her that he was proud to have been able to take part in the patriotic act of recovering the Islands. "They encouraged us; they congratulated us and told us that they were praying for us. During those first days everyone was happy."

Ten days after arriving in the port, the chief of the Apostadero sent Peralta with a team of seven men to build an air raid shelter in a piece of waste ground. Very soon they had to use it. Hearing the unmistakeable sound of the siren announcing a red alert on May 1st, everyone piled into the air raid shelter they had just finished building. Sea Harriers flashed by and bombs thundered. "That day I had my baptism of fire," Daniel Peralta recounts proudly.

Peralta and the other seven were billeted in a carpenters' shop where they were living off typical navy rations consisting of tinned corned beef, water biscuits and a bar of dark chocolate.

Before dawn on May 8th, Peralta and his mates were still drowsy from broken sleep when an officer announced that a small group of them would be sent to Speedwell Island to look for a boat and bring it to Stanley. Those chosen would have to board a helicopter immediately. The officer read out a list of names, which included that of Peralta. Also named was a senior rating whom Daniel did not know. While this announcement was being made another senior rating came out of the gloom and asked to be sent on the mission in the place of the unknown sailor. Some of those present were surprised at this at this turn of events, but Peralta was not. He had already recognised the voice of the volunteer as that of his friend and companion from their student days: Naval Construction Technician, Second Class, Carlos Contreras.

* * *

Carlos Contreras was working in the NCOs' School when they told him he was going to the Islands. A week had already gone by since the landing; enthusiastic crowds had already filled the Plaza de Mayo to applaud the de facto President, General Leopodo Fortunato Galtieri, who was thinking of himself as the new Perón. The US Secretary of State, Alexander Haig, was already shuttling between London and Buenos Aires and the Plaza de Mayo was filling up again with people cheering Galtieri's bellicose rantings.

As soon as he learned that he would be going to the Islands, Carlos Contreras asked permission to go home to say goodbye to his family. He boarded the last train to the distant suburb of José León Suárez at midnight on April 11th. He walked ten blocks because the buses had already stopped and said goodbye to his wife and their two-month-old daughter. The police had already been to his house looking for him and his wife had the papers they left ordering him to report to the Edificio Libertad, which was the naval headquarters. He closed his door and walked towards the Pan American Highway, from where a police patrol car took him to his destination.

At dawn a large group of officers, NCOs and conscripts came out of the Edificio Libertad and boarded a bus heading for the El Palomar air base. On April 12th they flew to Río Gallegos in an Air Force Boeing 727. The cabin didn't have any seats and the soldiers were piled up on top of one another. What he most remembers is that it was very cold.

The plane landed on the runway at Río Gallegos airport, where Contreras drank a hot coffee before taking the last aeroplane towards the unknown. "When we were almost there the plane made an abrupt turn and we could see the Islands from the air."

From the runway of the airport to the south of Stanley a lorry took the group to the place where they would spend their first night: a gymnasium between Ross Road, the avenue which runs along the edge of the sea, and the gravel shore. There Carlos met his friend Daniel Peralta, about whom he had heard nothing since he left at the end of March with the group which took the Islands. From then until the end of the war they were inseparable.

The following day the cargo ship *Bahía Buen Suceso* arrived under the command of deep-sea captain Osvaldo Niella.

As a member of the Apostadero, Carlos worked as a stevedore for the first time among the large group of sailors and conscripts who had to quickly discharge the boxes and bags from the ship's hold. We met each other during this task. I remember him as being thin, short, and wiry, with a very cheeky face. With these weapons he kept up his morale in whatever situation. He was born in Azul deep in the interior of the Province of Buenos Aires where he still had family and hoped to live when he left the Navy.

Contreras remembers that they spent several days in the carpenters' shop once the ship's cargo was finished with. When the party ordered to look for a boat at a remote island in the Falkland Sound climbed into an army lorry, it was already complete. Besides the two friends there were two more senior ratings, a petty officer, a lieutenant, who would be the vessel's captain and a blonde conscript with a strange surname who was to be the group's interpreter.

* * *

On April 10th, a naval lieutenant called over Engineer-Boatswain Second Class, Guillermo Ni Coló to tell him that he had to go to the Islands "on a three-day mission." Ni Coló was 21 and was working on the maintenance and repair of the Naval NCO School's boilers, where he shared watches and jokes with his friend Contreras.

It wasn't three days, but 64, which he described with restrained emotion in his memoirs, *64 Days Dead.* Guillermo, an acute and sensitive observer, was the only one of the *Penélope's* crew to keep a diary during the war.

The first thing he did after being told that he was going to the Islands was to talk to his mother, whom he had already called three times from Saladillo. To calm her he repeated many times that he was only going for a few days. "We never stopped saying goodbye. She was giving me a lot of advice and saying many tender things and I was doing the same, till at one point I felt a lump in my throat and couldn't utter a word. The fact is that I was crying, but I didn't want her to know. When I was able to resume the conversation, my mother wasn't there anymore. She must surely have thought that I had hung up," writes Ni Coló in his book.

Next morning just as he was about to leave on his "mission" Guillermo met up with his friend Carlos Contreras in the guardroom. When he was leaving, little Contreras poked fun at his friend. "I paid him back in the same coin and asked him to take care of himself because perhaps we were going to meet there."

Guillermo tells me that in reality he entertained no hopes for the possibility of peace. To quote what he wrote in *64 Days Dead*: "A few hours later, when the Plaza de Mayo was already full, I remember that I said to a big civilian chap of sixty or more who was employed in the workshop, "This seems crazy to me. It's going to end badly. This is England. There's going to be war there." I felt this from the first day. From then on I began to think that I would be called up, that I was ready..."

Before leaving, Ni Coló witnessed with surprise the way that they chose the men who were going to be sent to the Islands. "A captain was doing it. He was sitting down with a card index on his knees. He flicked rapidly through the cards and every now and then he extracted one at random and that person was called up."

In the end there was no plane available for Ni Coló's party until three days later. He spent the days of waiting at the family home of his then girlfriend, now his wife, María Inés. On Tuesday April 13th, at ten o'clock at night some buses took Ni Coló's group from the Edificio Libertad to the El Palomar air base. "I remember that during the whole of that trip we kept saying goodbye to everything we saw in passing. It was the last goodbye to the buildings, to the cars, to the people who passed; definitely it was the last goodbye to life."

At dawn on the 14th, getting his first glimpse of the Islands from the plane, Guillermo felt his chest swell with excitement and pride. On the runway, under a grey mist, a priest celebrated mass and gave everyone a rosary.

The first surprise out of everything that Guillermo encountered was that his friend Contreras, who had made fun of him when he was picked to go to the Islands, was already there to welcome him. When they hugged each other on the port's wooden jetty, the friends' laughter helped ease the recent arrival's worries a little.

As his first mission, Guillermo Ni Coló was sent to supply a fuel dump from a barge anchored in Port Stanley.

Guillermo remembers that one day an officer from the Apostadero called together the crew on the *Buen Suceso* and said to them, "Up until today we have just been working. From tomorrow, along with carrying on with the tasks assigned to each one of you, we will begin to prepare for war." After this he explained the meaning of the alerts: red for aerial attacks and yellow for naval. That day the senior rating began to do night watches and met with many nervous conscripts who saw shadows in the night and got their passwords confused.

Nor did they enjoy the chance of calming their nerves with a cigarette. "We were forbidden to smoke during the hours on watch. Popular wisdom says that with the third cigarette you are a dead man. When you light the first, they discover where you are, when you light the second, they take aim and on the third they shoot you," says Ni Coló's autobiographical account.

On April 29th, when the British attack was imminent, Naval Command decided to send the *Buen Suceso* out of the port and all the members of the Apostadero disembarked. It was very cold and raining continuously. They couldn't see anything and the NCOs and conscripts clung on as well as they could to the cat ladders to get onto a launch, which deposited them on the jetty. As he arrived there, Ni Coló was surprised to see a priest with a 9 mm pistol hanging from his belt.

Guillermo Ni Coló's "baptism of fire" came in the shed where they were billeted along with some marines. The bombs caused the first deaths and Guillermo began to fall back into the same state of depression that had attacked him before his departure. "Many times I had thought that my fate was prescribed and that I could not escape death, but that night I was definitely convinced that I would die."

Guillermo found reason for sadness in even a few fleeting moments of cheerfulness. As he tells it in his book, "We found ourselves in the carpenters' shop on one of those sad and rainy afternoons. Suddenly someone came in and broke the silence. Jumping about joyfully and shouting so that we could all hear him, he said that it was all over, that they had just signed a peace agreement and the war had ended. We all sprang up and went out to celebrate. We were hugging each other and some were firing shots into the air. It was a real party. We were very happy because we were going back home. But it did not last long. Soon the Captain in charge of the Apostadero came along and energetically put an end to our celebrations. He told us it was all a lie and that no one had signed anything to do with an end to the conflict. Hope had lasted only for a moment before sorrow overwhelmed us again."

His last day before embarking on the little ship Guillermo spent painting a sign to cover that of the traditional FALKLAND ISLANDS COMPANY sign, which was attached to the building which looked out over the Stanley jetty. Ni Coló painted the wood and the conscript Claudio Guida drew in white the letters 'APOSTADERO NAVAL MALVINAS'. On the night of the 7th an officer informed him that he had to go to Speedwell Island to bring back a boat that was to be found at a farm. After finishing his painting job, Corporal Ni Coló went to bed thinking about the new adventure that was about to begin and once again going over the letters he had received from his family.

* * *

The first thoughts that Chief Petty Officer, Oscar Luna, had when he stepped onto the Islands' soil, were not at all like the metaphysical meanderings of his subordinate Ni Coló. When he saw the black soil, he thought, "Great for growing radish and cabbage! And it must be especially good for potatoes!" It is not at all strange that Luna should have noticed these things, which passed me by unregarded. 'Uncle' Luna, as we called him on the *Penélope,* was a big solid man, with dark complexion, drooping shoulders and round face. On land he walked with bent legs, as if he was swaying easily along the deck of a ship.

In 1982 Luna was 43 years old, which is younger than I am today, however we saw him as a calm and enigmatic older man.

He was born in Cachi in the Calchaquí Valleys of Salta. Luna remembers that when he was four or five he caught a glimpse of a cousin who was in the Navy and turned up dressed as a sailor. "I was thinking, 'When it's my turn to do military service, what am I going to do?' I wanted to be called up by the Navy. I went to the city, to Salta, where I stayed with some members of my family. There I worked as a bricklayer's mate, but I didn't give up. I was 16 or 17. It was 1958. Every week they gave me a few pesos to squander. I remember that one day, a Monday, we were going to work with another boy, and it was raining, so as we worked in the open air, there was no work. We sat down in a café where there was an advertisement for the Navy. We asked ourselves, 'What if we join up?' And why not, except that you had to have your father's permission."

Oscar's dad didn't want to sign although his mother and older brother insisted. "The paper didn't come and it was getting near Friday when it had to be signed. My friend had an uncle who worked in the police and in the end the policeman signed as proxy and that's how I got in." He travelled on a train for two days and nights, sleeping in the baggage car. He didn't spend long in Buenos Aires because shortly afterwards they sent him to Martín Garcia Island where he did the six-month training.

"At that time I was very thin and because of this nobody thought I would get into the Navy. 'This one won't last even a fortnight' they said, but in the end I was there for more than 25 years."

His first posting was the old frigate *Hércules*, which was followed by other frigates. "They were beautiful those ships. I remember that we used to set sail in the evening and they would play music for us. We went to the cinema every night, any time that we weren't on watch … I liked cowboys films and films about cops and robbers … We used to sleep in hammocks which would tip you onto the floor if you turned over a little and we had off-duty shoes. Put those shoes on after wearing boots and they were so light..."

One of Oscar Luna's ineradicable memories of his time in the Navy was the voyage he made in 1970 in the frigate *Libertad*, the historic tall ship in which recently commissioned officers made their end of course voyage. "It was very long. We took part in a race from New York to Spain. We cruised up the coast from Argentina to New York, crossed to Spain, all the Mediterranean, went through the Suez Canal, came out in Africa, went south, turning round by Cape Town, to Portugal, crossed the Atlantic again to the Panama Canal, Mexico, went up to Los Angeles, Canada, Vancouver, Victoria Island, Hawaii, then we followed the Pacific coast down to the Strait of Magellan … we got back to Buenos Aires six months later." He paused for a moment and looked back with a smile at the exploits of the frigate. "When the wind blew it seemed that we were slicing through the water, with all sail..."

In the seventies Luna made several voyages to Antarctica and spent almost a year going to and from the USA, from where his ship carried ammunition and weapons. He also spent some eight years in the naval base at Ushuaia. A few months before the conflict in the Islands blew up they sent him to the recreational club that the Naval Centre ran on the banks of the River Plate.

"On the second of April I thought that it was going to be a transient thing" says Luna. "They could have sent a group from the Coast Guards, but to occupy the Islands like that was to declare war. And afterwards they were saying that the English weren't going to go ... from schooldays they always told us the Islands were Argentine, but you get there and you find out that the English have had them since eighteen hundred and something..."

Chief Petty Officer Engineer Oscar Luna was the last of us to set foot on the Islands. He says that he hardly remembers what he did before they chose him to join González Llanos's group to go and pick up a boat in a southerly island. He does remember that he thought about his family a lot. "I had eight children and the youngest was very small and didn't understand what was going on. I sent them letters and told them that what I was doing wasn't

FIVE NCOS at the Malvinas ariport in April, 1982. It's the only photo I have of three of my Penélope shipmates. From left to right, Daniel Peralta, Guillermo Ni Coló, two seamen called Oliva and Guerrero, and Carlos Contreras (Photo courtesy of Guillermo Ni Coló, from his book *64 Days Dead*).

bad, that we were defending the motherland. But afterwards you see that there were no Argentines there; all there was was an airstrip and some fuel tanks."

During my long interviews with 'Uncle' Luna he asked me more things than I asked him. "Many things aren't what I remember, but what I read in Ni Coló's book," he tells me. But every so often some of those phrases appear in the recording, which remain endlessly floating in the air and leave me thinking and diving into memories and ideas. "It would be hard to live in the Islands, don't you think?" he asks me. "I was in the south for many years and the wind isn't as constant as in Río Gallegos, but can be stronger. Who would want to live there?"

To this day I don't know how 'Uncle' Luna's name appeared on the *Penélope's* crew list, but the experience would have been so much harder without his calmness, his few but forceful words, and his memorable stews.

* * *

Retired captain Horacio González Llanos says that becoming a sailor "was a family thing. I suppose you are attracted to your father's profession. In my case, my dad was a sailor; he lived for many years in naval quarters in Puerto Belgrano, on the base. The whole patriotic business excited me a lot: military marches and the flag; those things that they used to inculcate in you formerly. Nowadays the feeling for country and nationality doesn't appear to be so strong in the schools. I felt all those things and when I heard a military march I used to get excited."

To have a part in the Malvinas action as a naval lieutenant and to have command of a vessel there – even though it was the smallest one – was the culmination of a dream of at least two generations. Horacio passed out from Naval School as a midshipman in 1971 (Promotion Number 100) and later served in the aircraft carrier ARA *25 de Mayo,* the patrol boat ARA *Thompson,* the hydrographical launch ARA *Cormorán* and, above all, the submarine ARA *Salta,* where he spent three years.

April 2nd found González Llanos working in the Operative Analysis Service of Naval Operations Command. One day after the disembarkation of Argentine troops in the Islands the naval lieutenant was summoned to Naval Operations Command where he was ordered to mine Port Stanley harbour from the ELMA ship *Isla de los Estados* to prevent the entry of British submarines. He travelled to the Islands on April 9th on an air force Hercules, with a petty officer and four senior ratings.

Meanwhile the *Buen Suceso* took on 25 mines and the Puerto Belgrano arms workshop was preparing another load to send on another ELMA ship, the *Córdoba,* which never arrived in the Islands after the establishment of the British naval blockade. So it happened that they could only lay two of the four minefields they had intended to lay and no mines exploded, because in the end no enemy submarine entered the harbour.

At the time of laying the mines the Argentine Naval Command could not be sure that British submarines were not lurking about. Because of this, in order to conceal the movements of the *Isla de los Estados,* Naval Command sent out the *Forrest,* an auxiliary vessel, to provide an anti-torpedo acoustic curtain. In the *Forrest,* the sailors and conscripts had to try to make as much noise as they were able, so that the radars of any possible submarines could not detect the manoeuvre.

The first day that they went out to lay the minefield with the *Isla de los Estados,* González Llanos's team had installed a platform which projected from the vessel's side and lifted each mine with a crane. The lieutenant was directing operations, standing on the deck, looking down on the members of his team who were working in the hold. "Theoretically the mine had to be dropped into the water, but it wouldn't drop." Then one of the most dangerous episodes of the lieutenant's whole war happened. "We are trying to get the crane to work and at this point the mine falls right into the middle of the hold. My heart stops." Horacio knew that mines have activation systems so that they don't explode when they shouldn't, but accidents are always possible. After some interminable seconds the mine did not explode and the lieutenant's team disconnected the cables, while on deck the *Isla de los Estados's* conscripts held their breath.

The following night, April 26th, the mine-laying ended and González Llanos was called back to the continent to deliver the chart indicating where he had laid the mines. However, more officers were needed in the Islands and he was ordered to stay and transferred to duties in the brand new Information in Combat Centre (ICC) where there were officers of the Army, Navy and Air Force.

On April 7th, while he was on duty in the ICC, the naval second-in-command in the Islands, Captain Antonio Mozarelli, called him to say that they had found a vessel on Speedwell Island. On May 5th a naval reconnaissance aircraft had spotted the small ketch *Penélope* tied up to a jetty on this small island situated to the south of the Falkland Sound, where there were only two houses with two families and a scattering of sheep. With the fleet stationed on the continent after the sinking of the cruiser *General Belgrano* and British ships and submarines closing the naval blockade of the Islands, this civilian vessel could be useful. "Mozarelli tells me, 'Get a crew together and go and look for this boat!'"

How was the *Penélope* group formed? González Llanos says that just as he didn't know the people in the Naval HQ, none of the names presented to him as possible candidates rang any bells. "I didn't know anyone; I believe that's how they were assigned to me."

There had been two petty officers in his submarine mining group that he had confidence in, but Horacio decided not to take them. "My reasoning was as follows: it was a small craft and of course I could do with the experience of petty officers, but thinking about it, it's a dangerous operation, with lots of movement and effort, so I've got to take some young men with me. That was my thinking, right? So I didn't choose those guys, but took some younger men with me like those two from naval construction." So that was how Contreras and Peralta ended up on the *Penélope*. He also needed men who would look after the engine, so out of the names proposed to him, a certain Luna and Ni Coló would appear good.

And he also needed an interpreter because he had been informed that the Kelpers who currently were running the boat could explain its workings to the new crew. The first candidate was a familiar name.

We are sitting in a cafeteria in Vicente López when he tells me the story: "One day I was in the Naval HQ when Captain Numer called me – do you remember Numer? You maybe didn't know that under his gloomy and serious appearance there lurked a funny guy? – Anyway he called me one day. We used to play rugby together. 'Horacio' he always called me, 'Come here Horacio, I have a surprise for you.' I don't know what, so 'Good' I say and go. 'Let's see. Come here sailor.' The sailor approaches with his helmet covering his face, 'At your orders Lieutenant, Sir.' I know that voice and after hearing it I can hardly believe it. My brother's here! What a mess! Because immediately I had a feeling ... May 1st had gone by and the bombardments had already started, or perhaps it was a presentiment that something could happen where they would send him and that I was a little responsible. Remember, he's my younger brother, I've got twelve years on him, and he's my godson..."

Fernando González Llanos, an architect today, was doing his military service in the Navy and had volunteered to go to the Islands without his older brother finding out about it. Of five boys, Horacio was the oldest and Fernando the youngest. "My mother was more distraught about him than anything; she was very worried" he tells me.

"For a moment I thought about taking my brother with me. They told me that both he and you were available. But I thought, well, if I take him with me and it gets dangerous and something happens to us, we die together. All these things begin to pass through your head and after a little the experience one has of boats doesn't allow that there should be two members of the same family aboard, whether father and son or brothers. It's a logical precaution to be taken because you are a military man and in an emergency, if you have two people and you can only save one, you have to choose whom to save. You know that if you save one person, the other will die, yes? So, whom do you choose? All these things made me think and I said, okay, I'm taking Herrscher."

He is saying this to me. I am the journalist interviewing him, but at the same time I am the former conscript who has just now learned how he came to be chosen to join the crew of the *Penélope.*

* * *

Eduardo Rivero, whose time on the *Penélope* has probably left him with most consequences, is the only one who wasn't part of the original crew.

During the *Penélope's* stay at Fox Bay, González Llanos swapped Able Seaman Carlos Salles for Rivero, a submarine weapons rating, who had been with the lieutenant during the mining of Stanley Harbour. In this exchange Rivero who had remained aboard the *Buen Suceso* came to swell the ranks of the *Penélope's* crew and Salles joined the ELMA cargo vessel.

Rivero had ended up on the Islands thanks to an officer's curious sense of humour. The story goes like this: He was serving in the destroyer *Domecq Garcia* when the news of the taking of the Islands arrived. On April 3rd at 11am the second-in-command made the eighty members of the ship's company assemble on the deck and asked for volunteers to go to the Islands.

The second-in-command told them: "All those who wish to go to the Malvinas, take one pace forward!" In Rivero's division, made up of eight NCOs, only Rivero and two of his best friends stayed where they were. Of the eighty members of the crew Rivero calculates that only about fifteen did not step forward.

A lieutenant came up to them and asked angrily, "Can we be told why you did not step forward?" "And we said to him; 'We are in the navy, so we obey what we are told by our superior officers. It's not up to us to take decisions whether to go or not.' He left then, but at the end the three of us were sent to the Islands. They didn't send a single one of the others. And those that went were those who hadn't stepped forward."

This anecdote shows something of the essential character of Eduardo: his incorruptible common sense and his rejection of ostentation and grand gestures.

He was born in San Juan in 1958 and was brought up in Washington in the Province of Córdoba. When he was thirteen he went to live with his family in Godoy Cruz in Mendoza, from where, aged fifteen, on February 1st, 1974, he left to study at ESMA. "I wanted to leave home" he explains. "I wanted to get on, to prosper." When he was fourteen he had gone to the city of Mendoza to work in a bottle stopper factory. In October 1973 he journeyed by train to Bahia Blanca to present himself for the selection tests at Puerto Belgrano. There for the first time he saw the ocean, which seemed to him enormously big.

One of his reasons for taking the decision to enlist was that it wouldn't cost his parents anything. In fact he had lodging, clothes and food and they paid him a small stipend. They sent him to naval aviation but he was clear about liking to sail so he changed to submarine weapons. He was posted to two destroyers and in 1980 he passed the Leading Seaman's course at ESMA. In 1982 he was posted to the *Domecq Garcia*, which was where he happened not to take that blessed step forward.

The day after this episode they told him and his two friends to report to an officer they didn't know: Lieutenant Horacio González Llanos. This officer seemed both serious and friendly.

He explained to them about the mine-laying they were going to do and sent them back home. "He told us, 'We are going by plane, but I don't know when, so I want you to tell me where you will be.' I remember that during this interval I went to a house with a few friends; it was the weekend. They came to get us, but the plane didn't leave. 'Everyone home and back tomorrow.' I am just arriving back at the house and I see a green truck. I start running and they say. 'Come on, come on, we've got to go' 'Just as I am?' 'Yes.' The only things I was carrying were the documents. We took hardly anything with us; just what we had on and a day bag, toothbrush, trousers, underwear. I didn't enter the house."

"Did you have a greatcoat?" I ask him.

"Only the jacket that I had on. Horacio was in the truck. From there we went to look for the others: Miguel Angel Sosa and Juan Carlos Ledesma. We went to the Comandante Espora air base. We flew out of Puerto Espora in a Hercules in which were two army lorries which were carrying fuel and around thirty army conscripts, together with NCOs and officers, altogether about forty five people."

The Hercules took them directly to Stanley. "We had no seats, nothing. And as the tail of the two lorries stuck out, the back was open. The lorry was tied down with slings and we were sitting on the floor in the front part of the plane. There were tie-downs, some of steel, to lash all the material. We didn't have anything to tie us down. The pilot says, 'Hang on we are going.' There was the pilot, the mechanic and the assistant. The plane speeded up but when it began to lift off it was very heavy, like a pile of rocks, going very slowly. We were saying, 'this is falling...' The flight lasted between two and three hours. Through the back we could see the sky and sometimes the lights of the cities in the south."

The cargo plane arrived at its destination at one in the morning. No one was expecting us and we had nowhere to sleep. In the airport an officer told us, 'Boys, there's a shed over there.' Do you remember that there was a shed at the airport? We got into the shed, all four of us. There was nothing there, only a few guys sleeping. We almost slept sitting down."

The second night they slept in a better place: some kind of a shooting range that the locals had. And the third night they were happy in bunks on the *Buen Suceso*, where Eduardo Rivero assures me that they slept "like kings. We had sheets and everything and we ate first rate food."

The first mission was to move the mines they had brought in the *Buen Suceso* to the *Isla de los Estados*. "They were big; the boxes would be about 60 cms across and 40 cms deep, with the round mine inside. When it was pulled out, the mine was like this and the cable here..." Eduardo does me a sketch in the same note book where I am writing down what he says. In the sketch you can see how the mine is lowered until it is submerged halfway between the surface and the seabed.

Following this Eduardo tells me the same story that González Llanos told me about the mine that fell into the hold, but from his point of view down below. He was with Ledesma, Sosa and Ovidio Bertorello loading mines when they saw one that had just been lifted out wobbling dangerously over their heads. "When we lifted the mine with the crane, we put it into position and there was a cradle with a base in the well of the ship, so that the mine's weight would cause it to fall from the crane into the sea. But the first one falls on the other side and into the hold where we were. It had a whole series of mechanisms to prevent it exploding, but all the same...! Ovidio jumped in with some pincers to cut the cable. He passes us the pincers and we begin to cut all the cables one by one like mad ... sweating ... there's a riot starting on deck with all the conscripts looking down. I was helping to get things we needed ... It was very dangerous, particularly because all the other mines were in down there ... and there were fuel tanks in the hold."

"I had my heart in my mouth" he explains, but by the gesture he makes with his hands, I don't think it is his heart he is talking about. Anyway, that was the end of mine-laying for that night.

The following night an engineer with welding experience from the *Buen Suceso*, rigged up a couple of rails that they found around the port, so that the mines could be lowered from the ship's stern. Rivero keeps on making sketches in the notebook and tells me the end of this story. "We put all the mines there, tied them up and when we were in position to lay them we cut the tube to loosen them with pincers, and having a drop of some five to ten centimetres, they shifted and fell into the sea. And that's how we did all the mine-laying."

They finished the job they had come to the Islands to do at around four in the morning of the second night. When González

Llanos was sent to the command team the following day, Lieutenant Commander Héctor Zukowski of the *Buen Suceso* offered the rest the chance of continuing to sail aboard the ship. So it was that on April 29th, a little before the first air attack which kicked off the hostilities, Rivero left Port Stanley and began a voyage around the Islands. It isn't strange that Eduardo should not have had a clear idea of where he was going. Captain Niella says that the only order he received was to get away from where the bombs were likely to fall. A few days later the crew began to find themselves running out of drinking water and they decided to enter Fox Bay where there was a small wooden jetty which had never received any ship as big as the *Buen Suceso.*

I ask him if he remembers the *Penélope's* arrival in Fox Bay.

"Yes, I remember. I saw it. It was so small. They put it at the back, in the bay where the *Buen Suceso* was aground, behind the army's house where the communications were. Do you remember?" Rivero had studied with Ni Coló at ESMA, but most of all he was delighted to see his mine-laying boss again. González Llanos thought that Salles wouldn't be as much use in the small boat's crew and offered Eduardo the chance to join it.

"I was on land with the people from the *Buen Suceso.* I was chatting with Sosa, Ledesma and Bertorello … and Horacio calls me and asks, 'Do you want to come with me?' 'No problem' I say and I tell him he should talk to Zukowski. Zukowski calls me and says 'Llanos is asking for you. Do you want to go?' I say, 'If I have to go, I'll go. I do what's necessary.' I grabbed all my stuff and installed myself aboard the *Penélope.*"

That same night Eduardo Rivero met his companion of the watch, a clumsy, spotty and talkative conscripted sailor.

CHAPTER 3

The Conscript Translator

That conscript, obviously, was me.

I had travelled to the Islands on the same flight as Carlos Contreras, though we had only just found that out twenty-four years later, when I asked him to tell me his story for this book. However, the hours before the flight were very different for him than for me.

The police also came to look for me, I told him. I was doing my military service in the same building, Edificio Libertad, but that Sunday April 11th I was on leave for Holy Week and we had gone with my parents, my sister Carola and Carolina, my girlfriend at that time, to the cottage on one of the islands of Tigre in the Paraná Delta. When my dad's Chevy hit the hairpin bend and we saw the policeman sitting on the house's iron gate on our Vicente López street, fanning himself with a piece of paper, all the doubts and premonitions that we had felt all week ended.

I would like to remember that we said profound things to each other, but all that I recall of that conversation are practical things. What to take? Which overcoat? How much underwear would fit in my blue going-away bag? My mother came into my room with some chocolate eggs left over from the Easter share-out. She put them in my bag and hugged me as if she was the one going to war.

I didn't know it at the time, but my family and I were getting ready for two parallel wars.

I didn't have to walk in the night or take any last train. My dad took me in the Chevy. It's funny, but often when I told the story of how the police came to look for me, I used to go on to say that the policeman who came with the letter took me to the Edificio Libertad. Having said this so often, I almost remembered the scene of the policeman in his patrol car driving me along Libertador Avenue. But it wasn't like that. When the policeman asked if I was me and I said that I was, he ceremoniously handed me the paper, made me sign something and off he went. My dad and I made the journey to the Edificio Libertad to report for service in the Islands, that night of April 11th, 1982.

Only many years later, talking about the Islands to a group of secondary school pupils who had grown up in democracy, one of them asked me whether it hadn't occurred to me not to go, but to escape. I could, for example, have gone back to Tigre and taken the Cacciola Express, which crosses the Paraná into Uruguay, without needing a passport. No, I told them. The truth is that it didn't occur to me nor to any member of my family that it was possible, that it was even thinkable, not to do what the paper said.

Now I think about this drive to the Edificio Libertad, in silence, with my dad and the goodbye kiss, without dramatics, without imagining what was coming. And, for the very first time, as I write, I think about my dad that Sunday night driving home alone along Libertador Avenue.

* * *

I shared that night with Carlos Contreras and some thirty others on the hard floor of a corridor in the building. I'm sure that no one slept. "And don't you remember that officer who said to us, 'When you return, if any of you do, each one of you goes to your former posting'?" I asked Contreras during the Saladillo barbecue. He didn't remember. Several times during these months while composing questions, I was surprised by memories of scenes, smells and shapes that had been buried within me for decades. Like the memory of how I got official confirmation that I would be going to the Islands. In the office where they made us wait at the Edificio Libertad, lying casually on a table was a sheet of paper with a list of names under the heading 'Malvinas'. The second name on the list was mine.

ME AND MY SISTER Carola, joking with my sailor's uniform some six months before the war.

At six in the morning on Monday 12th we left, half asleep, dirty and dishevelled to get on the bus which would take us to the El Palomar air base. The bus was in the entrance to the Edificio Libertad and my military companions and I were forming up there for roll call, when we found ourselves face to face with the civilians and conscripts from the offices who were arriving to begin another week of bureaucracy. I remember supportive applause, worried hugs and hardly concealed expressions of relief. We were going, but they were not.

At El Palomar I saw the first of many sights that I remembered from the war films I watched on the Saturday afternoons of my adolescence. Now the runway was full of soldiers with their green kit bags, their black boots and their guns in shoulder slings.

It's incredible how quickly the group acts on the individual, absorbing and transforming him. Something as random as the military service lottery had sent me to the Navy and now, a year later, I regarded the army boys as strange and was taking refuge in the little customs, the ridiculous codes by which the Navy – like any other force, tribe or political party – identifies its members. They were saying 'My Captain' or 'My Lieutenant'. We had been told in training that 'my' was only for one's wife or, of course, for one's lover. In the Navy it was 'Captain Sir' and 'Lieutenant Sir.' In these tiny expressions we recognised a familiarity with our own kind, which was vital to keep us from dying of loneliness, anguish or fear in the middle of these hundreds of troops bound for some unknown islands.

We of the naval group spread ourselves out in one corner of the immense belly of the stripped-out plane. In Río Gallegos airport many of us had our first encounter with the merciless cold of the South Atlantic. I had done a lot of back-packing in the mountains of the Cordillera from San Martín de los Andes to Bolsón, but always in summer and in the shelter of the forests. This seemed like a much more inhospitable Patagonia.

We sat on the runway, the majority smoking, with our backs against a corrugated iron shed. The wind was getting at us from all directions. I think it was afternoon when we climbed into the Fokker and, like Carlos Contreras, I also saw the sinuous silhouette of the Islands. The landscape was flat, with lakes, which reflected the aircraft's shadow, without trees, without roads, without villages or lights. Many compared it later to the imagined landscape of Mars or the Moon. I don't remember what I thought; I believe I was too cold to think anything.

The shed where we spent the first night seemed like the improvised field hospital of some natural disaster, with a wooden floor, camp beds and a very welcome hot meal. There I spoke with some of those who had taken part in the April 2nd landing. They told tales of heroism, gunfire and danger. They had only been in the Islands for ten days more than us, but we crowded round to hear them as if they were veterans of three or four wars.

* * *

When the cargo ship *Buen Suceso* arrived, every available body was called on for the unloading and stowage of boxes, packets, sacks and apparatus. The frenetic day and night activity of unloading and carrying things filled your whole mental space, or at least it did mine. However, at night when we collapsed on our bunks to sleep until we were woken to go on watch, we listened intently to anyone who seemed to have fresh news.

In March, the *Buen Suceso* had taken part in the extraordinary episode in South Georgia. The Argentine businessman Constantino Davidoff had chartered it for the dismantling of a rusty whaling station in South Georgia and someone had hoisted an Argentine flag. Faced with the requirement of the colonial authorities that the flag should come down and that the ship and its crew should present itself at Grytviken, Captain Niella finished the unloading operation, left the civilian workers in desolate Leith Harbour and sailed for Ushuaia.

The following day the Argentine Navy's ship *Bahía Paraíso* arrived in South Georgia with a detachment of commandos under the command of the infamous naval officer, Lieutenant Alfredo Astiz, later found guilty of human rights abuses in the 'dirty war'.

The episode of the flag in South Georgia heated up the front pages of the Argentine press during the week preceding the landing on the Islands, in such a way that the taking of the Islands, which had been decided on weeks before, was presented to the Argentine public as a reaction to the humiliation which Davidoff's patriotic workers had suffered.

Meanwhile the *Buen Suceso* was leaving Ushuaia and arriving at Puerto Belgrano when the Islands had already been taken. What with the change of the crew, who had already spent three months on the high seas, the loading of weapons and supplies and the sailing time, the ship arrived in Stanley, only a few hours before Margaret Thatcher's naval blockade around the Islands came into effect.

The merchant vessel was bringing arms, stores and food and we members of the Apostadero slept for some nights in its bunks. By day we worked feverishly unloading numerous boxes and sacks.

What did we know about what was being cooked up in London, Buenos Aires or New York? Almost nothing, except rumours. We wanted to believe that the peace talks were going well, for which reason we gave more credibility to those who said that the negotiations of the Pope, the President of Peru or the Secretary General of the United Nations were on the point of bringing peace. And we were just boys; we laughed all the time, had mock fights, made jokes. We still moved with all the elegance and the clumsiness of late adolescence. We ran about and shouted, but deep down I believe we were dead scared.

The most adolescent and most lively of all was Juan Ramón Turano, sailor Turano. We always tell ourselves things, on the basis of the knowledge that we have today, but I am convinced that I wouldn't remember Turano in Stanley, if it were not for what happened later on that terrible night in Fox Bay.

Turano was seventeen and had just left ESMA. Like the other brand-new career sailors, he was – and looked – younger than us conscripts. I remember him always running about cracking tedious jokes, which nobody ever minded because he was just a kid. Rivero remembers him always talking about death, "he used to tell me that he was going to die, but I wasn't; that we were all going to return and that all this would stop." At these times when he would talk about death while smiling and clowning around it seemed to us that he was taking it lightly. Perhaps we just wanted to believe that because he was always such a joker he wasn't really taking it seriously.

I have the feeling that all of us to a greater or lesser degree had our moment of going into ourselves and thinking about what could happen to us. The worst time for having terrible thoughts about the future was during the night watch. Several of my companions fired crazily on unwary seals, thinking that they were divers coming to plant mines on the *Buen Suceso's* hull.

I did early morning watches and to give myself something to live for I kept the bars of chocolate that they handed out in the afternoon. Round about four in the morning I would go down through the metallic labyrinth of the ship to the bakery where they would be just finishing baking the bread which a good part of the troops scattered around Stanley would get to eat for the next couple of weeks. The baker knew me already and would give me a hunk of bread. Its heat would loosen up my hands which the cold wind of the watch had seized up. I would cut the bread in two with my campaign knife and put the bar of chocolate in the middle where it melted slowly.

Many years have gone by and now bangers and fireworks don't make me crazy as they did in the first years after the war. Every so often, though, I walk at dawn through the Barrio Gótico in Barcelona and when I pass a bakery the smell of newly baked bread assails me unexpectedly. Then an infinite anguish rises in my throat; I am nineteen again and once more on watch at night on the *Buen Suceso.*

When the cargo ship put some distance between itself and the coast, we were put in barracks in the port zone. On May 1st, when

THE ANTI-AIR RAID hole in Puerto Argentino where we took refuge during the first red alert, in May 2, 1982. Photo courtesy of Daniel Gionco.

the red alert for the first Harrier attack sounded we scurried into the hole which Contreras, Peralta and Ni Coló had dug in April. They had placed wooden planks over the sodden earth of the floor. We entered through a hole and over our heads were more boards covered in earth. Little trickles of earth kept falling during the three or four hours we were in there, like the sand clocks of ancient times. A conscript from the Apostadero, who was always looking for others' weak points and laughing at everybody, made a big impression on me. On the afternoon of the bombardment I found myself next to him and at one point he grabbed hold of my arm as if he was drowning. He was pale and tense.

The moment came when the need to pee was stronger than the fear of bombs. I was one of the desperados who couldn't take any more and if they didn't let us out I was going to pee myself. The last red alert was around half an hour before and the petty officer in charge let us out for two minutes. For some the most urgent need was to smoke but I hardly had time to get up against a wall and relieve my bladder. I had just finished when I saw a lady come round the corner with a pram and a baby. I signalled to her and when she came near I asked her in English what she was doing out on the street with her baby while the aeroplanes were bombing.

Then, with surety but in a matter of fact way, the lady told me that there was no danger for her and her baby because the British troops would know that she was one of their own. And she continued with her walk, while the petty officer shouted himself hoarse at his men to get us back into our air raid shelter.

By a bitter and ironic twist of fate at the war's end, the only Islanders who were killed died as a result of 'friendly fire.' Her Majesty's gunners were not so infallible after all. However, it seems to me that what distinguished the greatest empire of its day and still lingers in the collective memory is, amongst other things, the absolute confidence and blind faith of its subjects that their own troops will perceive their 'Britishness' with precision from kilometres away, even from a jet speeding by like a burning meteorite.

* * *

I had entered military service on April 2nd, 1981. I learned nothing of the things they wanted to teach me during training in Puerto Belgrano: military discipline, blind obedience, informing on one's comrades, keeping one's head down, becoming a number without will or brain, and stealing if anyone steals from you to avoid being punished at the end of the day for being the fool who didn't steal, all that doctrine. However, I did learn a lot about my country and its lack of social equality and about myself. During training I lived together with kids from Jujuy who didn't know how to lace up their boots because they had never had shoes and kids from Formosa who got up from their bunks in the middle of the night to pee in a corner of the room (and afterwards we all got punished for it). In the eternal Sundays with nothing to do I had intense conversations with a Mormon from Córdoba, with an actor from the neighbourhood of San Telmo and with one of the most intelligent and scathing guys that I have known in my life, the ruddy-faced Juan Carlos Zangani, who later died on the cruiser *General Belgrano.*

I was sent to the Islands principally as a translator. The day that we began our military service, we had filled in the blessed forms that asked if we knew how to drive a lorry, how to type or speak another language. I thought that if I put that I knew English, I could end up working in an office and not cleaning latrines in some distant naval outpost. I had been to a bilingual college in San Isidro and spoke English well. Of course I was not the only one who boasted of his linguistic knowledge, but at the moment of truth, only three or four of those brought as translators could actually talk to the Islanders.

The chief of all naval operations in Malvinas, Admiral Edgardo Otero, arrived towards the end of April. He made his headquarters and personal accommodation in one of the houses used by the British Government for civil servants from the metropolis on the staff of the colony's Governor. Until the arrival of the Argentine forces, 10 John Street had been occupied by the First Secretary in the Governor's Office, Michael Growcott. On April 2nd Growcott was away from the Islands and his wife and children had only a few hours to pack up what they could carry by hand and take a plane to Buenos Aires and from there to London. Otero and three or four high-ranking officers took possession of the house and I was sent there as translator, house servant and cook with another naval conscript, Diego Pezzoni. Luckily Diego knew how to cook, because I was absolutely useless. Between the two of us, we cleaned, swept and made the beds.

We used to sleep in a room which seemed to be a store for old furniture and ironing next to the bathroom, with a window opening onto the garden. Among the many things that the Growcotts left behind was an interesting selection of English literature. I believe I was the only 'tenant' who enjoyed that reading material and at the beginning of May I took to bed and in my few spare moments began to read, a book which enriched me and left many impressions on me: Graham Greene's *The Heart of the Matter.*

With other conscripts from the Apostadero we dug an anti-air raid shelter in the garden. At the bottom of the garden was a green house with plants and vegetables, a common means of supplying fresh food in the Islands' hostile climate. From the kitchen window we could see the entrance to one of the town's most traditional pubs, The Rose. In the days I spent in this house I was able to talk to various locals. A Canadian came to complain because they had sunk his boat during the April 2nd attack. He told me that he had fought in the Second World War and had sought the most distant and peaceful place to live. He wanted to be in a place where wars would never happen and he thought that Port Stanley was ideal. And there he was with his hair standing on end and two armies hurling missiles over his head.

Another time a couple of captains who used to sleep in 10 John Street told me that they had decided to take another house. There were a lot of people in our one and a couple of blocks away they had spotted a cottage where they might spend the war very happily. Among us conscripts we swapped stories about the things that the chiefs had brought and the comparison with the cold and hunger that the boys in the mountains were suffering was frightfully ironic. One army officer came with his dog, another with a container full of furniture.

These two wanted the house on the corner and they made me knock on the door. The two old ladies who opened it looked straight out of an Agatha Christie novel. They were about to sit down to tea and a delicious cake and invited me to join them. I had to suggest to them that if they had family or friends in the countryside it would be better to leave town for a while because things were going to get ugly. The officers couldn't throw them out, but if they went of their own accord … In the end the officers gave up.

We ate well in the house – the pantry had stayed full and the officers brought provisions from the continent, for which reason we received frequent visitors: officers from the three services, civilians and military chaplains. Hungry conscripts also sneaked in without being seen and we gave them what we could.

Family letters arrived, but very delayed and all opened and bearing the stamp of the Argentine navy censor. Later I learned that many military wives and lady volunteers had been employed to cross out any attempt to demoralise, or any tepidity with respect to the necessary patriotic fervour, or any references to countries or cities which could be key military secrets if passed to the enemy. My mother, for example, told me that she was worried about members of the family who were in Los Angeles, New York and Paris. The sentence remained with the word 'worried' and the three cities crossed out with black marker pen, but in such a clumsy way that the words could still be read from the other side.

Re-reading my letters from that time now I can hardly recognises myself. With a lieutenant reading over my shoulder I almost didn't need naval censorship to paint a pastoral panorama. Did I just not want my parents to worry or was I really not affected by the climate of fear, the awareness of the notable military deficiencies and the ever more desperate state of the army's soldiers, scattered over the mountains around Stanley?

However it was, this strange domestic existence was interrupted for me on May 7th when they told me I must pack my gear to go on a mission to find a boat. I found it hard to sleep that night.

A Land Rover stopped at the gate of the house in the silence and darkness of the early morning and without turning off the engine, someone got out and knocked on the door. I left without making a noise and between sleep and awakening climbed into the jeep through the back door and greeted the people seated on their belongings in the seats in front. I had the impression that Peralta and Contreras were the only ones I had seen before. A helicopter was waiting for us at the Government House field.

What I most remember about the helicopter ride is the din of the engine. I covered my ears with my hands. The machine flew low and the south of East Falkland seemed even more strange and deserted than on the night of our arrival.

Reading Ni Coló's book recently, I discovered that behind his serious and intense expression, he was really excited. "I want to say that daily we were living new experiences, good and bad, sad, or as in this case, happy, at least for me who had wanted to fly in a helicopter for so long. On other occasions, it seemed to me that I was living a film, that such scenes only happened in the cinema, but it wasn't like that, this was real; I was in a helicopter and I was happy."

Neither he nor I noticed that the lieutenant at our side was pale and his pulse was racing. In mid-flight the pilot detected a British ship and González Llanos confessed to me that this was one of the most dangerous moments of the whole expedition. "These were not Argentine ships. The pilot told me 'We're going to get a missile for sure.' Anyone who knows about missiles knows that an aerial target at low speed is very easy to hit."

The incident passed and the helicopter landed in the middle of nowhere. The pilots wanted to check the direction with the maps. An hour after taking off, we finally put down on a little island where there were a couple of houses, a shearing shed and a wooden jetty.

Some marine commandos had arrived the previous day to check the boat out. While González Llanos talked with the marines, I approached the people of the house. They were all together, in a knot, looking at the helicopter with a mixture of curiosity and fear. There was a girl of about fifteen. She told me that two families lived there and that a teacher came every now and then to give her lessons for a few days and then went again. This girl surprised me a lot, alone on an island the size of one of the planets in *The Little Prince,* growing up with four or five adults, a load of sheep and nothing else. Every blue moon she went to Port Stanley. The port had a little more than a thousand people, but to her it was the big metropolis. I didn't think much about how other people's lives would be then, but this life of loneliness and wind made a deep impression on me. What would growing up in such a place be like?

From the house, we walked to the jetty and that is where we saw the *Penélope* for the first time, rocking between the silvery sparkles of the waves.

CHAPTER 4

Schooner at war

'Uncle' Luna says that when he got close enough to see it well, the *Penélope* seemed tiny, like a nut shell.

But immediately he adds that he liked the coal-fired stove, the wooden table where we used to eat and the bunks. He was happy to find the food locker full and remembers the first foray through the bowels of the boat. "The engine was good, wasn't it? You went down to it by a little ladder from the bridge. Do you remember that we went down together the first time and almost couldn't make it?"

By contrast, the first thing that Guillermo Ni Coló felt was fear. It was his first time on a boat. "I said to Horacio, 'Is this thing going to get us back?' I was expecting something different..."

"What were you expecting?" I asked him.

"I was imagining a more important boat, to go through a war in. I didn't understand what they were going to do with it. What are they going to do with this thing? What do they want it for?"

A little while ago, I too had to answer this question. Martin Virtel, the multimedia editor of the *Financial Times* German edition, who helped me so much as my guide in Hamburg, wrote an article about the arrival of the *Feuerland/Penélope* based on my experience and began by asking me about the moment when I saw the rough, rounded hull of the *Penélope* for the first time.

"I remember much more about afterwards, about the sailing," I told him. "So many things happened and I have gone on living with the memory of the boat for so long, that I have to strain to know if I thought anything at that precise moment. I have the impression that during this period I adapted myself to every new situation, tried to grasp those things that touched me and didn't hang on to any other kind of impressions. And, of course, I didn't imagine that this boat was going to remain part of me for such a long time. Evidently I never thought that it wasn't very suitable as a warship, because I simply didn't imagine that we were going to be involved in warlike situations, like attacks and bombardments..."

I also told him: "The war was far away. The truth is that at this time I saw it as a kind of adventure, like a voyage ... I thought that it was a boat that I had to sail in with this group of people. And I would prefer to be on the sea than stuck in a hole, or to be doing watches in a place where they could come and attack me. I think I had a good feeling about it from the start; I got on well with the local people and the same with the other crew of the boat ... above all with the seamen who were as young as me. Now that I talk to you about it, I think the best way to describe things is that I was playing at being a sailor."

I had never sailed; in fact I had never been on a ship, either during my training or my military service. My maritime experience was limited to some small boats on the Tigre Delta. But what struck me a lot during the interviews was that some of the others had never been on a ship either. The experienced one was the Lieutenant who was a career officer and had done a voyage on the frigate *Libertad*. He knew how to handle the *Penélope* in any circumstance, in storms, by night and by day. Really, looking back on it from a distance, this Lieutenant González Llanos was a good sailor."

Martin asked me if the boat had also looked very small to me. "Yes, but not too small. I thought we were comfortable in that boat; that it was old, but not abandoned. It looked much more infirm when I came to see it again in Germany. But, of course, twenty-four more years had gone by. She was comfortable; she was our home. If I remember anything, it is that it seemed nice, that I liked that boat."

The five crew members of the little boat that we were going to take were standing nervously on the jetty. Guillermo remembers that they were all unusually under-dressed for the weather, with shirts and pullovers, but no parkas or windcheaters. "Through the conscript Herrscher, who was our interpreter, our boss addressed an older man and they talked for a few minutes. He was asking him amongst other things about the condition of the vessel and whether it had a radio and told him that we were taking charge of the boat and that he and the engineer would have to sail with us for a few days until we knew how everything aboard the vessel worked."

In *64 Days Dead*, Ni Coló lists what we knew about the boat at this time: that it was an old German vessel, that it had a six cylinder Ford diesel engine that developed a maximum speed of four knots, two fuel tanks and two 200 litre drums, one with drinking water and the other for general use." It was also equipped with a generator which allowed us to have electrical power.

What else did the *Penélope* have when we went aboard on May 8th 1982? Jorge Muñoz, author of a fistful of works on the participation of the Coast Guard, merchant ships and civilians during the Malvinas war has the answers, and also writes about our voyage in his book, *Poker de Ases en Malvinas.* The book tells about the four auxiliary vessels used by the Navy in the Islands: the *Yehuín,* which arrived from the Argentine coast, and three small ships requisitioned from the kelpers: the *Forrest,* the *Monsunen* and the *Penélope.*

At the beginning of his chapter on the *Penélope,* based mainly on naval reports and the account of González Llanos, Muñoz describes it thus: "The last of the vessels incorporated into the Malvinas Naval Command was the *Penélope,* a double-ended schooner of German origin with a double-skinned wooden hull, 18 m in length (in reality only 16 m), 4 m in the beam and drawing four feet. It had two masts with boom and gaff sail, a hoist, echo sounder, radio, magnetic compass and just one engine which allowed the development of a five knot maximum speed."

Despite the fact that I was the translator who transmitted all of this information, none of it remains in my memory. Translating technical terms is an almost impossible task for a make-shift nineteen year old, who had never lived in an English speaking country and knew more about the insults used by kings and aristocrats in the works of Shakespeare than he did about booms, gaff sails and echo sounders. With such a translator it's a wonder that the boat did not sink.

The *Penélope* was full-bellied and rolled a lot (it moved constantly from side to side). It had two wooden masts, the tallest in the bow and the other shorter one behind the wheelhouse. It didn't have any sails so we could neither hoist them nor see how they looked. In the wind the metal rigging for the sails vibrated and whistled with a mysterious and ghostly sound.

I remember that the first impression that I had of Finlay Ferguson fitted perfectly with my idea of an old sea dog: short, solid, with hard wrinkled skin, bright, roguish eyes, and a cigarette hanging from the corner of his mouth. He wore a worn out blue and white chequered jacket and his round head was crowned by a blue peaked cap, even inside the cabin-kitchen-galley.

Around him stood the other four crew members. The helicopter carried off three of them together with the commandos. With Ferguson there remained only Brian Jaffray, called Jeff by everybody, the tall and taciturn chief engineer, who smoothed his dense black beard and analysed the situation with a frown.

The two islanders, the six sailors and I embarked and Ferguson began to describe the components and operation of his ship. The wheelhouse, a wooden box where four people could just fit with difficulty, held an old wheel of worn-out wood like a jewel. Steering was done standing up, just like in the movies. Behind the wheel was a shelf with charts and exercise books. A little metal ladder led down to the engine room and a little room into which a ramshackle bed barely fitted, with a space where you could put your feet. This was Ferguson's cabin.

In the bow, a little tower rose up like a pimple on the schooner's nose. This was the entrance to a companionway leading to the galley, the mess and the crew's cabin. The old coal-fired stove was a heavy iron brute, which filled the room with heat and smoke when 'Uncle' Luna was cooking. The four bunks were arranged around the table, which in its turn embraced the base of the main mast. Between the engine and the cabin-mess was a central area accessed by an easily opened door in the middle of the deck. This was the hold.

The first thing we did was to choose beds and leave our bags on them. In the centre bunks, which went across the ship from starboard to port were, on one side, Ni Coló in the top bunk and Salles, below, with the Lieutenant and I on the other side. Luna slept alone in the port bunk and Contreras and Peralta had the starboard bunks, with Contreras on top. Ferguson and Jaffray occupied the little room in the stern.

We sailed off to try out the boat. González Llanos and Ni Coló remained in the wheelhouse. Peralta prepared the lunch and then threw himself on the bed. The boat was moving a lot and to avoid seasickness he lay down to rest for a while. He had decided to take everything calmly. His rule was that the more difficult or complicated the situation, the more it should be faced calmly.

Meanwhile I went down into the engine room with Luna, Ni Coló and the local Chief Engineer. The four of us were stuck in this noisy and badly-lit cubicle with our heads together because of the din, looking at things stained with grease and dirt, while Jeff tried to explain how the engine worked and I tried to transmit to Luna and Ni Coló the little I had understood. Guillermo and I were also beginning to feel ill. Before coming back from this short excursion most of the sailors were bent over the gunwale. This was the moment when I realised that nearly all of them were novices, just like me.

When the boat stopped moving, Daniel found a treasure which would accompany him for the whole voyage, a bulky recorder and a collection of Elvis Presley songs. From this moment on the soundtrack of his quiet moments was the King's catchy rock.

This is how Guillermo records the scene in his book: "During the short time that we were sailing, the boat moved a lot; the sea's waves were high and for those who were making their baptismal voyage as sailors, things looked pretty ugly. Contreras, Salles, Herrscher and I went to the stern and hugged the deck rail. We couldn't stop vomiting. I had a terrible headache. I begged for the boat to get into the shore because I couldn't take any more. Finding some courage I went to the cabin. Peralta was lying down placidly listening to music from a cassette player belonging to the English. When he saw my face and how little of me remained, he began to laugh and could not stop."

That afternoon we sailed around the most southerly point of the Islands towards the Bay of Harbours. We could not navigate at night because we had neither radar nor sonar. González Llanos recalls that he saw a ship's lights and ordered that the *Penélope* should hide in the bay. Later we realised that it was the *Buen Suceso* heading for Falkland Sound.

Peralta was on watch that night and was alarmed when by the light of the moon he saw the black shiny heads of some sea lions appear. "He woke us all up, shouting, 'Mates, there's someone in the water'" relates Contreras with a grin. "Some of us got up and went out on deck with the gun."

I spent some of my nights on watch with Mr Ferguson. We talked a little, he smoked and I asked him questions. To be honest what remains with me more than anything in particular that I might have said is a feeling of cordiality, of a few words which would open a little window onto an unknown world for me. Long minutes would go by without him saying anything, and then a question would occur to me that he would answer with very few words, but nicely.

He told me that he had lived all his life in the Islands, that he had a wife and daughter in Darwin and that he had only left twice for health reasons to have operations. He had spent a few days in Buenos Aires and a few more in London and that both cities seemed to him the same, like insane, unhealthy anthills of people, vehicles, smoke, noise and buildings. For many years he had been involved in the transport of sheep and wool between the small islands and from them to Port Stanley.

Ni Coló remembers something else that I told him at this time from my conversations with the Kelper captain. He says that Ferguson told us that each May a ship arrived from London and there were parties and they organised dances and football matches and horse races and "that the Falkland Islands Company (FIC) was owner of the whole island and the source of all the work."

* * *

The voyage from Speedwell Island to Port Stanley, which was due to end the night of May 9th, was postponed when an order from above commanded us to go in the opposite direction and enter Fox Bay. Then began a series of missions, voyages and adventures, which would last nearly a month and terminate near the end of the war.

Guillermo, Daniel and Carlos were on watch in the wheelhouse when from the radio they heard a strange message: 'Lizard, Lizard, this is Concert, take pencil and paper immediately. Note: All civil and military personnel to skate immediately to Uranus.' The ratings understood it to require them to disembark, but when Peralta woke up the Lieutenant, he translated the message to mean that they had to find and then follow another of the Falkland Islands vessels used by the Argentine Navy, the *Monsunen.* González Llanos took the radio and answered that we could not "skate" by night, so the sailing was postponed till the following morning. The Lieutenant recalls that at that moment we made out the *Monsunen* coming out of the dense mist. They, of course, had radar.

The first and one of the most dangerous incidents happened that night at the entrance to Fox Bay when a terrible storm blew up without warning. The *Penélope* was leaping around buffeted by huge waves, the dishes and cans in the pantry fell with a clatter and we all fell on the floor or onto our companions. The bow rose and fell like a roller coaster, but after having vomited everything we had inside the previous day, we were already veteran sailors and no one was sick.

In pitch darkness, the *Monsunen* berthed alongside the *Buen Suceso,* which had arrived some hours earlier and we tied ourselves up alongside the *Monsunen.* But the waves and wind made the wooden hull of our little 'schooner' crash against the metal hull of our neighbour and with the most serious expression on his face that I had seen up till then, Ferguson said that if we didn't separate, the *Penélope* would break up. We had to cast off and head for the interior of the bay, where we dropped the anchor to spend a dog's night.

When we got ashore, we encountered our old companions from the *Buen Suceso* and the *Monsunen* and also a glimpse of the Islands landscape. It seemed that the only productive activity was the raising and shearing of sheep, because the hills covered with grass and bushes showed no form of agriculture other than the gardens for the use of the scattered inhabitants. Inside Fox Bay were groups of cottages, sheds and shearing sheds – Fox Bay East and Fox Bay West – where a few local families lived. They appeared to be all mixed up together in one big house. Later I learned that each one had his own house, some several kilometres away, but they had come together for support during the occupation.

In the hills round about, there was an army regiment and the soldiers were living in fox holes. As I never was in the mountains around Stanley, these were the only fox holes I got to see in the Islands, but they were enough to give me an idea of what those boys were going through; they were freezing, with a pond in the bottom and insufferable dampness. I only spent one night in one of those holes and I could hardly sleep for the needles of cold which were driven into my feet.

But that first day in Fox Bay, the tragedy which awaited us was much worse: the transport ship, *Isla de Los Estados,* from which González Llanos had mined the bay and with whose crew we had fraternised in Port Stanley, had been bombed the night before in the middle of Falkland Sound. After the sinking there was no signal and it was feared that they had all been killed.

Naval Command then divided the Sound into three sub-sections and sent out the three local vessels: *Forrest, Monsunen* and *Penélope* to search for survivors or the remains of the shipwreck. Two civilian sailors asked to come with us and Ni Coló and Salles remained on shore. One of the sailors, a big weather-beaten man with suffering etched on his face, was José Manuel Martinez, a sailor from the *Buen Suceso* and one of the missing was his nephew, the cook on the *Isla de los Estados*. Like a lot of the ship's company, Martinez was a Galician. The other sailor who came with us was called González and was part of *the Isla de los Estados* crew. He had been disembarked at Fox Bay and was now looking for his shipmates without much hope.

This was the first mission in which I could put to the test my new calling as 'lookout.' I stayed at the bow with a pair of powerful binoculars and looked with all my might. On this rugged coast there could be some survivor, maybe collapsed, with no strength to move. Between the wave crests out to sea a windblown raft might perhaps be awaiting rescue. I scanned this unpopulated corner of the Islands for hours and hours, but without success. The mood of the civilians became darker and darker as we followed the coast inch by inch and saw no signs there of human life.

There was, however, a great quantity of fascinating wild life. With my binoculars I followed the acrobatics of dolphins playing chase in front of the *Penélope's* bow, sea lions frolicking in the rocks and penguins proud and erect like executives at a cocktail party. Albatross glided over our heads with immense wings outstretched. I lost myself in ecstasy, with the war and fear and the poor conscripts, naval ratings and the civilian sailors that we were looking for, all forgotten. In these circumstances the enjoyment of nature was a guilty but irresistible pleasure.

Other times they put me in the wheelhouse. When we were near rocks or in difficult passages, Ferguson took the helm. He could leave a cigarette forgotten on the edge of his lips and take a puff every now and then. When the ash was about to fall on the floor he would cup his calloused hand and deposit the white powder in his palm. Later he would stand in the doorway and throw the ashes in the sea.

That night when we got back to Fox Bay, we found that the *Forrest* had picked up the only survivors from the *Isla de los Estados*: the army captain Alois Payarola and the civilian sailor Alfonso López. The other 22 crew members perished. Among them were 15 merchant seamen, some of Spanish nationality, an officer and an NCO from the Army, naval ratings, an airman and one sailor from the Coast Guard.

According to what López and Payarola told their rescuers, they received four hits and the ship sank so rapidly that they hardly had time to lower a raft. Payarola, López and a sailor called Sandoval swam towards the raft, but Sandoval sank. The First Officer, José Bottaro and the civilian captain Tulio Panigadi did manage to get on, but the Captain threw himself back into the sea to stabilise the raft and disappeared under the water. They reached the shore, rowing desperately, but Bottaro died on the beach for all his effort. When the *Forrest* discovered them, López and Payarola were shaking with cold next to their companion's corpse. I couldn't get out of my head the farewell dinner that we had given to the *Isla de los Estados* crew in Stanley.

González Llanos recalls that we didn't have any general duties to perform while we were at Fox Bay, but the 'schooner' was given various specific missions. "One was to carry this patrol to look into the possibility of helicopters being at Port Edgar. There was a crowd of people, some army and two guys from the Air Force with SAM 7 missiles, like a bazooka that you put up against your shoulder."

When the Lieutenant saw some of these bazookas fired at Fox Bay, he was left with a bad feeling, not because of the deadly power of these weapons, but precisely for everything to the contrary. "It was horrible, because while I knew that these guys were there, I was thinking, 'That's good, we are protected against aircraft. We will at least shoot one down.' When we were attacked by the same planes that attacked the *Isla de los Estados,* that was when this guy comes out with the SAM 7 and goes fiuuuuu...," and he makes a gesture with his hand like a flying drinking straw falling to earth in spirals and makes a low whistling sound with his lips.

After a pause and a sip of coffee, 24 years back in time, the Lieutenant looks at me and says: "That was a 'here we are in God's hands' kind of feeling, because what we had previously thought would be fine for bringing down aircraft, didn't bloody work."

The second day in Fox Bay, 'Uncle' Luna revealed himself to be an amazing cook. Ferguson had made the first few meals, because he wanted to have something to do and because he knew what was in every jar. The *Penélope's* pantry was a living museum of a robust and rural culinary tradition with its roots in Scotland, from where the majority of the Islands' old sailors had come. Of course, they cooked a lot of mutton, both roast and in soups and stews with plenty of potatoes, carrots and cabbage. They also ate meat with sauces and creams and finished each meal with abundant quantities of whisky or rum.

That morning when he entered the galley Luna had an inspiration and asked me to translate to Ferguson that he would take charge of lunch. "There was everything on that boat" he remembers today with a picaresque smile. "I made that stew with part of half a mutton carcass that was hanging outside, with potato, chilli, paprika. I put in a lot of oregano..."

We sat down at the table and Luna arrived with a steaming saucepan. Finlay Ferguson's eyes lit up at the first spoonful. Summoning up all his reserves of Spanish, he attempted a eulogy in that language. All that emerged was "*Cochinero mucho bueno*". We all fell about laughing.

At night I used every available moment to continue reading *The Heart of the Matter.* When I discovered this orange coloured Penguin book in the library of the English civil servant, I had hardly heard of Graham Greene, but he captivated me from the start. For years I remembered telling Ni Coló the story of this English colonial officer in Africa, his struggle with his conscience and the sexual intrigues of the novel's plot, though in my retelling I could not match the hypnotic style of the Master, his short precise descriptions, nor his dialogues, full of violence and irony.

In my memory, after my desperate attempts to convince him how good the book was, I promised Guillermo that when we got back to Buenos Aires I would give him a copy in Spanish. Also, one night of fear and distant bombardment the insane thought occurred to me that I had to hurry up and finish it, because if we were sunk I ran the risk of dying before I'd read the last pages.

In the decades which have passed since then I have read many of the Greene's novels of intrigue (*The Power and the Glory, The Honorary Consul, Our Man in Havana)* like a grateful disciple and every time that I begin one, I think of that first one and the nights in my bunk, using half of my few hours for sleep in making the voyage to Greene's sticky Africa, full of mosquitoes and moral ambiguity. The first thing I said to Guillermo Ni Coló, when we met more than twenty years later, was that I had not kept my promise to give him a Spanish version of the book. "What book? What are you on about?" he replied.

On that voyage I saw for the first time a very different flying beastie from the albatross and one which would torment my dreams for years: the Sea Harrier. The first ones thundered so low and fast across the Falkland Sound that by the time we could see them they were no longer there. They were silvery, with such a sharply pointed nose that you felt they were going to stab you in the chest. What the myths of the terrible Ghurkhas were for the boys on Tumbledown or the Two Sisters, for us it was the shout of "The Harriers are coming!" It felt as if they saw you, stopped in mid-flight, turned to point their cannons, fired a barrage at you and then accelerated away from nothing. By the time you looked up they had already evaporated.

The first Sea Harrier appeared in the middle of the fruitless search for the *Isla de Los Estados*. It didn't shoot, but just flew over us. In our wooden 'schooner' from the twenties, which slipped along at five knots and with our only defence our ancient FAL rifles – which I for one had never practised firing – the sudden appearance of this war machine from another century left us with our hearts jumping out of our chests.

The war and danger were drawing ever nearer to our 'schooner.' At night, Ferguson, the most distant and also most genuine of Her Majesty's subjects, continued to tell me stories of how the Islands had been before; how they had no roads or telephones and communication between the islands was by means of radio – every message being heard by everyone – and little ships like *Penélope* and *Monsunen*.

I remember him being worried, but never annoyed or aggressive with us. It seemed to me that he was taking it as a catastrophe that had befallen us all and we had to wait in the best manner possible to see how it would all work out. The word 'pragmatic' is used today as a synonym for calculation and a lack of ethics, but it's the first word that comes to mind to describe Captain Ferguson. He was a man far removed from big words and grandiloquent gestures, who looked after his own people and, like a good man, also looked after those who for whatever reason were round about him.

On May 14th, before returning to Fox Bay, Ferguson proposed to González Llanos that he and Jaffray (who had rarely been seen during the voyage and with whom I had hardly exchanged a word) should be left at a place called Egg Harbour. From there, they would walk to Darwin, crossing East Falkland.

This Egg Harbour turned out to be a jetty and a little house in the middle of nowhere. I watched the two Islanders getting off in the wind with their bags and their chequered shirts. Where would they walk to? There were no roads in the Islands at that time. I couldn't imagine that they would know this country literally like the palms of their rough hands, but they seemed sure that they would arrive at their destination. We shook hands and wished them luck and when I returned to the cabin I felt that the boat was lacking something. Nearly a quarter of a century would go by before I would learn the end of the story of Finlay Ferguson and Brian Jaffray in the Falklands war.

* * *

In his book, Ni Coló recounts that he thought a lot about his family in those days and that his friend Carlos Contreras had stuck up over his bunk a picture of his wife and another showing her and their little daughter, to whom he had hardly managed to say goodbye that night when he took the last train to José León Suárez. "He used to spend a lot of time looking at the photographs and stroking them," writes Guillermo in *64 Days Dead.*

From the time we left Puerto Argentino, practically from the imposition of the naval blockade, none of us had received any mail from home. I was writing letters to my parents, to my sister, to my girlfriend, to my aunts and to my grandparents, but I didn't know when I was ever going to be able to give them to the postal clerk. There was one handy: Daniel Peralta, but he wasn't much use in that place.

Reading some of these letters again at a distance, I don't think they would have said much even if they had arrived at their destination. On the one hand, the attacks were so unexpected and continuous that the only thing that the cards guaranteed was the pathetically useless knowledge that the sender had still been alive and in reasonable health a couple of weeks before. So many things could have happened between the sending and the arrival of the letter in question. So many times we could have been killed and meanwhile the letter would have continued its slow bureaucratic journey carrying its pathetic good news.

On the other hand, my letters didn't say much either. I limited myself to reminding everybody how much I loved them and to telling them obvious things which would get past the censor and reassure them. With my girlfriend Carolina, I was a little more melodramatic. I asked her to remember me for ever, if did not return, but not to be too sad. With my parents, as always, I tried to show the most positive side of everything. I talked to them about the experiences I was living through, about the dolphins and the penguins and about the excellent group of humans that I had met on the boat. It all sounded as if I had gone camping.

* * *

The second Sea Harrier visit nearly ended my life.

It happened during the first voyage after our return from Egg Harbour and this time it was my turn to stay ashore. The *Penélope* carried a group of well-provisioned army commandos to a remote farm to see whether any reconnaissance or advanced enemy troops were there.

I was in the open-sided shed where the *Buen Suceso* crew were quartered when the red alert sounded. We all ran out to put ourselves in fox holes, but the planes were too quick and we didn't have time. If I were a believer I would imagine a punishment from God to be like this. I am running through a spongy quagmire in uncomfortable and leaky boots and suddenly the sky opens and silver arrows appear. They stop in the air, turn round and bombs begin to explode on all sides. I throw myself head first into a crater left by a previous attack and when I lift my head from the grass, there is the monster returning to the heights.

Many years later, I read, dumbfounded, *Sea Harrier over the Falklands* by Commander Sharkey Ward. Ward was the leader of 801 Sea Harrier Squadron, which operated from the aircraft carrier *Invincible* and it was he who directed that attack on Fox Bay.

"When the flare went off it seemed to be in the right place – right on target. Now, for Fox Bay. The second target was well covered in thick cloud, but that made no difference to the attack profile. My radar confirmed what the Navhars was telling me and I had no doubt at all when I pickled the bomb-release button that the Lepus was again bang on target. It was easy as riding a bike. Having seen the glow from the flare through the cloud, I turned to the east in the climb and set off on the long dog-leg home."

In the book, the real enemies of Sharkey Ward were the dusty bureaucrats of the British Navy, who would not let him wage war in his own style. In his almost 400 pages the flying ace compares himself to a Formula One driver performing marvels with a prodigious toy. It is not strange that the first names in his list of thanks are those of the designers and builders of his Sea Harrier.

I had no idea of any of this while the grass and the peat and the fear were getting to me through my jacket – rigid with so much dirt – in the leaden hills of Fox Bay.

Luckily there was no one aboard *Penélope* because in this attack a piece of shrapnel damaged the main mast and another broke the radio, as a result of which all communication with Puerto Argentino was lost.

That attack was also in part responsible for taking the *Buen Suceso* out of combat. From when it beached the week before, the crew members had little else to do but fetch water and keep themselves sane.

The transport ship had been left stranded without any chance of moving since the storm on the night when we arrived at Fox Bay. The jetty to which it had been moored was a little wooden construction which moved like an accordion under the pounding of the ship and finally gave up. The propeller and part of the stern remained aground with no way of moving them. Captain Niella saw that they were going to run out of drinking water and ordered rainwater to be stored in empty fuel tanks and the rationing of what was left.

Eduardo Rivero, the Able Seaman from González Llanos's mining team, who was on the deck of the *Buen Suceso* that day, remembers the Sea Harrier attack like this: "I was on watch in the bow of the ship and I see something coming down from a mountain in front of Fox Bay and I say to Ovidio Bertorello: 'There's a plane coming over there.' Before he could agree, it was already, that second, over the ship. I remember that Ledesma began to fire with his .45 pistol and I say to him: 'You think you will hit it with that?' It was a reconnaissance flight, round about eleven in the morning. The attack with bombs came afterwards, but we were already on land. Luckily they made us disembark."

Captain Niella told me in Buenos Aires that after the reconnaissance flight he had a feeling that they were going to attack and managed to get nearly everybody ashore before it happened. "At the side of the Kelpers' house, some hundred and fifty or two hundred metres from the ship, was a place used maybe for keeping one of their vehicles, which because of its location and condition lent itself for some of us to stay there. When lunch was over, I proposed to Corvette Captain Héctor Zukowski that the men should go to these sheds as a matter of urgency. I told him: 'You get on with communications, while I will attend to getting the people ashore.'"

Niella blew heartily on the whistle which hung from his neck at all times and Rivero and the rest went ashore as quickly as possible down the mooring ropes which connected the deck to the tiny Fox Bay jetty.

"That was at 13.00" recalls Niella, "The attack by the English planes came at 13.28."

Niella, Captain Zukowski and the able seaman responsible for communications remained on board. "That was where they got me. When I was crossing the passage that leads to the ship's side to go up onto the bridge, a piece of shrapnel like this (and he shows the size with his fist) entered my thigh and various pellets hit my face.

The able seaman was worse; they had to take him off the ship on a stretcher. Once on land the regiment's nurse took care of him. From this moment on the crew of the *Buen Suceso* slept under a corrugated iron roof, practically in the open air.

This is how Rivero remembers it: "That wasn't even a stable. We were shitting ourselves with cold, and eating once a day, taking lunch and dinner together between four and seven: some kind of meat stew for which we caught a lamb. We were about eighty men. I remember we played football. We put together a ball from rags and paper." The NCOs and ratings took turns to do watches on the ship. In those circumstances, Eduardo managed to get near to his old boss from the mining operation and asked if there might be a place for him on the *Penélope*.

* * *

The middle part of May was a time of much anxiety and tension. After the sinking of the cruiser *General Belgrano* (May 2nd) and the last "no" from Galtieri to Alexander Haig, there was no margin for peace negotiations. The British fleet was already stationed around the Islands and would establish a beach head for the disembarkation of the troops who would advance on Port Stanley. But where would the attack come? From the North or from the South? The army regiment stationed at Fox Bay was preparing for an attack there and we would find ourselves in the middle of the fighting.

There was a serious problem with the transportation of food, munitions and supplies to the troops scattered around the islands. The *Córdoba,* which should have brought González Llanos the mines he lacked for mining the capital's outer harbour, never left its base. The *Buen Suceso* was unusable and the *Isla de los Estados* sunk. On May 16th a formation of Sea Harrier bombers went after the one transport ship that they lacked: the *Carcarañá.*

The *Carcarañá* was another ELMA cargo ship with a civilian crew. Unlike the *Buen Suceso,* the *Carcarañá* left Buenos Aires after the 200 mile "exclusion zone" was imposed around the Islands by the British forces and entered Puerto Argentino on April 26th. In anticipation of the imminent attack of May 1st, she had left two days before.

During the same Sea Harrier attack on Fox Bay, part of the formation dropped bombs on the *Carcarañá,* which was cruising the Falkland Sound. The ship was not seriously damaged and no crew member injured, but the Captain decided upon an immediate urgent evacuation before the possibility of another attack.

All the crew members climbed down ropes into an inflatable raft and two lifeboats. As Jorge Muñoz mentions in another of his books, this one about the civilians who participated in the War (*Civiles por Malvinas*), the formation of Sea Harriers passed over the rafts without attacking them, and the crew landed on a rocky promontory on East Falkland. Before nightfall the *Forrest* came for them. This little ship had already picked up Payarola and López, the survivors of the *Isla de los Estados.*

The following day we went in the *Penélope* to inspect the *Carcarañá.* Ni Coló mentions that: "once alongside, the Lieutenant and one of my comrades climbed up and went around it rapidly. There was nobody on board and to our surprise we made out two English aeroplanes flying at low height, which disappeared behind the mountains after passing close to us."

That comrade was me. From the scraps of memory that I conjure up while writing these pages, one of the times that I best and most vividly remember is that climb onto the deck of the *Carcarañá,* in a complete downpour, in the middle of a storm. The *Penélope* was banging against the hull of the enormous transport ship (measuring 180 m, almost double the length of the *Buen Suceso*). From the rail of the *Penélope* we climbed up the cat ladders (two ropes joined every half metre or so by bits of wood which made steps), which the crew had left when leaving the ship after the aerial attack. We were hanging from these ropes in the middle of the sea, our hands numb with cold. The 'schooner' and the rough waves looked further away and further down with each rung.

When we finally reached the deck, the *Carcarañá* seemed like a ghost ship, moving slowly in the storm without a soul on board. I went from cabin to cabin, picking up some of the personal belongings that the crew had not had time to take with them when they made their impetuous abandonment of the ship.

There were unmade beds, socks and vests on the floor, spectacles, books, framed photos; all the domestic relics of a life spent on the high seas and of men who construct their own little familiar worlds in order to spend months away from home. Their colleagues were now feverishly stuffing these things into bags so that even the least talisman that would make this or that sailor feel himself less homesick should not end up at the bottom of the sea. On one bed lay a book of pacifist essays about the First World War, by Herman Hesse, which, along with many of his novels, my father had encouraged me to read when I was an adolescent. It was the same book in Bruguera's pocket edition which was waiting for me in my room in the now so distant family home in Vicente López.

Back on deck, I discovered that the storm had got even denser. For a while I thought that if it got any worse, we weren't going to be able to get down onto the *Penélope.* When once again we stepped onto the cat ladders, the movement of the *Carcarañá* was making the ropes snake about and strike against the steel of the ship. We were carrying the most valuable and fragile things from the cabins in bags on our shoulders.

When everybody was finally on board the *Penélope* once again and we drew away from the drifting ghost ship, we followed the coast looking for the *Carcarañá's* crew, but only found the lifeboats and some petrol drums. That night we slept in Egg Harbour where we had left the Islanders.

Guillermo remembers a lot about that night because González Llanos honoured him with a post at his side during the voyage. "When the Lieutenant went to the toilet or left to walk about on deck, he told me the course to follow and the steering of the ship was in my care. I felt very useful and proud to be able to do it."

When González Llanos read this paragraph in his able seaman's memoires, he told me his reaction: "It made a big impact on me to read in his book how he felt that day and all that the confidence invested in him meant to him, when I told him 'OK, Ni Coló, take the wheel.' I never would have imagined all that was going through his head at that moment."

"Reading the book" I told him, "while the rest of us appear, especially Contreras and Peralta, you are the most important character..."

"OK, normally in a ship the captain is very present and when you are young, thirty-year olds seem like ancient mariners. Now I am fifty, with children in their thirties, I would regard someone like I was then as a baby, wouldn't I? It's all about image."

On the 19th, several sailors from the *Carcarañá* boarded the *Penélope* to check the state of their vessel and to find out if it was able to sail and to unload food and provisions for the hungry navy and army population that survived at Fox Bay.

This time, we of the *Penélope's* crew stayed on our 'schooner' and hoisted the *Carcarañá's* crew members onto the cargo ship. While some went down to the engine to see if it would move, others quickly got food from the store room. Back on deck, the sailors had dragged out a load of bags and boxes and were throwing them overboard. Down below, we were picking them up and putting them in our hold. The sun had already set before we got back to our refuge in the interior of Fox Bay.

The biggest part of the provisions from the *Carcarañá* were for the boys at Fox Bay, but some tins and above all some succulent steaks went into the *Penélope's* diminishing store cupboard. The day after the boarding of the cargo ship, 'Uncle' Luna made us some tremendous beef sandwiches.

During these days, I went several times to talk to the owner of the house where the few remaining locals who had stayed in Fox Bay were taking refuge. He seemed to be the only one who went outside and the first time that I saw him hanging out washing to dry on some wires behind the house I approached him. He was tall, stout, and seemed to have a weight on his shoulders, as well, as I recall, a lot of concerns. He told me that he was called Richard Cockwell and was not born on the Islands but regarded them as home. He said that he had no hatred or animosity towards the Argentine people, but that the Islanders felt themselves to be British and wanted to continue being so. He was the only one of the many Islanders I talked to with whom I dared – and he also dared – to talk about these matters.

When I saw Cockwell hanging out or taking in clothes and I didn't have anything to do, I used to walk to the house to ask him what he thought about the war and what was going to happen. While he used to complain that the British government had not paid attention to them, he hadn't been surprised by the reaction of Margaret Thatcher and the rapid dispatch of the fleet. He said that they were coming to fight, not for the Islands, but for national pride and he was sure that the conflict would be short and that Her Majesty's forces would win rapidly.

On something like my second or third visit, when he realised that I would not report him, he told me that it seemed to him that the Argentines would have difficulty in convincing the Islanders that they would be well treated, when they treated their own soldiers like dirt. He said that from his window he had seen army officers punching and mocking their soldiers and was appalled that they had organised nothing to allow them to sleep and eat decently. Cockwell spoke very eloquently and my biggest surprise was when he began to tell me what was happening in Buenos Aires, Córdoba or Rosario. He had statistics from human rights organisations and was the first to tell me about the disappeared and the tortured while the wind shook the drying washing in his farm at Fox Bay. His argument was that besides feeling and wanting to stay British because of culture, tradition and language, his people had a very real fear that the Argentine dictatorship would do to them the same as it was doing to us.

From what I was telling him about these conversations, Guillermo writes in his memoirs: "A Kelper approached to hang clothes on the clothes line and spoke a little to the conscript Herrscher. He said that they wanted to live a tranquil life, in peace, as they had always done. They didn't like the English or the Argentines, but if they had to choose between the two, they would doubtless opt for the English. In the back yard of this man's house were his children: two blonde boys, very good looking and about six or seven years of age. One of them was getting his hair cut."

On May 21st, Guillermo recounts a change in the personnel of the *Penélope.* The Lieutenant made Seaman Second Class Salles disembark and "in his place came Seaman Second Class Eduardo Rivero, a submarine weapons technician."

The nights of the 20th and 21st finally saw the landing of the British marines and paratroopers in the Islands, but at the opposite end to Fox Bay, in San Carlos Bay, on the north of East Falkland, where, for some reason, no one was expecting them. In a fragmented manner we learned that a landing craft had been sunk and another seriously damaged and that the brave Pucará pilots had performed great feats. However the British troops had achieved their objective of setting up a beachhead, were making themselves a defensive position there and in a little while would begin their march towards the Argentine positions. As we didn't have a short wave radio, we had to trust the reports that the crew of the *Buen Suceso* and the army came to tell us. In general, Radio Carve from Montevideo was most listened to, because even the officers realised that little came from the Argentine radio stations that could be accepted with any degree of certitude.

That day, in the middle of febrile rumours about the landing, the 'schooner' carried out another mission for the army; we took a corporal and two conscripts to a place called Carcass Bay, where they were to keep watch from a cape in case the attack came that way. The previous days had brought a number of day time attacks by Sea Harriers and night time bombardments from frigates, stationed far beyond the firing range of the Argentine anti-aircraft batteries.

On another occasion we took army personnel to Port Edgar, where they were sure that they had seen a helicopter brought down by fire from their regiment. Guillermo remembers: "When we were nearly at the entrance to Port Edgar the Lieutenant told me that we should take up our rifles and be on permanent alert because we could be going into combat. We covered all the area of the bay close to the coast very well, but we didn't find the remains of the helicopter. This didn't surprise us, because we were completely sure that it hadn't been touched by a single bullet."

On the 24th May in preparation for the celebration the following day of First National Government Day, we entered a house where there was running water from a tap. We went to the bathroom in twos, stripped off, and threw water over ourselves from a jar. It was our first chance for a wash, almost from the day before we left for Stanley and we had been sleeping in our uniforms and many times with our boots on. During the first week the smell of our bodies seemed worse each day. After that, as the days passed by, we always smelled the same. On the *Penélope* there were two theories: one that our noses had got used to it and the other that there is a maximum limit of filth, and that after that it doesn't matter how many days go by, it won't get any worse, because we will have already reached rock bottom. I held to the second theory.

The thing was that after this wash, I at least experienced several hours of indescribable well-being. It was like being a baby again, wrapped in perfumed towels, but the following day the feeling was worse than if we had never bathed. Once again began a week of feeling oneself smellier with every passing day. Our sense of smell, which after three weeks in that tigers' cage had lost all its acuteness, began to suffer from the nausea-inducing nature of our aroma all over again once reawakened to the smell of cleanliness.

I got on well from the first with my new watch companion. Rivero was just as pleasant to me and more talkative than Salles, with whom I had exchanged few words during our nights on watch in the wheelhouse. During it all, Peralta never tired of hearing Elvis's songs, nor Contreras of looking at his family photographs nor Ni Coló of reading the letters from his family and his girlfriend for the umpteenth time.

I was already near to finishing my novel and I didn't want to get to the end, because the hero, as I saw each time more clearly, was at the point of deciding to kill himself. The literary works that I had read and learned to dissect at my English college – like George Eliot's *Silas Marner*, E M Forster's *Where Angels Fear to Tread*, Shakespeare's *Macbeth, Merchant of Venice* and *Henry V* – had prepared me for Graham Greene's world. On one hand, the precise and virile poetic language, where each description and each speech takes the reader further and further into the internal universe of the author and into a complex and lucid vision of human nature and on the other the constant preoccupation with the themes of piety, empathy, cruelty and guilt so characteristic of English literature.

At the beginning of the Second World War, Henry Scobie, the novel's hero, was falling head-long into hell in the insufferable heat of a small British colony, in the most lost part of East Africa. In another distant British colony, forty years later, an Argentine conscript was fleeing from the nightmares of war and drawing strangely close to the enemy, as a result of a moral tragedy which he had found in the library of a colonial officer in Port Stanley.

The morning of May 25th, National Holiday, 172nd anniversary of the establishment of the first national government in 1810, found us in good spirits. The day dawned brightly and we were clean – although still in the same filthy clothes – for a military parade which was, as Guillermo says, "a simple ceremony made even more emotional because of the circumstances in which we were living."

That day, González Llanos suggested to Naval Command in Puerto Argentino that the *Penélope* could take some thirty drums of JP1 fuel for helicopters from Fox Bay to Darwin. The drums had been delivered to the main outposts in the Islands in anticipation of the arrival of the helicopters which the ELMA ship *Córdoba* was going to leave in those places. But the *Córdoba* and its helicopters never arrived, the drums were of no use in the South and by contrast, it seemed that they would be necessary in Darwin given the imminence of an attack by land forces.

As soon as he received the go-ahead, the Lieutenant called us together and explained the way in which we were going to put the drums in the *Penélope's* hold. It wasn't an easy task as the little ship was anchored in the middle of the bay, joined to the beach by a thick steel cable and it would be necessary to get the heavy drums, which were presently in the mountains, first rolled onto the beach, then floated out to the boat. This manoeuvre would need to be repeated several times, because there were a lot of drums. Eduardo Rivero believes he remembers that there were 43.

* * *

With the dinghy, a little wooden life boat that we always kept tied up behind the *Penélope*, we had to transport the drums from the beach, tied on with ropes, till we could lift them up one by one with ship's primitive hoist. I was in the group which waited to put the drums in the hold and stack them. From there I could see neither Guillermo, nor Daniel nor Carlos. In his book Guillermo says that this was the day when he earned his dinner. "All the time that this manoeuvre was going on I was sleeveless and with water up to my elbows; I was cold, completely frozen. When we finished I ran to the galley and put my hands on the stove because I could scarcely move my fingers."

The one who definitely had the worst time was Peralta, who fell in the water in the middle of the operation. "At one point, I saw a drum which was about to fall on top of one of you, I don't remember who. I tried to grab it from the little wooden jetty and went in the water. It was very deep, I couldn't touch the bottom." We got him to the *Penélope* as quickly as possible and came close to putting him almost whole into the oven. He was shivering, but as always, smiling and calm. As he didn't have any more clothes, the Lieutenant lent him an overall.

That night 'Uncle' Luna's stew seemed particularly nutritious, and thinking of the long and dangerous day's sailing ahead of us, everybody went to bed except Rivero and I who had to take the first watch. After midnight we were falling asleep. Eduardo, who needed to go to the toilet, asked me if I would stay on my own for a little while. The so-called toilet was a little room without lights, stuck onto the wheelhouse, which hardly left any room to pass from one side of the stern to the other. In this cubicle there was a tin, like those in which you might mix paint, crowned by a toilet seat. When each person finished his business, he took the tin, removed the seat and threw the contents into the sea. As it was attached by a cord, it was lowered into the water, rinsed out and then filled again to leave ready for anyone who might need it.

That time the needy one was Eduardo, who entered the room at the back a minute before hell broke out. "I was taking off my overall to do the necessary, when I felt that everything was moving. I said: 'Hey, they've begun to fire' and I shouted, 'Jersch (for Herrscher) where are you?' You said: 'Here I am.' I felt glass jumping on every side and little bits of severed sling and there you are stretched out at the side of a fuel drum and I was splashed by something that fell like water. It was a liquid from your side, which turned out to be diesel."

"And where was I stretched out?"

"Behind the diesel drum, don't you remember? You were behind the drum. We had asked the *Buen Suceso* for that drum; it was fuel for our ship. And in the hold and above were 34 drums of JP1. I say to you, 'look, wait here' and I wake everybody up and I tell them: 'they are firing, we've got to disembark! They say 'Don't fuck about,' but they stick their heads out and it's an inferno. Those on land were shouting: 'Disembark, *Penélope*, disembark!'"

Daniel Peralta was sleeping. "The explosion broke the hull and some shrapnel passed over my head. The flashes lit up the night through the hole in the ship's hull. I lifted my head. I saw everything red and then everything went dark. I started to dress calmly."

Able Seaman Peralta did everything calmly.

This is how Guillermo remembers it: "I was dressed. I sat on the bed for a minute, made the sign of the cross and ran out, bumping into Contreras and Luna who were putting on their boots. I climbed the ladder and was running across the deck towards the stern when another bomb went off. They were making one hell of a din and lighting up the whole place."

As for me, I have wiped from memory the seconds which followed the first bombardment which broke the windows of the wheelhouse. The first thing I remember is being stretched out on deck, covered with broken glass and the following second, with a great racket, a piece of shrapnel burst a fuel drum which was almost next to my head. The noise and the shock wave made me giddy and that's how I was found by the Lieutenant who had emerged like a cat from a cave. He says that when he saw me, he was sure that I was wounded.

* * *

The others were already putting weapons and blankets in the dinghy to take ashore. Nobody doubted that if the thunder and flashes of the bombs were to continue like they were the *Penélope* would soon be at the bottom of the bay, or worse, flying through the air with all its cargo of barrels of helicopter fuel.

Before leaving the 'schooner', González Llanos asked Eduardo to go to the engine room with him and from there to the hold to see whether any of the drums were already breached. "We went down with Horacio to see the cans below. I'm just going down the ladder and with the shock wave from another bomb, I fall on my back on top of the engine. I lift up my head and he says: "Are you alright?" and I say, "Yes, I'm here."

"And you fell onto the engine?"

"A big shock wave like a wind grabbed me from in front; I fell backwards and bashed my spine. But I say, 'I'm OK, I didn't bang my head.' We had a torch and we got back into the boat again. Then you all fell on top of me, remember? It was terrible, bombs were falling all around and everybody was falling on top of me, in the pitch darkness, in the midst of the bombardment..." Because of the adrenalin and excitement Eduardo wasn't thinking about his back and the fall onto the engine, but at that moment he felt an unbearable pain.

Guillermo Ni Coló was one of the first to jump on top of poor Rivero. "When I got to the boat, Rivero was already there. I jumped and I don't know where I landed, whether on my feet or my head, I don't know, but Rivero was underneath. I don't know if it was me that hurt his back. I was the first to jump and I fell on him. Later I went off to look for guns and bring them to the boat."

"Are we all here?" the Lieutenant asked.

Peralta was missing.

"I got to the dinghy and everybody was saying; "Hurry up Peralta, we are waiting for you." Daniel remembers. "The bombs continued to light up the night, as if there was fire in the sky."

We were getting away from the *Penélope* and stunned and silent we began in turns to pull on the metal cable, which tied us to the beach. That was the moment when I looked up and saw the red and white planking on the starboard side of the schooner, from down below, at sea level: the same image which I recalled in Hamburg in Christian Bauer's little wooden skiff, a whole lifetime later, in July of 2006.

All seven of us were whole, but we were still not safe.

CHAPTER 5

Meeting again in Saladillo

Guillermo Ni Coló comes in through the door into the garden with a tray overflowing with sausages and black pudding. Later he would bring in barbecued ribs, steaks, the lot. The meal is stupendous, especially for an Argentine living away from his own country. Guillermo tells us that he hired an old barbecue chef from Saladillo, who keeps sending miracles to the table from the bottom of the garden. I sit down between Contreras and Ni Coló, but the owner of the house hardly stops coming and going until it is time for dessert.

Without anyone arranging it, the seven of us from the *Penélope* are sitting at one end of the long table and all the families are at the other. At one point I observe that the manner of the NCOs who are still in the navy is more formal towards their old lieutenant than that of Rivero and Ni Coló, who both left the service years ago.

Peralta and Conteras address him with the formal 'usted' and Horacio protests and says that they should use the less formal 'vos' like the others. González Llanos tells us that when he started his post military career with a car firm, it took a while to adjust to being called 'vos' by everybody. Now he was so used to it that it came as a shock, when old companions from his former existence returned to the use of 'usted.'

Just in time, when the last meat is brought in and it's time to dismantle the barbecue, the drizzle turns to rain. Several of us go out with Guillermo to get what remains, and there, surprisingly, an old vision of a dreamed childhood is hoisted before my eyes.

At the bottom of the garden, perched on a tree, I see an authentic play house made of wood. It has been half destroyed by a storm, but this only gives it a certain air of childish adventure. It is the tree house that Guillermo built for his children.

When it comes to time for coffee, the seven of us sit in the living room. I leave my notebook resting on my knees and start to try to put together the whole jigsaw puzzle of our voyage. A good portion of this old story that I am telling comes out of those hours of recollection together in Saladillo.

At one point Peralta comes up to me and putting his hand on my shoulder, says; "Roberto, mate, you never sent me the book." "What book?" I ask in surprise. "The one you were reading."

* * *

Now I understand everything. The person I had talked to about Greene's *Heart of the Matter*, the one to whom I told the story with its moral dilemma and to whom I promised to send it, was Peralta and not Ni Coló. I think that when I met Guillermo and found out that he had left the navy to work in the Chamber of Deputies and had finished his law studies, something inside me decided that it was with him that I had all those conversations about the book. Now, not only do I feel relieved of my confusion, but also about the fact that Guillermo, who has a good memory, could not remember the book at all. In some strange way, I end up learning the last lesson of my military service.

When dessert time arrives, we are all already bursting with so much good food and my Falkland Islands cake has to compete with others of much more presence and more vibrant colours besides. As Guillermo had taken charge of the barbecue, almost everybody else had brought cakes. However we all find a small corner to sample this taste which comes from the far away islands and the ladies make packets of the large portion remaining so that everyone can take home some of this cake from the Malvinas. My parents try it the following day and it seems to them, says my mother, that its sweet taste is like when an internal wound is beginning to heal and when on passing your tongue around the inside of your mouth you don't feel the sour taste of blood as much.

Peralta, Contreras and his family have to undertake the long journey to Punta Alta, so the three cars leave a little after six and we all begin to return, each one to his own world. González Llanos leaves me in Puente Saavedra and continues on to the capital, to take Luna and Susana home.

The lights of the end of Sunday are blinking in the shop windows. People pass by without stopping to look at the goods on sale, with their hands on their bags and with steam issuing from their mouths like the dragons of their own nightmares. As I walk, this time without my cake, I can't stop thinking that Puente Saavedra is where the naval bus dropped me off that 21st of June, 1982.

From the Falklands, the English ferry *Norland* left us in Puerto Madryn where we got on a bus belonging to the navy, which took us to the naval base at Trelew. From there, a commercial aircraft flew us to Ezeiza and afterwards a naval bus distributed us around, throughout the Buenos Aires night. I didn't want, I couldn't, arrive at the door of my house and ring the bell. Is it still here? Is the war over? Have I returned and does life go on?

I wanted to return, but first I needed to walk and to breathe. I felt in some way that I would not be able to explain, that I wasn't prepared to deal with embraces. Even today I don't know how to explain that need, however I may keep on recognizing it. A little time ago, when I was telling my mother about that walk she could not understand why I would want to delay for those extra minutes, and if I were her, I wouldn't understand it either.

THE SEVEN OF US posing in front of Ni Coló's house in Saladillo with the families of Luna, Rivero, Contreras and Ni Coló.

The bus dropped me in Puente Saavedra. I walked the fifteen blocks home looking at people with infinite strangeness. I first went down Maipú Avenue, which I remember as dark and grey and then I skirted the paving of Roca Street, with car lights glinting off every cobble and the so familiar sound of tyres against that mattress of granite blocks. After every war, those who return remember their amazement that life in cities has gone on the same, while they were under fire and their companions were dying. I had already given up trying to understand my country on April 2nd, when everything went crazy and now I didn't understand how everything had gone back to normality.

Normality! In that instant I already knew that I was carrying within me a sleeping volcano. I had to calm down. I had to arrive whole and ready for all the questions. I had to forget about my pain and the past to meet with my family, my girlfriend and my friends once again.

First, however, I had to be alone. I had to walk from Puente Saavedra by a route, which I knew very well, because half of it had been my normal way to go to college. I had to arrive, but little by little. From that time on, I now go walking whenever I feel a new piece of shrapnel might explode in me, or when, from time to time, the same old piece of shrapnel returns: the one from the oil drum on the night of May 26th 1982.

* * *

This account of our meeting came out in *La Sintesis* of Saladillo the day after our barbecue:

TOGETHER ON DRY LAND JUST AS THEY WERE AT SEA

"A windy cold morning, like many in the south of Gran Malvina. But not as impious as in those places where the *Feuerland*, later renamed *Penélope*, sailed. It is Saladillo and the host is Guillermo Ni Coló. "It wasn't easy getting all the *Penélope*'s crew together; two of them live in Bahía Blanca and another one in Barcelona."

"Today with Guillermo Ni Coló (left of photo) are Roberto Herrscher (centre) Carlos Contreras, Horacio González Llanos (right of photo) Eduardo Rivero, Julio Peralta and Oscar Luna."

"Herrscher teaches journalism at the University of Barcelona. "We are among colleagues" he says. "This meeting moves and excites me. I was in the Islas Malvinas last week. The people respect us. I can't say how I found the Malvinas, because I didn't know it except during the war. I can't compare these two occasions. They are 3,000 people with the characteristics of a village of 3,000 people."

"Between hugs and tears, memories emerge of days impossible to forget, when the ever constant presence of death prevented them from getting to know each other, Ni Coló said: "We didn't know each other; we didn't know who each one was, because we didn't talk of the future or of any plans after the war. We couldn't do it. Because of that, this is now permanently post-war and all in good time we can keep on getting together and, of course, getting to know each other and closing wounds."

"Horacio González Llanos, ex commander of the *Penélope*, told us that "the joy is in all of us being able to get together. I live in the centre of Buenos Aires, but this is a place for living. I am very happy sharing this occasion, which will surely be repeated. We will go on doing it in different places."

"A present from Malvinas: Roberto Herrscher visited the islands a few days back and brought with him a gift which yesterday served as dessert: a cake from the Malvinas. It was something both unexpected and tasty."

CHAPTER 6

A small bitter victory

The shells kept on falling around the rowing boat and filling the night with red. The *Penélope* had remained alone, forsaken, at the mercy of the bombardment. The beach was boiling with men running in every direction. We were pulling with all our might on the cable that joined us to the land.

Rivero says that he remembers we had not brought the oars. "I was in the bow then and I jumped out to set foot on land, but fell in the water and you had to rescue me. Because of this I spent the whole night sleeping wet."

On land and more or less safe, Rivero's stomach reminded him that he had still not been able to go to the toilet and his need was now much greater. "I asked everyone if they had any paper and Mi Coló told me: 'The only paper I have is my girlfriend's letter. Don't even think about it!' 'No' I said, 'I'm not going to use the letter, but at least let me have the envelope.' The thing is that I had wanted to go to the toilet since the bombardment began, but then I no longer could. I went off to a corner. We were on the shore with the guys from the *Buen Suceso* and others from the *Carcarañá* and at about half past three or four o'clock in the morning they began to say that someone had died.

There was a death, our first death.

The stories were at first a little confused. While we were flattened against the freezing sand of the beach, in a hollow which made an improvised refuge from the bombs which kept reddening the sky and filling our heads with noise and fury, a conscript came to tell us that a column which was pulling or carrying something from a position in the mountains had run into the bombardment in open country. They began to run, but one was killed.

Little by little I got the full story. They were running in indian file and it seems that someone began to fire sending a bullet through the helmet of the man in front. He then tripped and fell, and in the process shot himself in the neck. Later, when a bigger group came to occupy our hollow, I learned the name of the dead man. It was sailor Turano.

Turano's death made a big impression on me. Every time that I meet war mongers, both those who were in favour of this absurd war and those who were in favour of all the much bloodier others, which followed and keep on following, I picture the face of this cheerful, tireless boy, full of nervous energy. His death filled me with bitterness and rage against those who had sent us to kill and to die in this cold corner of the world, without either trees or compassion.

When the British frigates stopped spitting shells Lieutenant González Llanos took the rowing boat and returned to the *Penélope* to get blankets for everybody. Some soldiers appeared in our hole and I remember especially a military chaplain, who didn't stop muttering the rosary all night. I had frozen feet like two blocks of ice, whose pain kept me from sleeping and the litany in my ears, far from lulling me to sleep or tranquilising me, filled me even more with hatred and rage against the god of battles, the lord of fundamentalism and intolerance. I can repeat on this page the endless prayer that I was forced to learn that night at Fox Bay, listening to the officer cleric with a pistol in his belt and a crucifix round his neck.

"Hail, Mary, full of grace. The Lord is with thee. Blessed art thou among women and blessed is the fruit of thy womb, Jesus. Holy Mary, mother of God, pray for us now and at the hour of our death. Amen. Hail, Mary, full of grace. The Lord is with thee. Blessed art thou among women and blessed is the fruit of thy womb, Jesus. Holy Mary, mother of God, pray for us now and at the hour of our death. Amen...," and he went on and on and on, and with each little plastic ball, the hour of our death returned in the cleric's arrogant and frightened voice and the memory that I want to shake off, but which returns, brings me back to the steam which issued from his mouth with each repetition.

Rivero remembers another prayer from that night, this time from a seaman that he knew: "There was this seaman, who it seems was a bit of a wife-beater and while the rain of bombs continued, all night he was saying: 'my love, I will never hit you again.'"

* * *

The next day Peralta, Contreras and Ni Coló got to work making a proper shelter, since the Lieutenant had decided that we should go back to sleeping on the beach. Daniel remembers that about ten metres from the shore they chose a spot, "on a mountain of earth. We went off to look for tools and came across a pneumatic hammer which worked with petrol. We made the hole and covered it with metal, but everybody else got into it before we had a chance." The three ratings stayed outside, "in tremendous cold which got into my bones and didn't let me sleep."

Before dawn, Peralta saw González Llanos getting up and the two of them went back to the *Penélope*. "I'm sure he couldn't sleep either."

That day Peralta and I went to get water from the tap where we normally filled the buckets, but once there I had a great shock; there was Turano's body covered by a green blanket. The blanket was short and his brown boots stuck out from under it. The day was bright, without clouds and almost windless. I could not get over how still the body was. While so many other things slip from the memory like grains of sand through the fingers, I can still see those seconds of walking towards the watering place, in nightmares, awake or asleep.

Guillermo remembers that he was busy making the fox hole: "and I went over to where Contreras was and he showed me the body, which was on a stretcher and half covered up. I was annoyed with Contreras; I didn't want to see that kind of thing. I knew that from the first day when I arrived in the Malvinas; that if there was no need for it, I wasn't going to go to see things … I didn't want to bring back sad memories from there. I was lucky enough to get home and I was going to try to avoid the worst of it. I have more or less managed to do this."

A little while ago, I was working in my office in Barcelona, when some mail came for me from Martin Virtel, the German journalist. This was before he published his article on my adventures on the *Penélope* and looking for information on the internet, he had come up with the report by the operations commander of the British Special Boat Service (SBS) on the attack on Fox Bay on May 26th.

"With British forces firmly established on East Falklands the Argentine battalion stationed at Fox Bay on West Falklands could, it was supposed, entertain the possibility of attacking the British flanks, while they were preparing to attack Stanley. Something had to be done to harass the Argentine forces in the area and keep them occupied. Trying to avoid having to dispatch a significant troop contingent to attack Fox Bay, the planners decided to use a deadly combination of naval fire and special forces."

The special forces were 148 Commando SBS, who disembarked on Knob Island to guide the fire from HMS *Plymouth*. This was surely the landing that the army commandos had gone on *Penélope* to look for at Port Edgar, without success.

"With the corrections given by 148 Commando, *Plymouth* bombarded the Argentine fuel and ammunition dumps. Naval artillery is much more accurate than land, thanks to the fact that the guns are stabilised gyroscopically and have computerised aiming systems. Also a ship's main gun can fire repeatedly, taking many shots per minute. The effect of such a powerful weapon under the direction of well-trained men strategically placed on land caused much consternation and confusion in the Argentine positions."

I continued to work preparing my classes at the university, but I couldn't get out of my head those two words, *consternation* and *confusion*, inserted in a cold technical report.

Yes, that was that night: consternation and confusion, and many other things from which we will perhaps never recover.

* * *

The next day we began the voyage.

I don't recall the farewell to Fox Bay. Like so many other times during the war, all my senses were taken up simply with doing things well, with surviving.

This is how Jorge Muñoz describes the beginning of that long voyage: "once the loading was finished they decided to attempt the crossing of Falkland Sound, which was made impossible by the presence of two British frigates, which on the night of May 27th came into the southerly entrance of the strait to head for Fox Bay with the intention of shelling our positions. After other frustrated efforts, due to the possibility of detection by enemy ships, or by their intense air patrols, at a speed of four knots, the *Penélope* crossed Falkland Sound, which had already cost many lives with the consequent loss of several ships in similar circumstances. Hiding in inlets and creeks almost inaccessible to ships of larger size and the protection of darkness were the only guarantees on which they counted for a slow voyage, without cover of any kind."

With no radar, no sonar, no radio and no good charts and with a total armament of a pair of pistols and a couple of old rifles made rusty by the sea water, the *Penélope* undertook the long trip half way round the Falklands, crossing the sound between the two islands on the widest side and afterwards sailing very close to the coast to the capital in the north-east of the islands. The first night the Lieutenant decided to put into Low Bay, in front of the small Bougainville Island. The distant flashes of the battle in Goose Green could be seen in the dark and faint sounds of explosions and gun fire were heard. Ni Coló, Contreras and Peralta were awake nearly all night.

The following day only the constant wind could be heard. The rough sea would not even let the Lieutenant go ashore in the rowing boat. In Guillermo's account the three ratings managed to go ashore in the afternoon with the sea already calmed down and González Llanos asleep in the cabin. When he woke up and saw them on land, he reprimanded them for having gone without his authorisation. He told them: "that he knew our keenness and our determination for getting tasks done, but he was in charge of us all and if anything happened he would be the one held responsible."

That night Guillermo covered the first watch with the Lieutenant. "He was telling me that he didn't see any likelihood of spending his birthday at home with his family, so I asked him when his birthday was and he told me it was June 12th. I retorted that he should have no problems because by that date we were going to be on our way back. I wasn't sure of anything, but I showed the optimism that we all thought was necessary to prevent depression overcoming us. Later on he sat in a corner and remained for a long time in silence looking from side to side."

After many incommunicative hours, Horacio took the radio and succeeded in contacting Puerto Argentino; "You saw all the time that I was sitting there without talking? I prayed a rosary that the radio would work again and it got results," he said.

The fragments of Ni Coló's book where he describes González Llanos with admiration are among the most moving. While I was bottled up reading my book, Guillermo was noting in his diary things which he was to write many years later in his book: paragraphs like this: "I already knew the Lieutenant a bit better and noticed when he appeared worried and nervous and this indicated that we might have some problem. While we were sailing that afternoon he seemed that way again. He was clinging to the wheel, but straining to look ahead, first through one window and then through the other, as if wanting to identify something. I asked him what was going on and he answered that he thought he had seen a ship at the entrance to the bay".

So as not to run into a vessel which might be an enemy, González Llanos steered the 'schooner' towards Bleaker Island, and we spent a quiet night there, without storms or the noise of bombs.

That was May 28th. In Goose Green they were fighting hand to hand and we were lost, alone in what seemed to me to be the ends of the earth, sailing along steep coasts inhabited by peevish penguins and over confident sea lions. That night the war seemed – or I wanted it to seem – as far away as Buenos Aires or the 18th century. I think it was on that night when the Lieutenant, who was on watch in the wheelhouse, asked me to fetch him a coffee. Every one of those days we were working like donkeys and only sleeping half the night because the other half we were on watch. I was dropping with sleep and in the darkness of the galley and the confusion of tiredness, I threw two good spoonfuls of salt into the coffee.

I came slowly out on deck by the bow companionway. It was very cold and the wind was hitting me in the face, but the moon and stars lit up everything with a magical halo. I reached the wheelhouse and handed over the mug. The Lieutenant grasped the handle, thanked me and took a sip to get the cold out of his body. Immediately he stuck his head through the door and spat energetically. I still remember the second he delayed before reacting. His reaction was a burst of laughter and I flew to the galley to make him another coffee, this time with sugar.

Why do I remember this irrelevant anecdote of the coffee with salt so much? There are things which have no rational explanation and in my case many years later I got to thinking about why so many of my strongest memories of the islands have to do with tastes and smells – the *Buen Suceso*'s bread, 'Uncle'

Luna's mutton stew – and not with meditations and chats about life, courage or patriotism.

On the following morning, I came out on deck, and from the bay where we were anchored a crystalline clarity on the choppy surface of the sea welcomed me. I clung to the rough beauty of the landscape as if to an interior world where the war and fear could not make an impression. I was continuing to write letters to my parents and to my girlfriend without knowing how or when I might send them. In the letters I tried to write minute descriptions of the dolphins, the penguins and the seagulls of the coast.

In a joking tone, the Lieutenant commented at dinner that perhaps we should stay on this island until the end of the war – which could be months – and 'Uncle' Luna and the ratings, also jokingly, began to imagine life in this lost corner of the world, hunting and fishing and installed in an abandoned house that I remember not very far from the jetty. The house had boarded over windows. Inside, I remember, like in a mist, the kitchen with cans – the majority out of date and rusty – and on the wall, a buckled and yellowing calendar from 1979.

"We were without radio and one of those nights the attack on Darwin happened, I don't know if you remember," Horacio González Llanos says to me. "We were listening to the artillery fire because we were relatively close, just a bit to the north. Suddenly we were listening to some radio as well and we said, 'we are dreaming' because Darwin must be full of English ships. I remember that when we were in this house I climbed up to the top of the hill and when I got there I looked and I saw ships, which afterwards they said could have been the *Irízar* which was sailing to Puerto Argentino. I saw the ships a very long way away, or at least one ship. What with this and the landing, we already came up with the idea of staying on the farm with a lot of sheep."

Daniel Peralta remembers that the sea was very lively that day and that he went onto the island with Guillermo and Carlos. In the house they found a bow, some arrows and a target.

As Guillermo tells it in his book: "We disembarked, armed that time, and went slowly towards the house. The doors were shut. Then I went round to the back and there I could get the wood off one of the windows, which opened and made getting in easy. It had already been abandoned and was very comfortable. The only furnishings were three beds and there was some food in the kitchen cupboards."

Contreras, Peralta and Ni Coló said that we didn't have much food and went off to catch a sheep. I don't remember which one of them said that he knew how to butcher sheep and that they would kill one with a bayonet and then we would have fresh lamb to dine on.

The ratings came back two hours later. I remember them telling me that they hadn't been able to catch a single sheep. But that night – and this is one of my strongest memories of my three months in the islands – the idea of staying on this little island for ever returned and this time it didn't sound like a joke. I wanted to stay; I didn't want to return to the war. I even started to imagine spending months with Lieutenant González Llanos, with 'Uncle' Luna and the four ratings in this paradise, so cold, so lonely, so peaceful, so far from the world. From the distance flashes were seen and bombs heard and everything seemed unreal and far away. Why not? Escape, flight, just meant staying immobile on a little island that perhaps was not on the maps.

That was the best night's sleep that we had on the *Penélope*. Warm, with the stove lit, and just a gentle rocking motion, I closed my eyes tight to imagine that we were staying there; that we were fleeing from the war.

Recently, 24 years after that day, I finally find out what really happened when the three ratings went out to run after sheep. I am in the Congress bar where we meet with Ni Coló. The former able seaman, in the flesh a robust, smiling person with grey hair, tie, coat and scarf, leans his elbows on the marble table and gets ready to tell me what happened that day.

"It's a lie that they got away from us," Guillermo begins, playing with a teaspoon. "We got hold of at least three, but we couldn't do it." He pauses and takes a sip of coffee. The three sailors had bayonets in their hands, but none of them could bury one in the animal's neck. The first sheep was fat and between the three of them, they decided that it must be pregnant. The second was thinner, but Guillermo says that neither he nor his companions had the courage to kill an animal which was baaing for its life and looked at them with such big eyes. They let it go as well. They returned with empty hands and heads bowed down as I remember, and 'Uncle' Luna had to open cans and heat up the usual soup.

And that was the moment when he said it. He looked at me and shook his head. "But who were we going to kill, if we couldn't even kill a sheep?"

For a few seconds the two of us remained in silence, smiling gently.

* * *

On Bleaker Island I felt myself very distant from my companions, despite the closeness in which we slept in that snug cabin, where Peralta continued with his Elvis cassettes, no matter what, and 'Uncle' Luna tried to cheer us up with more variations of the same stew.

"Then the Lieutenant called us together and said that we had only three drums of fuel left and that we could try to get to Puerto Argentino, or to home territory (the coast of Patagonia)" is how Peralta recalls it. "We told him that we could get to the coast with sails, but he remained firm and told us 'We are going to try to get to Puerto Argentino, whatever the cost' but we knew that the fuel might not last."

González Llanos explains to me: "We didn't have fuel for the *Penélope* and there were some drums of fuel on the farm, so I ordered Luna to see what kind of fuel it was. Luna analyses it by sight and touch, and says: 'yes, it's the right fuel for the boat.' We didn't need to use it, but when we got to Puerto Argentino we saw that it was the same as that for the helicopters, which we couldn't have used. We noticed this only when we got to Puerto Argentino. Luckily the fuel on the boat was enough to get us there."

"We had thought about staying on that island," remembers Eduardo Rivero, "but Horacio told us, 'No, we're going' and we set sail, coasting further along the Darwin Strait and there were aeroplanes. I think we left that day, June 2nd at five in the morning".

Eduardo narrows his eyes when he remembers the glassy calm of that last day's sailing. "We were making three knots. We saw the lights of a ship and thought it was one of the English ones, but it was our own hospital ship. Their ships were also passing by there."

That morning the Lieutenant had said to able seaman Ni Coló: "This time I am not stopping anymore, so you can crash into the *Hermes* (the british aircraft carrier)."

"We had left a rucksack in the stern with some food in it to take with us in case we had to abandon ship" Guillermo remembers. "We were also towing the dinghy astern on a rope. We joked that if we had to abandon ship and all seven of us got in the dinghy, it wouldn't support our weight and we would sink."

Without radio, sonar or radar, with an engine coughing gently and almost out of fuel the *Penélope* advanced towards the blockade of the capital and the Atlantic full of enemy destroyers, glued to the coast where the British paratroops were advancing after having taken Darwin. Analysing it now, in retrospect, the chances that the little 'schooner' would arrive at her destination were minimal. We still didn't know that the naval command in Stanley had already given us up as disappeared.

* * *

"We had to arrive at seven, in the dark. We passed close by the lighthouse. Do you remember the lighthouse?," enthuses Eduardo. "And we were afraid that those guys in the lighthouse would shoot at us with their rifles. Finally we were able to tell them not to shoot, that we were us … boats were an easy target to shoot at."

Ni Coló remembers repeating the message time and time again on the radio, without knowing whether it was received and whether the Argentine batteries had understood that one of their own was approaching. "We went on a little further and then on the radio we heard a voice coming from we knew not where, telling us the following; '*Penélope, Penélope,* don't reply. Skate close to the coast because there are tunny in the bay.' 'Tunny' were helicopters".

After this order, the Lieutenant said every one should get his rifle and wait on deck. Guillermo knows how to reconstruct this scene as if he were witnessing it: "I remember Peralta sitting on the hold cover. I took my gun and went to the bow. There was Contreras, sitting down with his gun between his slightly splayed legs and his hands interlaced. Surely he was praying. I sat down at his side and did the same."

González Llanos recounts that "when we arrived nearly at Puerto Argentino, ready to turn north and enter the inner harbor, we heard the radio telling us that that there were English helicopters about and we heard the helicopters – chucu, chucu,

chucu, chucu – I don't know if they were searching for us or for something else. So, well, we went ahead until we were in Puerto Argentino."

When finally, after nine at night, we made out the lights of Stanley and slowly entered the harbor, it seemed like the end of a dream. We knew that what was coming was going to be terrible, but we were about to meet our companions from the Apostadero again, get letters from our folks and be among the familiar.

We jumped ashore and the sailors tied us up at the jetty where the *Buen Suceso* had been a little more than a month ago. We hugged the conscripts from the Apostadero and in between mate (a traditional and popular argentine drink) and chocolate we told them about the exploits of the *Penélope* as if we were the heroes of an adventure story. I, an asphalt kid of the Buenos Aires middle classes, who grew up reading the adventures of Sandokán in the garden of my house, felt like a sailor, adventurer and Malaysian tiger.

Eduardo says that when the radio operator Manuel Escalada saw us arrive he could not believe it: "We had given you all up for dead" is what Manuel told him, he says.

We lay down on our bunks to enjoy our letters and messages. The girl from Mar del Plata, amongst others, had written to Peralta. She was sending him chocolates and sweets. Our families, wives and girlfriends were writing to all of us. I counted 27 letters, from between family near and far, my girlfriend, college friends, the Edificio Libertad, and childhood friends that I had not seen for years.

That night the feeling of all of us was that we had done something special and we slept in the round cabin in the bow, like young men in boys' stories who grow up to do heroic deeds; going over the most dangerous moments, exhausted, but satisfied at having been able to get to the end of the road.

The following day General Menéndez and Admiral Otero came onto the *Penélope*. González Llanos remembers that they emphasised the courage of the crew and the fact that, against all probability, the little ship had accomplished its mission. Guillermo with his prodigious graphic memory recalls Menendez slowly surveying the galley, mess and bunks compartment, "while holding his baton of command in his right hand and hitting his other hand with it. Later he briefly referred to the importance of our work, congratulated us and left."

"General Menendez still calls me now and then," González Llanos tells me. "I meet him frequently at the Malvinas war veterans' reunions that the Patricios Regiment holds in June. I go over to chat with him and he always remembers the *Penélope*. He remembers the day we arrived. For them it was an Argentine victory that a ship should have entered Puerto Argentino on June 2nd."

He remains pensive for a minute and suddenly says something for which I wasn't prepared: "It didn't do any good, because I remember doing the calculation of how far a helicopter of the kind that has two rotors and lifts tanks can go and the fuel that we carried was enough for about four hours flying time for such a helicopter, so ... that's nothing. But, well, it was the act of having broken the blockade with a little wooden ship under the noses of the English. That fundamentally was the triumph that the guy saw which made him so euphoric. It showed that anything was possible."

"Four hours?" I explode. We load drums that almost blow up, one of us falls in the water, one freezes his hands, one damages his back, we do this epic voyage with those drums of helicopter fuel, crossing enemy lines between the paratroopers in Darwin and the ships along the coast, they give us up for dead, we arrive safe and sound, all so that one of those helicopters could fly for four hours?

Of course the ARA *Penélope's* voyage was not for those four helicopter hours. Everyone has his own deep reasons be they love of country, to show others or to show themselves that they were carrying out their duty, to get to the end, or as the Lieutenant says, to show that anything is possible.

Now I stay silent, I take a sip of water and I ask González Llanos, still trying to digest it, "but are you sure that it wouldn't give more than four hours flying time?"

The day after our arrival I returned to 10 John Street where the officers of the Naval Command lived. My companions remained on the *Penélope* until the surrender, ten days later. I went to visit them when I could. Nothing was far away in a village of a thousand people and the jetty where the 'schooner' rested was about five blocks from the house.

The first thing they did was to paint the entire 'schooner' black. The last thing that Ni Coló did before going to look for the *Penélope* was to paint the sign APOSTADERO NAVAL MALVINAS. Now this sign was hanging in front of the jetty in the place previously occupied by the one which read: FALKLAND ISLANDS COMPANY. Once again, brush in hand, Guillermo and the other ratings applied themselves to painting black the deck, the wheelhouse, the hull and even the masts. That's how I found them when I dropped in hoping to taste again one of 'Uncle' Luna's glorious stews.

Every night, the *Penélope, Forrest* and *Monsunen* patrolled the harbour.

Guillermo includes in his memories that every so often the Lieutenant would take his binoculars and scan the night, leaving him in charge of the wheel. One of those mornings, Peralta asked to take a day's leave to accompany the commandos who were taking food to the forward positions. The British regiments were drawing nearer and nearer to the mountains that ringed the port and the atmosphere was gloomy and tense.

Back again in my room at the house, I saw officers coming and going with serious faces. The war was overtaking us and the rumours that penetrated the kitchen, where the conscript Diego Pezzoni and I spent most of our time, were confused, contradictory and in some cases, terrifying. It's difficult to reconstruct these rumours from a distance, trying to put myself in the place and the time when a 'mantle of fog' covered everything. Some said that there were a couple of regiments of paratroopers who would descend at any moment behind the British ranks which continued advancing, and that the navy would sail out from Puerto Belgrano when all the attacking forces were occupied with these paratroopers and that the war could still be won.

Others, especially the conscripts in the mountains who had spent two months waiting for combat and surviving half-dead from cold and hunger, said that no one would come out of this alive, that the British were excellent soldiers armed with the ultimate in technology and that in the first line of attack were the Ghurkhas, short Nepalese men, strong and fearless, who had curved swords with which they entered fox holes at night, cutting the throats of whole companies.

I have the exact image of a time when I was in the kitchen peeling potatoes and looking through the window at the ridiculous anti-air raid bunker in the garden and at the bottom the street and the Rose pub, while a couple of conscripts from the mountains were telling us stories about the Ghurkhas. At around that time Menéndez had made a speech to the troops on the radio, in which he said that nobody was going to surrender, but would fight on to the last man. In three or four days we would be behind sand bags, shooting our rifles in the streets of Stanley, against blood-thirsty Ghurkhas who would run at us screaming like lunatics and waving curved swords in their hands. The hour of combat was drawing near.

* * *

On one of those last days when we could already hear shooting in the mountains round about, one of the officers had the brilliant idea of disguising me as a kelper.

In the house there was still some of the outdoor clothing of the British civil servant who used to live there. Leading from the kitchen was a porch, typical of the Islanders' houses, which served as a kind of antechamber to the back door. There people took off their muddy shoes, hung up their heavy coats and, I think, there was also a washing machine. There were some overcoats, pullovers, woollen shirts and flannel trousers there.

As the authorities didn't want to leave the locals without provisions, they had forbidden the Argentine military of whatever rank to buy things in the shops or the community's supermarket, the West Store. With military and civilian personnel the population of Stanley had quintupled and obviously since April 2nd the food and supplies from Great Britain that the locals were used to receiving had not come in.

However, that night the High Command was going to meet at 10 John Street and had to have something to drink. It was then that this officer thought that I, being blonde and with a northern face (really I look more German or Slavic than English) could put on the clothes that were in the house, go to the West Store to buy as many bottles of whisky as I could carry and return whistling. As the Argentine civilians (journalists, postal clerks and radio people) were allowed to shop, it was possible to use Argentine pesos. The officer gave me a wad of notes which I put in the wide pocket of the trousers.

The plan allowed me to take off my green overall and experience what it was like to be a civilian once again. I remember that at the time I took it more as a game than a crime. After all, I was obeying the orders of a superior. The trousers were a bit tight on me, but the checkered shirt and the anorak fitted me well. With a tartan cap tilted to the right over my already long hair and a red scarf flung back, my disguise was almost complete.

I had walked many times through those cement streets – the only ones in the islands that weren't of earth – in the month and a bit that I had spent in Stanley, but always wearing the green uniform of a naval conscript. In the street I came upon military personnel from the three forces, but having already had a year of military service I had learned to recognize the ranks and insignia so that structured world held no secrets for me. Each movement in the occupied town had an order and a purpose. From the moment that I went out into the street disguised as a kelper, I noticed for the first time how strange it was to walk through streets full of soldiers and military police, with army lorries and jeeps everywhere.

I couldn't stop much; it was dangerous in case anyone recognized me. I arrived at Ross Road, went past the Catholic church and the Post Office and walked resolutely to my destination. I was walking with my cap pulled down and looking at the ground. I went into the West Store, which was a modest little market, but with cans and packets of food that I had never seen before and whole shelves of alcoholic drinks. I had clearly in my head the brand of whisky they had asked for and the number of bottles, so there was nothing to detain me. The cashier asked me if I was a sailor from one of the Polish fishing boats which used to fish in the autumn and I believe I said I was. The lady was talking with another and the two of them tried to start a conversation with me. I just wanted to get away as soon as possible; I was afraid they might denounce me.

I went out onto the street with a bag in each hand, both very heavy and full of bottles and had only gone about fifty metres when a couple of military police told me to halt.

They had discovered me because I was still wearing my usual brown boots, my feet being a different size from those of the previous occupant of the house. Those military boots were unmistakable.

Shouting throatily and separating every syllable, they ordered me to leave the bags and stretch out on the cement of the street with my arms and legs extended. The ground was very cold. The minutes went by and groups of soldiers passed in all directions and looked at me thoughtfully, some with scorn and some with pity. The police seemed to be waiting for someone. Finally the officer in charge arrived and asked me who I was and what I was doing there. I told him the truth and asked him to ring the house and speak to the officer who had sent me.

The military police officer communicated with my boss by means of an immense black walkie-talkie. "I don't know him; I don't know who he is," the naval officer assured him. Was that a bad joke or was the punishment for military who went to buy things so severe that they were leaving me here, staked out on ross road with three guns pointing at my head?

The suspense did not last long. The naval officer explained the situation and somehow persuaded them to let me go. A military policeman escorted me to the house. I didn't feel in such a good mood as a few hours before, when I was trying on various shirts and trousers to assemble my disguise.

Twenty four years later I nearly fell over when I read an anecdote told in a chronicle of the war from the civilian point of view (*Falkland Islanders at War* by Graham Bound). In the penultimate chapter, Bound gives a couple of examples of how the islanders, who as a result of living for generations in a community of less than 2000 people, knew everybody, began to see unknown civilians of British appearance and arrived at the conclusion that the Secret Services of Her Majesty had skillfully infiltrated the community without being detected by the Argentine forces.

This is what the radio telephone operator Eileen Vidal declared: "I was coming out of the store when this chap was coming up the steps. I thought: 'who the devil's he? He's a stranger.' He was dressed in a parka. I stopped in my tracks when I saw him. He just gave me this grin, then he went on and I went on. I'm sure he was an SAS (Special Air Service) man. Definitely a stranger."

I read and reread this fragment and I am convinced that the fellow that Eileen Vidal saw at the entrance to the West Store was me.

* * *

On June 12th, the war was already lost. The British destroyers were bombarding our positions day and night and the battle-hardened attacking soldiers were advancing on the mountains that surrounded Stanley: Longdon, Kent, and Two Sisters, where soon they would be involved in the most terrible battles of the war. From the landing in San Carlos on May 21st, the war was no more than a rapid British advance and a slow Argentine retreat. The ultimate horror was still to come and the prevailing mood was black and hopeless.

That day was Lieutenant González Llanos' birthday. Guillermo made a cake and Luna and Peralta added meat – where from no one remembers – charcoal from the *Penélope* and a braided wire that made a grill. Daniel remembers that the barbecue was ready, when it occurred to him to add salt. "Someone, most likely 'Uncle' Luna, had already salted it, so it ended up like brine."

Alternatively, Ni Coló remembers the surprise that they gave the boss: a table with a candle and the number of years he had attained, a cake and a bottle of whisky. "We prepared everything and went to look for him and asked him to come out to the boat because we wanted to talk to him. When he came down and saw all that, he was very surprised and told us that he had never expected to be celebrating his birthday in that place. We presented him with a parchment we had made as a gift and two handkerchiefs."

That day the hospital ship *Bahía Paraíso* arrived at the Apostadero jetty. It had passed through the British blockade because it was on a humanitarian mission with the flag of the Red Cross.

I went with the captain in a little car to look for food and clothes for the house. We parked at the port and boarded the 'schooner'. It was the last time that I sailed on the *Penélope*. Painted black as she was, she seemed a different boat, smaller and a little sinister. The *Bahía Paraíso* was anchored in the harbour and with the 'schooner' we came and went with clothes, food and medicines.

I climbed onto the deck of the enormous hospital ship. They threw down parcels from above and we from the Apostadero then threw them down to the men on the *Penélope*. When the war was practically finished, here came part of the protective clothing that the people of Argentina had sent us: thousands and thousands of scarves, woolly hats, gloves, socks … all that we had dreamed of during two hard months of cold. I carried off a pair of 'long johns', the kind of underpants that go from your waist to your ankles. My legs had frozen on many nights of guard duty.

"There were some tremendous parcels!" Daniel Peralta remembers. "They completely filled *Penélope's* hold. There were vests, pullovers, sweaters, some very beautiful clothes. I had a couple of those clothes for ten years: a brown sweater and a black pullover".

The captain I had gone with came back from the bridge with a pile of cigarette cartons that almost obscured his head. He had not been able to resist: now he was going to smoke. We got back into the car and the captain made a terrible mistake; he threw the cigarette cartons onto the back seat and seated in the front ones we set off slowly along Ross Road.

We could only go a little way. We were coming across hundreds of soldiers approaching us, walking heavily and dragging their rifles on the ground. Thin, with uniforms in rags and eyes on fire, they were the vanguard of the scattered troops.

The first ones raised the alert that the car was full of cigarettes. They surrounded us submissively, asking, begging us to throw them some packets. The captain pursed his lips, stretched his hand over to the back seat and made his second mistake; he got two packets of cigarettes and put them into the nearest blackened hand, then closed the window, ready to drive on. The boys did not go and the circle began to close. Begging changed to demanding, to shouts and threats. They began to throw themselves against the car and could have easily turned it over. They were coming from another more horrific war without the comforts that we had enjoyed. They were coming from hell and the captain was trying to deny them cigarettes.

The situation became intolerable. Haggard and furious faces howled at all the windows. When they were at the point of breaking the glass we opened the windows and bunches of arms came in, desperate to carry off the prized cigarettes. All this was over in a few minutes and we soon arrived at the door of the house with the food and clothing which were in the boot, but the scene continues to give me the shivers.

On the 13th and especially on the 14th, the town filled up with these walking skeletons, which were coming down from the mountains. I found their intense gaze, as if of men who had seen the depths, almost unendurable.

* * *

The first snowfall came on June 14th. Dozens of veterans still suffer today from damage caused by extreme cold: feet amputated because of gangrene, noses broken by the cold ... and when the war ended, the winter had still not begun!

The snow fell in smooth flakes and covered the silent march of the boys who were coming down from the mountains defeated in spirit like a mantle. In the officers' garden we spent part of the morning burning papers and documents in the hole which we had dug as an anti-air raid shelter. Later we left the house and set off towards the jetty. Above everything else, Pezzoni and I put warm clothing, a blanket or two and tins and biscuits in our white bags... I didn't know where they were going to put us nor for how long and the first thought was to be prepared to fight hunger and cold. In the house freezer we left the meal we had prepared for that night: some very tasty milanesa steaks ... as always, my contribution had been peeling and frying the potatoes, because my kitchen skills didn't allow me to do more, but Pezzoni was a good cook and his milanesas were the last of the joys that we were leaving behind in the Naval Command's house.

My first destination as a prisoner of war was the *Yehuín,* the only one of the little auxiliary vessels that had come from the continent. The *Yehuín* was built of steel and a little bit bigger than the *Penélope.* During the first two post-war days it was used to take the wounded to the hospital ship. It was aboard the *Yehuín* that I learned the details of the surrender. Menéndez had signed it that same morning with the British troops surrounding the town and also entering it. In fact, we were chatting with some British soldiers in the port before the end of hostilities was announced. It was said – and afterwards the media confirmed it – that Menéndez had asked the British commander, General Jeremy Moore, that the document he would sign should say only "surrender" and not "unconditional surrender." But what were the conditions? If there were any, we never knew them.

For us, the Malvinas war was over and we were going home. In the port a sailor wept as he took down the Argentine flag, but in the following days the expressions that I saw were all of pain for so much suffering and relief that the senseless atrocity of war had ended.

Ambulances, stretchers and Land Rovers were arriving at the jetty carrying soldiers with all kinds of wounds, bandaged with shirts and socks, shouting and bleeding. Some could hardly walk. Some were using their gun as a crutch, but after throwing their arms in great heaps in the street, they had to grip their companions in order to advance over the snow. I remember one who gave a shriek with every pace he took. They were being taken on board the *Yehuín* and the whole deck was full of stretchers and grey blankets where the wounded lay in twos and threes.

In the ship's dining room a group had formed which was looking intently at something on the table. Going close, I saw one of the military chaplains, a captain cleric with an aquiline nose, hard features and fine white hair. The chaplain was drawing for the conscripts around him the naughty picture on a packet of camel cigarettes. Inside the camel, between the head and the front foot, the priest was assuring his audience that you could see in profile the figure of a man with an erect penis. To demonstrate, he took a pencil and traced the outline of the man. And there it was in the drawing that he was making, the crouching evil that these wounded conscripts would have to guard themselves against.

I left to go on deck, where with every blow of the sea, the boys were complaining, imploring and swearing. Passing between two of them, one grabbed my foot as if clinging to a life raft.

The next trip with wounded was to the *Almirante Irízar*, a naval ice-breaker being used as a hospital ship. For this voyage Peralta, Contreras, Ni Coló, Rivero, 'Uncle' Luna and Lieutenant González Llanos had embarked on the *Yehuín*. The sailors told me that they had abandoned the *Penélope* that morning with all that they could fit in their kit bags. We were on deck and the impact of salt water on our faces and the movement of the waves took me back nostalgically to the voyage in our 'schooner'.

The Lieutenant recommended to the *Penélope's* crew that they should pass themselves off as wounded and board the hospital ship. That is what the five of them did. I belonged to the Naval Operations Command and had to return because Admiral Otero had told me that I was needed as an interpreter. On the *Yehuín's* deck we took our leave of those who were already going home.

I try to remember the farewells to my companions on the *Penélope*, but the scene doesn't come to mind. I have the feeling that we were so concentrated on the moment, on the next minutes, on the dangers and surprises of what was happening, that stopping to construct memories for the future was a luxury. Now the journalist from Saladillo's question about whether in the islands we had ever dreamed of a meeting twenty-four years later comes into my mind. I believe that exhausted and shivering with cold as we were, I was only thinking about what would await me back in port, in my new role as prisoner of war.

The sea was getting up and the job of getting the wounded on board was difficult. We had to pass people up by climbing a net. Some stretchers wobbled dangerously in the short space between the ships. Finally we left the *Almirante Irízar* behind. The *Yehuín's* deck was almost empty. The wounded had gone, but continue to haunt me from that time on. The chaplain went, classed as one of the wounded, no doubt so that he could continue enlightening the crew with his vision of hell until they reached Río Gallegos. We returned to the jetty where the big sign reading APOSTADERO NAVAL MALVINAS was no longer there and that of the FALKLAND ISLANDS COMPANY had taken its proper place once again.

The British ship's company for the *Yehuín* was already lined up on the jetty. They were bathed, ironed and incredibly clean. We got off and the group split up. They took me to a club where senior officers of the navies of both sides were meeting. It seemed like a comradely meeting. Admiral Otero 'handed me over' to Captain Brown of the Royal Marines, who was in charge of the prisoners. There were thousands of prisoners scattered around the islands and thousands of soldiers guarding them, but they didn't understand each other. As interpreter for Captain Brown I spent almost four days without sleeping.

We went round the camps where the soldier prisoners were crowded together, In a Land Rover. I had to intervene very little because the majority of my compatriots were motionless and dejected. Nor did the Royal Marines guarding them seem to have any desire to fight. The vast majority of these 'gaolers' had just got off ships. It was rumoured that for the triumphal entry into the streets of what had gone back to being called Stanley, they had lined up those neat and smiling soldiers who had not fought and not those who had crossed the island and fought in the mountains. I only remember having to intervene in one dispute between some British paratroopers and some terrified Argentine conscripts. One paratrooper said that he had come across the prisoner with a watch belonging to one of his own companions who had died in combat. He said that the Argentine soldiers had taken the watch from the body of his dead companion. The soldier denied this vehemently. He said that the watch was a present from his father. Captain Brown confiscated the watch and ordered an investigation to begin.

The airport was like a refugee camp in Africa or the Middle East, but with snow and frightful cold. The state of the soldiers was lamentable. They were sleeping in little cloth tents, heating water in cooking pots and holding their freezing hands in the slowly rising steam in order to feel their fingers. The British officers told Captain Brown that they would shortly run out of water and that they must hurry up the movement of prisoners to the ships for their return home.

One of the images that most often drifts into my memory is the opening of the store full of sweet potato jam cans. I have told it in at least three articles and it still seems to me today to be a metaphor for so many things which happened in the Falklands. With his athletic pace and professional smile, Captain Brown directed a group of marines to one of the port's warehouses that had not been opened. One cut the padlock with bolt cutters and three of them went in with weapons at the ready. Nobody was there, but what they found surprised them and the Captain called me over to explain the phenomenon. In that shed there was food up to the roof and above all, tin after tin of sweet potato jam, in those cans as round as a plate, some with and some without chocolate.

The marines hadn't a clue about the marvelous nature of sweet potato jam. I explained to them that on its own or with fresh cheese it has for generations been the delight of old and young in my country and that my mouth had watered at the thought of a pudding of sweet potato jam since I was a kid. "But what are so many cans doing here?," Captain Brown wanted to know.

I didn't know what to say.

CHAPTER 7

The future takes its course

The last image of the Falklands that Daniel Peralta has is of helicopters arriving with dead bodies, unloading them and then returning for more.

Eduardo Rivero remembers what was nearly their last meal in the Islands. "'Uncle' Luna had got hold of a little turkey, ready to be cooked. I think it came from the *Irízar* ... and he was putting it in the pot when Horacio says: 'Grab your things, everything, they are going out to the *Irízar* in the *Yehuín*.' We left almost everything behind, just took some kit bags. Remember, we had night vision goggles; we left them there. Pistols, we didn't take them either, only the rifle, the green belt and the sword. The *Yehuín* was alongside and we got out of there. It was the last time that we saw the *Penélope*."

Guillermo Ni Coló recounts that on the *Almirante Irízar*, "many wounded came. The holds were full of beds and all the interior passageways. While leaving Puerto Argentino we went past many English vessels in the harbour. We sailed for over a day and when we arrived in Comodoro Rivadavia the disembarkation began".

In Comodoro Rivadavia they got on a plane bound for Buenos Aires. The plane made a stop at the Comandante Espora base in Puerto Belgrano. Oscar Luna says that they had to get off the plane at the Espora base and when they got back on again their seats were occupied by officers going to Buenos Aires. "There was a captain that I knew and I said to him: 'Excuse me sir, but these men are returning from the Malvinas.' They got off to wait for another plane and left us to ourselves."

Luna arrived at his house in Santos Lugares at three in the morning. His wife hadn't been able to sleep and was watching television. His youngest daughter threw herself into his arms. "She kept on asking me, Where were you? Where have you been, daddy?"

Although some were stationed in Puerto Belgrano, they made them all go on to the Federal Capital, to report to Naval Command and from there they gave them a sealed paper to take to their unit and from there they were given post-war leave.

Eduardo Rivero, for example, got off the plane in Puerto Belgrano (his posting), got back on the plane again, reported to the Edificio Libertad and the next day travelled the 600 kms back to the naval base in a bus. He didn't even go back on board the destroyer *Domecq García, w*here three months ago he had had the blessed idea to not step forward when they were looking for volunteers for the war. On the deck of the ship those that had stepped forward were bustling about and cleaning as if nothing had happened.

Not being able to greet his companions, they give him a free pass to go home to Mendoza. Almost two days spent on a bus later, when he opened the door to his house, his mother fainted.

"What a fright! I didn't die, but my old lady was going to." Luckily, she recovered very soon. His father was working and ran home when he heard the news. "When he got there, my old man also started to cry... Nobody asked me anything for fear of finding out how it was. I told them that I had had the knock which was hurting my spine."

Daniel Peralta remembers that when they arrived at Ezeiza and before getting on the bus that would take them to the Edificio Libertad, they had a little bit of cheer. "When we arrived at Ezeiza, Argentina was playing in the World Cup in Spain. We had a wash there, they gave us something to eat and then we watched the match, which I think was the only one that Argentina won in that world cup."

In the Edificio Libertad, Peralta took off his military uniform and dressed in civilian clothes. All around him was a hubbub of rumours and news. Several admirals were going to the Casa Rosada (the President's Palace) to ask for Galtieri's resignation. Not involved in the political conflict, Daniel took two flags from the bottom of his white canvas kit bag: the British one which he had picked up from under some rocks on April 2nd, and the Argentine one from the *Penélope*, which he had remembered to haul down and save before abandoning the ketch on the day of the surrender. "I left them in the Edificio Libertad, because it seemed to me that it was what I had to do," he reflects.

As he was also heading for Puerto Belgrano, he boarded a bus in Constitución to take him to Punta Alta. "In the seat next to me was a girl from some town or other. I was feeling bad; I'm not sure if I didn't cry. She gave me a hug and companionship. My whole body was hurting until I fell asleep. When I woke up she had already gone."

In contrast, they took Carlos Contreras by bus to the door of his house in José Léon Suárez, but his family wasn't there. "As we arrived before the rest, being the first, they weren't expecting us. My wife had gone to visit her sister in La Plata, so there was no one at home and I went to my sister-in-law's house, where there is a long passage before you get to the door."

He appeared at the window and his brother-in-law spotted him, but did not recognise him. Carlos signalled to him not to tell anyone because he wanted to surprise his wife. The brother-in–law, who still did not recognise him, began to think the worst when this unknown, with a face like someone who had just returned from a war, made strange signs to him, while continuing to advance along the passage. Soon everything became clear and Able Seaman Contreras was able to embrace his wife and hoist into his arms his son, who meantime had just reached four months old.

"I had thought many times about how my return home would be," writes Guillermo Ni Coló at the end of his memoirs. "I imagined jumping for joy, running to meet all my folks, but it wasn't like that. I remember that I was very sad and almost speechless. I felt as if they had killed all the joy I had carried in me. Today, when so many years have passed, I still feel the same. I think that I am still on the ship asking myself what was happening to me."

Guillermo returned to Ezeiza with the rest. He could ring his house from the Edificio Libertad, but preferred to get a friend to ring his mother to say that he was well. He thought he would arrive at dawn and give them a surprise. However the friend finished up by asking the lady he was talking to if she would like to talk to her son. "When my mother heard my voice she could only answer with an endless shout full of tears, pain and joy."

When he returned to his beloved Saladillo at five in the morning and finally met his mother, she "was motionless, pale and didn't utter a single word. In time she asked if I had killed anyone. I answered, no, but she continued asking this question several times all the same. Later I sat on the bed with my parents who told me it was the first night they had been able to sleep in two months."

The one who was last to return was Lieutenant González Llanos. After the last trip with the wounded and after making sure that the five NCOs from *Penélope* were bound for home on the *Almirante Irízar,* he, along with some other officers, was taken by order of the British to a smithy where they spent their first night as prisoners. "At first they let officers keep their pistols, I remember, because they said it was up to us to maintain order among the troops, but when they put us in the smithy, they took them from us."

Horacio says that he spent the worst night of his life in that smithy. "It was that kind of cold which gives you no chance of sleeping anywhere; it was a freezer." The following day they made them walk to the heliport, where a British helicopter took them to San Carlos. "We got off where they had landed on May 21st. There was an unfinished freezing plant there, for sheep I think. It was built of cement and had underground chambers where they checked you out and then assigned you somewhere to be. We were there for fifteen days."

In San Carlos there were some four hundred military from the three services, almost all officers. "There we ate out of tins, all combat rations, which you eat to survive. Afterwards, we got a wash every three days, more or less in those improvised showers, which were fairly cold. For other necessities we had drums which we had to carry, drag, clean..."

What the Lieutenant found hardest was that they had to sleep on cement.

"And that I was thirty years old, eh? Well, fine, sleeping on cement is one thing for two days or three days, but by the fourth day you don't know what side to lie on because your little sweet bone hurts, your shoulders, everything. Those days were rough for sleeping."

After two weeks, another helicopter took the group to the ship the *St Edmund,* where they stayed for a further fortnight. Although six officers slept in each four berth cabin and used the bunks in rotation, the situation was much better than in San Carlos. They were finally disembarked exactly one month after the end of the war.

They had almost nothing to do with the British officers, but one day they were made to assemble and were given a surprise.

"They had called us together to give us our pay as prisoners of war. I remember that they gave us each eight pounds sterling, which was what was established in the Geneva Convention. With that we could have access to the canteen on board, so we could buy chocolate, that kind of thing..."

Horacio continues to be amazed by how scrupulous his gaolers were with the weapons, cameras, or radios that they confiscated. "Everything that they confiscated during the inspection, the fellows punctiliously noted down what it was and to whom it belonged. My Nikon camera, a knife, a penknife belonging to such and such ... and the day before we arrived in Puerto Madryn, they returned to us everything they had confiscated. Very organised, you see."

When González Llanos arrived at Puerto Madryn, the country had changed. After the fall of Galtieri, the military had appointed as president a retired general called Reynaldo Bignone, who had announced that there would be elections. The country was living in a state of effervescence. The naval personnel who arrived on the *St Edmund* went to the Naval Hospital at Rio Santiago for a complete examination. There we received our back pay and they sent everyone to his previous unit. "They sent me to the Espora base in Bahía Blanca and there I met up with my family. At that time I was married with three children of seven, six and the youngest, two years."

* * *

My last day in the Falklands was June 20th. Six days had passed since the end of the war and my family didn't know if I was alive, dead, wounded or hopelessly insane. Every day, every television bulletin, every telephone call was torture. My mother wore my vests, my sweat shirts and pullovers to feel near to me, although they were too small for her and squeezed her heart. My father was coming and going to his office with a tragic face that he couldn't change day or night. My sister tried to console them, but she herself felt sorry and inconsolable. She didn't pay attention in college and began to get bad reports. My girlfriend, Carolina, went to visit them and felt the atmosphere charged with the weight of the uncontrollable and the unknowable. The war had already ended; there were dead and there were survivors. I had to be in one of those two groups, but the days passed and still no news came.

It took me years to leave my own centre and to see them as they were, to see how each night for three months they ate with an empty chair and a vacant place, how they jumped each time the door bell rang and to begin to understand their war.

Recently, some months back, in the middle of my interviews with my old companions from the *Penélope*, my sister told me how she had spent the war and the waiting. How she had waited in vain for the call from her college tutor. Carola was fifteen with a brother at war. Of course she didn't want congratulations, but neither did she want to feel shame. She wanted them to be concerned about her, not only because of her absent brother, but she didn't know what to ask for. Her class tutor called her in in November, when it was her turn according to the plan drawn up at the beginning of the year. "I don't need anything," my sister spat at her with the pride and sense of justice that she has always had. I heard her tell me this story twenty-four years later and asked myself why I had not wanted to know it before.

To be in the middle of a war is a kind of fear, of anguish, of tension, but to be at home, surrounded by all the usual things, with a son at war, is another kind of suffering which at that time I was not prepared to understand.

When I scribbled my home telephone number and address on a piece of paper for one of my colleagues at the naval headquarters who was going home on the *Canberra* on June 19th, I hadn't imagined what the result of his appearance would be. They received him like an angel of providence. They kissed him till his cheeks were red, they asked him a thousand times to tell everything he knew and they heaped blessings on him when they said goodbye.

Meanwhile with the prisoner crisis already over with the departure of more than 4,000 on the *Canberra,* I went to sleep in a cold, inhospitable loft, without food and almost without water. They told us that we would be embarking the following day, but we already had learned that rumours depend much more on the wishes of the messenger than on the trustworthiness of his information. However, so it was. On the morning of the 20th they made us line up at the port. It was the Day of the Flag, the day in which we raise the light blue and white flag at college while singing the march which begins with the words: "Here is the flag we love so much." Formed up like prisoners of war on the point of boarding an enemy ship to go home, the patriotic anniversary seemed like a bitter coincidence.

In front of three brick houses from the end of the 19th Century, some British soldiers were searching us before we went on the ship which would take us back to the continent. This was the ferry *Norland,* which normally plies the route between the North of England and Belgium with its hold full of cars. The soldier searched my kit bag and came across the piece of shrapnel the size of an eggplant which had accompanied me since May 26th, the day on which a drum of fuel exploded just a metre away from my head. It was the shrapnel which nearly killed me, but I suppose that it was capable of breaking someone's head open, if held by one end, so my souvenir went back to being a dangerous weapon and, as such, was confiscated. The souvenir of the day on which I was reborn had to remain on the heap, with knives, bayonets, pistols, helmets and all the metal or cutting objects that they were finding.

I moved along in the file of prisoners like an inflated doll, because as everything would not fit in the kitbags, we had put on several uniforms on top of one another. I was wearing a double-breasted green tee-shirt, a white sweat shirt, a woollen pullover that I got from the hospital ship, the green overall which on the *Penélope* I had only taken off for the bath on the 25th May, a camouflaged jacket and, on top, the parka with four pockets. On my legs I wore the long johns and two pairs of trousers. Below all of that, I was wearing several layers of dirt. From that file of prisoners I could see the *Penélope* for the last time. She was painted black and swaying gently against the jetty as if expecting something, with nobody aboard.

On the *Norland* they located us on the rusty floor of the car deck. My hands and feet felt very cold and with my clothes one on top of another I felt like a wrapped mortadela. However, the night didn't last long, because around about two they came looking for me to perform my last duty as interpreter.

There was a row between the Argentine soldiers and the British marines in the dining room. Escorted by two military policemen, I went among those who were sleeping on the dining room carpet, under the tables and asked myself what these people were complaining about who didn't have to sleep in the car deck. In one corner Argentines and English were shouting hostile instructions at each other. There was nothing to translate because neither group had any intention of understanding the other. If they had been shouting in the same language it would have been just the same. The marines went and were replaced by others who opted not to reply and so the thing was calming down. When they let me return to my hard corner in the ferry's belly, dawn was already breaking and the coast of Patagonia was visible.

The *Norland* moored at the big jetty belonging to the Aluar aluminium plant in Puerto Madryn. It was very cold and I was tired, hungry and wanting to go home.

Three years before, I had been in these parts on a family summer holiday. We had seen thousands of penguins squawking in Punta Tombo and hundreds of sea lions romping about on the Valdés Peninsula. With binoculars we had followed the strange dances of whale tails and later had descended to dive among the remains of a sunken ship, where my sister Carola had moved about the bottom of the sea like a mermaid. The world then was agreeable and understandable.

Now I was returning to Puerto Madryn like an old man of nineteen.

The wind rocked the branches of the trees and combed the grass of the hill which was becoming visible to the north, beyond the jetty and Aluar's warehouses. Some buses were waiting for us on the hard concrete platform. The jetty guards were waving to us. I was looking at it all as if I was swimming in murky water in some kind of dream.

I walked over to the naval bus that would take me to the base in Trelew, to Ezeiza airport, to my family, to the post-war, to adulthood, to nightmares, to the profession of journalist, to trying to understand what happened, to living and suffering a further crisis in the country, to the time of going to work and starting a family in Costa Rica, to the clouding over of memories, to the return to university in the United States, to teaching journalism in Spain, to my son growing up and beginning to ask me how it was and what I did in the war, to the reappearance of the *Penélope* after 24 years and to this night, sitting in front of the computer, struggling with the words to construct that old adolescent, confused but alive, standing on Aluar's old wooden jetty, taking the first step towards the bus that was just about to leave.

SECOND PART

The years of the *Auxiliary Ketch Penelope*

CHAPTER 1

Confrontation with Question Seven

With a professional smile, the air hostess hands me the immigration form. While I am descending through the clouds which I see through the plane's windows, I open the folding table, get my pen out of my pocket and begin. Just the usual questions: name, surname, address, passport number ... until I reach Question 7.

"*Have you been to the Falkland Islands before?*"

I spend five minutes looking at the form, staring at Question 7, as if there was a way of looking at it which might help to find the easy, bureaucratic answer to such a question. It's mid-day on Saturday the 19th June, 2006; I am sitting in seat 17A of the Lan Chile flight which is bringing me from Santiago in Chile to the military airport of Mount Pleasant in the Falkland Islands.

The flight left in the dark early morning of Santiago and in its first part – to Puerto Montt and Punta Arenas, flying over all the impressive white spine of the cordillera of the Andes – is the same flight which daily unites the capital of Chile with its distant south. On Saturdays, however, the plane carries on to the Falkland Islands, making the flight international. From the hundred or so sleepy people who got on in Santiago, only about 35 of us go through immigration and get back on the aircraft in Punta Arenas.

My travelling companions are Falkland Islanders returning from Chile or from the rest of the world and there are also some Chileans who work or run businesses in the Islands. In the depths of winter, without cruise ships to board or penguins to see, there are no tourists. I seem to be the only one who does not fit on this flight. Some people look at me out of the corner of their eye as if not liking what they see. Do they look at me with disquiet or with interest, or is that just my imagination?

Back on the plane I sit at the window as if the silhouette of the Falkland Islands were not going to appear in a couple of hours, as if it was just another flight. I try to show the outward mask of a 'frequent flyer,' lost in a newspaper, or thinking of something else. Everything seems to be going well until I come across that wretched Question 7.

"*Have you been to the Falkland Islands before*?" The answer should be simple: yes or no.

It's clear that I was once in these islands 24 years ago. However, I didn't go through any immigration office, my passport wasn't stamped and my name doesn't figure in any file. I didn't come as a tourist, or as an immigrant, or as an English student. It's certain that I spent a week as a prisoner of war in the British Colony of the Falkland Islands, but that was a chaos. Clearly where I was for three months was the Argentine territory governed by General Mario Benjamín Menéndez. Where is that territory now?

But what is making me stare at this cold paper until my eyes ache is not, of course, the administrative problem. Nor am I afraid that they won't let me in. I already know that many Argentines, including among them several veterans, have visited the islands since they lifted the ban in 1999. No, the problem is in reality much more profound. Was I here? I look at the clouds which cover the sea like a sad, heavy blanket. I can't stop thinking about the "cloak of mist" from the celebrated 'March of the Malvinas' which became so popular during the war. What is that cloak of mist hiding? What is there down below?

As I can't put 'yes and no' on the form, I put 'no.' But that isn't the answer I came so far to find. Perhaps at the end of my journey I shall be able to answer the damned question for myself.

* * *

As the plane is so empty I go from the right hand windows to the left and back again, trying to see something and taking frenetic photos with a digital camera that my sister lent me.

The camera isn't the only thing I carry which belongs to someone else. My brother-in-law Juanjo, a seasoned television cameraman who travels to far more inhospitable places than me, lent me a pair of very hard brown boots, very like those I nearly destroyed in 1982. "Your boots walked on the Malvinas" I tell him when I return them and we both know they have been converted into special boots.

I have a typical grandfather's cap to cover my head with. It belonged to my grandfather, a Catalan, who emigrated to Bolivia when he was 18 and arrived in Buenos Aires in 1946. The old raw wool cap, like the one in Chaplin's *Poor Boy,* has been with me since I first went camping in the eighties. When I returned from the war my grandfather never stopped asking me if it had been cold. He died two decades ago, but I think that he would be pleased to know that I am now well-protected.

My dad lent me a warm blue well-padded jacket, mum some gloves with raw leather outside and wool inside, and my wife Pini gave me the most important thing: the Moleskine notebooks – just the right size for the pocket, without lines, hard-covered, and with an envelope in the back flap – where I write down everything and where I also make little drawings of things about which I cannot write.

Half an hour before landing, the chief air hostess orders us to put away cameras and videos as we are entering a military zone. At no time are the words 'Malvinas' or 'Falklands' heard from the loudspeakers, only the name of the airport. This figures in the pilot's notes as 'Mount Pleasant,' but it doesn't even sound like that when the air hostess pronounces it with her sing song Chilean accent. She says something like '*Monplasán.*' Isn't that where the Tigers of Malaysia had their hideout? *Monplasán?* It seems to me like an unreal, invented name. Will Monplasán really exist?

And the moment arrives. The plane descends through the clouds, but I still don't manage to see the silhouette which the maps show: the all too famous contour of the two ominous stains in the sea. When we pass through the clouds, we are already crossing Falkland Sound and flying over the south of East Falklands. Just as I remember it, there isn't a single tree. There are sheep and cows scattered about, but neither people, houses nor roads to be seen. Little by little the submerged city of the military base appears.

And suddenly I am thrust into a scene from *Star Wars.* Our ship is descending into a desolate and cold planet with a strange name. We draw near to a rust coloured semi-submerged city where a multitude of soldiers of the Empire, or the Business Federation, or something similar, guard the protagonists. Even the weather – fine and persistent rain making pools which shine as the plane passes – seems to have been lifted from George Lucas's saga.

The runway opens like a wound in the frozen landscape. It is very long, as if to receive transatlantic flights. The offices, arsenals and stores of the military base are scattered to one side. Here live some two thousand people, including civilian workers on contract, and members of the three British armed forces, who spend between three and six months stationed in the Islands. The main buildings are connected by closed corridors like long caterpillars and you can go through the whole of this military city passing from one corridor to another without going outside.

It snowed a little while ago and the land around the runway is white and spongy. The landing is smooth. The engines switch off with a light murmuring. I hang on to my note book, find my hand luggage and put on all my borrowed outdoor clothing. Now it is time to get off. We descend the steps from the front of the plane and walk from there to the terminal. There doesn't seem to be much military presence, but an old Argentine canon stands guard in front of the door of the terminal building. There are a couple of bored soldiers in the arrivals hall and the rest are officials.

I show my passport and my form, when my turn comes. In answer to the question about where I am going to live I have written the name of Celia Stewart's guest house, which was recommended to me by the tour guide, Tony Smith, whom I contacted in Buenos Aires. The round-cheeked and smiling official wishes me a pleasant stay. She has no idea of how I have struggled with Question 7.

There is a bus service for the hour-long journey between Mount Pleasant and Port Stanley. A pair of burly chaps grab suitcases at the terminal door and fling them in a truck. The few travellers not to be picked up by family or friends climb into a small bus like those that take children to school. The driver is wearing a black short-sleeved tee shirt and sun glasses in the midst of the frost. A ring shines in his left ear. The cold is visible in the vapour that emerges from his mouth with every breath, but this man does not seem to feel it.

The mini-bus runs past the bleak, grey city which forms the military base and leaves behind the officers' houses, all identical with gardens covered in snow. The asphalt road is one of the changes that the war brought. Before 1982 there were no roads in the islands.

The first road sign that appears is so unexpected that it surprises me; it is a picture of a coffin with wheels. In flaming red the sign asks: "DRINKING OR DRIVING?" It is obviously part of a campaign to persuade drivers not to drink, but also, of course, it shows that, even in the Falklands, life and death continue their course, far beyond our war.

With difficulty due to the bouncing of the vehicle, I draw a little coffin with a cross in my notebook, while the music of Jamiroquai issues from the loudspeakers. It is four in the afternoon and the BBC interrupts the music programme to give the eight o'clock news. "It is eight o'clock," says the news reader. Thousands of kilometres away the Israeli army continues its bombardment of Lebanon. Looking through the window it certainly seems like a quiet winter's night. Here it is four o'clock, but, as if the weather agrees with the BBC, it is already beginning to get dark.

* * *

The van leaves me in the middle of a snow-covered street at the side of a children's' park with a football pitch, swings, see-saws and a wooden boat. Everything is white with snow, empty and silent. From the lorry behind I get my suitcase with wheels – which are not much use in the snow – and then they go on to deliver the others to the only hotels that are open at this time of year: the Upland Goose and the Malvina House. I ring the bell of the house which the driver pointed out. A gentleman comes out in slippers and points to another house on Allardyce Street, up the hill.

I feel a little ridiculous pushing a suitcase uphill through the snow in an empty street in the Falklands dusk. Is this really the place where I was in a remote past life? This part of Stanley doesn't remind me, but as soon as I arrive at the door I recognise the typical front porch of the majority of these houses: a front patio full of pots with flowers and plants, with little square windows on three sides and at the back, in the centre, the front door. All the houses have these closed and windowed patios at the front, so that the interior of the house is not at the mercy of the wind and cold.

I move the door knocker. From the inner door appears a pink and robust lady with a welcoming smile. It is Celia Stewart, the owner of the boarding house. Inside it is warm and the floor is covered with a springy red carpet. A staircase leading to the upper floor dominates the hallway.

Sitting in the middle of the stairs, which are covered in the same red carpet as the entrance, a short, bald and well-built gentleman is painting the banisters with a fine brush. In a state of total concentration he is putting coats of white paint on the wood and the smell of fresh paint is mingling with that of newly baked bread.

The painter tells me that his name is Dennis Bolt and that he is finishing preparing the house to be a 'Bed and Breakfast.' He asks me who I am and where I come from and in a few minutes I get the first big surprise of the journey. Dennis is a former British Royal Marine, who took part in the taking of South Georgia, then came to the Falklands a little after hostilities ended and decided that this would be the place where he wanted to retire. Now retired, he had taken up working on the houses of his new neighbours, because it appeared he had a good hand.

"We were enemies, weren't we?" he threw at me with a frank smile, adding immediately, "and here we are chatting while the paint dries."

Dennis is much more concerned with avoiding getting white paint on the stair carpet than with re-launching his war memories. However, he tells me with delight that today he heard on the BBC that the British government had finally issued an official pardon to the deserters of World War One.

At first I don't understand what he is talking about. It seems that it is a subject which has occupied the London media for days. In the monstrous Great War of 1914-1918, the British came out of their trenches in France and Belgium in their thousands to be massacred by the German machine guns and many of these soldiers deserted from the trenches or never returned from leave. Before being shot summarily they were publicly degraded and humiliated. Of the 700,000 British who died in the First World War, 2,300 were shot as deserters. Their families had been taking legal action for more than ninety years to restore the memory and honour of these men.

"It could happen to anyone, couldn't it? What do these judges and the folk who condemn know about what war is like? They weren't less brave for having deserted. Who is the bravest?" He turns back to dipping his white brush and giving a third coat to the edge of the stairs.

These are my first minutes of talking to someone in the Falklands. Dennis continues concentrating on the slow movement of his brush and I fill up with questions. What would have happened to him and his companions in South Georgia, or perhaps in Iraq or Northern Ireland? Is he really talking to me about a recent deserter? Why had the pardon of deserters from the First World War made such an impression on him? What world lies behind his last sentence, his hurt rhetorical question: "*Who is the bravest*? And still I haven't unpacked!

My room on the first floor is big and cold but has furniture and curtains like you find in people's houses, not in hotels. In different ovens Celia is baking biscuits and sausage rolls as if for an army. She shows me where everything is, sells me a telephone card and returns to the ovens. For my first walk I put on the padded jacket, wrap myself in the scarf and put my grandfather's cap on my head.

* * *

It is still snowing in the street, but there is something new. Now in the little play park in front of the house there are two mothers with snow up to their ankles chatting while their children score goals, which open paths in the white foam. With their padded parkas, their hats and their gloves they can't play football with much fluency, but it's obvious that the ladies couldn't confine them to their houses any longer. I go downhill towards the sea. The water in the harbour is calm. A few Land Rovers advance along Ross Road with their lights on. The Post Office is as I remember it, but the gymnasium where we slept the first night is no longer in the next block. In its place they have raised the only banking hall in all the Islands.

Going east, past the West Store, I eventually come to the much photographed red brick Anglican cathedral and the equally famous arch made from the jaw bones of two blue whales. Everything seems strange, desolate and unreal. What is missing? Clearly I feel there is something missing.

I turn around, look in all directions and understand perfectly what is missing: the soldiers are missing. I never saw the centre of the city without hundreds of Argentine soldiers, combat vehicles, military police and officers from the three services in their jeeps.

The more that the war was being lost, the more soldiers there were each time and after the surrender there were even more.

I leave the sea and climb the hill, puffing – I'm not 19 anymore – towards John Street. Where was the house? I don't recognise it and none of the houses resemble it. Is my memory playing tricks? I go back down to the harbour. In the Capstan, the West Store's book and souvenir shop I buy ten books to begin to cover my lack of knowledge about these islands. There are only three subjects: the beauty of the Islands, the war of 1982 and Ernest Shackleton.

One case shows books, leaflets and CDs about the history and wildlife of the islands. There are large tomes with photos of beaches, mountains, cliffs and of the fascinating marine fauna of the small outer islands: penguins, sea lions, seals, dolphins and albatross. Scientists, photographers and tour operators compete to show the best landscapes and the most photogenic animals.

Another bookcase contains works on the '82 war. Illustrated chronicles of the battles abound for the war enthusiasts, punctilious drawings of armaments and uniforms for fans of weapon technology and analysis of strategy and the geopolitical consequences for those who play at being sofa Kissingers. There are also a few commentaries on how the Islanders lived through the conflict. The one which appears most complete is *Islanders at War* by Graham Bound and also there is the day by day account of the occupation by the old official historian of the Islands, John Smith: *74 Days.*

The only other subject – probably because the principal public for this shop are the passengers on cruise ships which go to Antarctica – is the exploits of the explorer Ernest Shackleton, who tried to conquer the South Pole in 1916, remained trapped in the ice in his ship, managed to reach South Georgia in a small boat and returned to the remote Elephant Island, where he had left his men. The glorious failure of Shackleton is a legend among Antarctic explorers.

The penguins, sea lions and albatross also dominate the postcard section in the stand near the door. I am looking over the postcards when one of them gives me a start. I bring the card up to my face, look at it then look at it again, but still can't believe it. It's a typical sort of card showing the most picturesque bits of a holiday resort, with four photos forming a square. In this one the top left shows the painted wooden tower of St Mary's Catholic

Church, below the church are the recognisable red phone boxes at the door of the post office and at its side the whale bone arch in the garden of the Anglican cathedral. And there in the top right square ... yes, there is no doubt, it's the *Penélope* at the Crozier Place jetty with her masts and her red and white hull.

The photo of the *Penélope* on a postcard! What is so special about this little ship for the Islanders to put it on a postcard?

I add a dozen postcards to the books and go out into the cold, loaded down with bags and questions which I hope will be answered in some of the books and the many interviews that I hope to make during my stay.

Further on, towards the East, the buildings of the port follow apace: the metal sheds, the jetty which trembles with every attack of the waves, that half skeleton of an olden wooden ship where I remember the Apostadero boys unloading the *Buen Suceso,* doing guard duty, telling jokes or horrific stories about the Ghurkhas. The jetty is just the same. This is where *Isla de los Estados* was moored, further on the *Forrest.* This is the exact spot where we arrived on the *Penélope* that June 2nd during the last days of Puerto Argentino.

I go into the warehouse. It is half a ship and at the same time one of the jetty's warehouses. It's empty, but during the war it served as a dormitory, workshop, store and armoury for our Apostadero Naval Malvinas. I know now that the old ship was called *Egeria,* that it was built in Brunswick in 1859 and that in 1872 on a voyage from London to Callao in Peru, it was shipwrecked in the Islands. After that, it was used for years as a wool store.

Inside there is a rusty wheelbarrow, with a tank and a hose. The wind and air creep in through various holes and the only things that seem solid enough to withstand the storms that sweep the coast are the roof beams. I go round the warehouse, looking without hope for some sign of our passage through this place. Many sailors and a lot of merchandise seem to have passed through in the last 24 years and I am at the point of leaving when I seem to see something. Some letters written in pencil on the main beam attract my attention. It isn't a painted thing which seeks to attract my attention. It doesn't shout, it whispers. It's difficult to see, unless one is looking very hopefully trying to see something.

As if they were written yesterday, the letters on the ancient beam say "VIVA YO." "Long live me," in Spanish, without a signature, without emphasis.

Commenting on the message to Alex Olmedo, the Chilean chef of a neighbouring restaurant some days later, he says that to him the message sounds very Argentine. "I have never seen any of us going down there and, besides, I don't think it would occur to a Chilean to write, 'Long live me.' What do you think?" After protesting that one should not generalise and that there are modest Argentines and boastful Chileans, I keep turning it over in my head. To me as well, for some strange reason, it seems that the author must have been Argentine and I have the conviction, although with no proof, that it was written during the war.

Now I think that 'Long live me' isn't an expression of youthful boastfulness. I don't think it's about pounding the chest or the fist raised on high. I believe it has about it much anguish, much hope, and much supplication. There could be so many meanings, so many tones in a message as simple as "Long live me." The wood, hard and rough, surviving since it was put into the *Egeria* almost 150 years ago, seems a symbol of what lasts, what hangs on and resists. We were 18 or 19 years old and each day that we were in the Islands could well be our last.

ME IN 2006, looking at the place we used as lodging at the Apostadero. Photo by Jane Cameron.

I walk back to Celia Stewart's house, thinking that the *Penélope*, whose history I came here to seek, is also a survivor, a hanger-on to life, like the anonymous author of "Long live me." Tomorrow I will begin to look for the pieces to put together the jigsaw puzzle of the 78 years of my 'schooner's' life in the Falklands.

There are almost no lights in the port, the sky is diaphanous and dry after the snowfall and millions of stars are threatening to fall on my head. In the intense blackness of the sky the stars shine as if there was a sun behind the cloak of night and holes open in the cloak through which seep needles of light. You have to walk with care, because the snow has turned to ice and anyone could slip.

Who was it who gripped the pencil to write those two words?

Of course, it could have been me.

CHAPTER 2

The arrival of the white ship

"Here it is! I have found it!" says Jane Cameron, the head of the Falkland Islands Government Archives, breathlessly. She is speaking in a low voice because it is taking nearly all her strength to carry a gigantic leather-bound tome from the historic book store. With a sigh of relief, Jane supports the old battered book on her office photocopier and the machine narrowly avoids collapsing from the weight and the surprise. The book which the Islands' official archivist is bringing is the record of all the ships registered in the Falklands since the 1860s. Each ship is described in two facing pages, which contain the information of the name, owner, tonnage, size and characteristics of each vessel.

Jane assures me that no investigator since she took charge of the paper memory of the Islands has seen pages 78 and 79 of this fat book, where a fine bureaucratic hand certified that on the 15th of April 1929 the prosperous landowner John Hamilton appeared in the registry office to enter his new purchase.

At the side of the vessel's official number (139450) appears its name: *"Penelope."*

According to the document, John Hamilton, a sheep farmer from Weddell Island brought the boat, which was his property, to the Islands. It was previously called *Feuerland* and registered in Germany. It weighed 46.11 tons and it measured 53.5 feet in length, by 16.8 feet in the beam. It was constructed entirely of wood and presented two masts of different heights, which technically made it a ketch. In the register it was also indicated that the boat could develop a speed of 8.5 knots with its original diesel engine, an Oberwünzel made in Frankfurt, and that it could use sail.

John Hamilton was born in Wick in Scotland in 1860. Like many young men with ambition but no money, when he was twenty he heard there was a chance of work on the sheep farms of the

Falklands. He arrived in the Islands in 1880. In the oldest document about Hamilton which still exists in the Islands – a list of wages paid in the Darwin farm in August of that year – the young immigrant appears to be receiving a salary of four pounds and seven pence, the lowest on the list. At that time Darwin farm had 100,000 sheep.

In June 1882 he had already risen to be second worker at High Hill, one of the Darwin farm's scattered shepherds' outposts. In a letter to his directors in London, three years later, the Falkland Islands Company's Colonial Manager, F. E. Cobb mentions Hamilton as a good worker of good character and says; "I am sorry to lose him." He was already about to lose him because five years after his arrival, Hamilton realised clearly that if he wanted to prosper he couldn't stay in the Islands. He had to cross the sea to Patagonia.

According to all the reports, John Hamilton was an industrious, intelligent and ambitious worker. He wanted to buy land and start his own business, but land in the islands wasn't for sale. It belonged either to the government or to big landowners, of whom the majority lived far away from the Islands – absentee landlords.

Hamilton arrived in Punta Arenas in 1885 and a year later acquired land in Río Gallegos. Together with four other Scottish immigrants he bought thousands of sheep and several horses in Necochea and drove them down the whole length of the Patagonian coast to Río Gallegos. This epic expedition lasted almost two years. They slept under the blanket of the stars. The legend goes that when he arrived, Hamilton made a shack of adobe and let his flock graze free until after the sale of the wool from his first shearing, when he could buy material to build a house and fence his land.

In 1887 he bought the estancia Punta Loyola and a year later, Pali Aike with 40,000 hectares. He also acquired land in the south of Chile and rented an estancia of 24,000 hectares in Tierra del Fuego. These were times when the Argentine government was selling land at very low prices to the Europeans who wanted to work it.

In *From the Falklands to Patagonia*, the exquisite account by Michael Mainwaring about another family of colonisers of the Patagonian coast: the Hallidays, who were neighbours of Hamilton in Punta Loyola, the writer picks up the story of the beginnings of his career. The author mentions that with his friends and colleagues William and Thomas Saunders, Hamilton founded the company Hamilton and Saunders and prospered in sheep rearing and the sale of wool.

In 1904, when already a forty-year old of good standing, he contracted matrimony with Olivia Heap, also a Scottish immigrant, who had worked as a nurse in the British Hospital in Buenos Aires. They had two children. They called the older one Olivia after her mother. On April 27th 1929, Olivia married Alexander MacKay Gaillie, also the son of a Scot, who had important business interests in Punta Arenas. At this point the Falkland Islands archives lose track.

His younger daughter, the apple of his eye, who stayed with John Hamilton until his death, was called Penélope.

Despite his growing interests in Argentina and Chile, Hamilton had never lost hope of returning to the Islands to acquire land and establish himself there. In the twenties he was able to begin buying some of the small outer islands. He acquired Beaver in 1922, Weddell in 1923 and afterwards the Passage Islands and Saunders. Weddell, where he fixed his principal residence, is the biggest island after the West and East Falklands. He built a great house on one of the four Passage Islands, which still stands, despite the hostile climate and the lack of money to look after it. It is still known as "The Hamilton Mansion."

On her computer, Jane Cameron shows me photos of the mansion's rooms. My attention is drawn to a small, narrow bed which seems built into the wall. "That must have reminded him of his childhood; his bed in Scotland must have been like that," says Jane.

John Hamilton threw himself into introducing Patagonian species onto his islands. His energy and entrepreneurial flair were proverbial, but he did not always triumph. He introduced guanacos and nutria to Weddell, which survived, but did not turn into the big business that the impresario hoped for. In contrast, the foxes enjoyed tremendous success and promptly became a plague, threatening the indigenous species. They are still trying to eradicate them today.

Already by the thirties a powerful and influential figure, John Hamilton became a philanthropist. He financed the Boy Scouts and the Girl Guides and subsidised the installation of two legendary marine lighthouses: one installed at Porpoise Point in 1930 and the other at Cape Meredith in 1934. The lighthouses are now in disuse, but old sailors still remember them with gratitude.

* * *

This was the man who in 1929 bought the ketch *Feuerland*, constructed two years earlier for the Patagonian expedition of the German explorer Gunther Pluschöw.

Pluschöw had taken almost a year to arrive from the port of Büsum in the North Sea near Hamburg to the Eden of his dreams, Tierra del Fuego. For eight months Pluschöw and the five members of his group had explored, sailed and flown over the extreme south of the continent, with the ketch and with the seaplane, *Silberkondor*. Short of money, the explorer was called urgently back to Berlin by the Ullstein publishing house, which was financing his voyage. In the early part of 1929 he had to sell his treasured ketch.

The *Feuerland* and the *Silberkondor* would be immortalised in the book and documentary that Pluschöw made on his return to Berlin. The President of the Republic, Paul von Hindenburg, attended the screening of *Silberkondor über Feuerland*, the silent documentary of his voyages. The *Silberkondor* waited a long year for its owner, stored in a shed in Puerto Natales, in Chile, at the mercy of rats. Pluschöw returned in 1930 to begin covering the heights of the cordillera.

During the time that the German was trying to sell his vessel, John Hamilton was looking for a boat of those dimensions to transport people and provisions to his islands. The ketch was in perfect condition, had a latest generation engine and came with a captain and an engineer besides. They were Paul Christiansen and Joseph Schmitt, two German sailors who had been living with the vessel since its departure from Büsum and had learned all its secrets.

The first thing that Hamilton did was to change the name of the ketch. In honour of his younger daughter, he named it *Penélope*. On March 22nd 1929, some three weeks before its registration in Stanley, the *Penélope* touched Falkland soil under the command of Captain Christiansen. That was in Fox Bay.

The most personal and complete account of the arrival of *Penélope* in Port Stanley is that told by the local writer Gerald H. Roberts. At the end of his well researched and even better related history of the vessel he recalls that one day in 1929, in the middle of their favourite game – not Cowboys and Indians, but "Royal Navy and Germans" – the boys of Stanley heard a worrying rumour: "A German ship is coming."

Hardly a decade had passed since the end of the First World War and the little Roberts had grown up with the conviction that the Germans were bad. His father said he didn't like them and stories were still told in the Islands about the legendary naval battle in which the British destroyers had defeated Admiral Graf Spee's fleet.

"I remember feeling scared, I was seven years old at the time," writes Roberts. "A few days later the ship arrived. I woke up in the morning to the plonk-plonk sound of her engine and then the rattle and splash of her anchor. When I looked out of the bedroom window there she was, a little ship painted white and anchored directly opposite our house. She had two masts, but looked so different from our familiar cutters and schooners. She was higher out of the water and her jib boom slanted upwards more steeply. Then there was that wheelhouse taller than a man right aft."

Gerald forgot all his fear when his father offered to take him on board. "It was a windy day, but bright and sunny." Once on deck, the father went below to the cabin and the lad remained in the charge of one of the sailors.

The sailor was talking to him in German, which he didn't like, but soon he realised that he was just being courteous. "I happened to look down through the skylight over the captain's cabin. I could see three men sitting around a table looking at drawings of the *Feuerland*. They were laughing, and joking and thoroughly enjoying each other's company. One of them was my own father, he who had said he didn't like Germans. I never forgot it and I always think of it again when I hear smug and unfriendly nationalistic myths, clichés and prejudices."

"After a while the little ship went to Weddell Island, leaving the Stanley children arguing as to whether she was called the 'Pennylope' or 'Pen-el-o-pea.'"

Whatever may be the correct English pronunciation, the ketch spent the next twenty years on Weddell. John Hamilton was already over seventy and didn't travel much to his properties in the Islands. In the thirties, the ship still made some trips to the continent. Paul Christiansen, the captain, soon left both the boat and the Islands and settled in Chile. Joseph Schmitt, the second-in-command, became the captain. The old people in the Islands like the owner of West Point, Roddy Napier, still remember the amiable captain 'Joe' Schmitt carrying sheep, wool, building materials and passengers from one island to another on the *Penélope*.

"It was 1934 or 1935 and I will always keep in my memory the day that Captain Schmitt took me on board" Napier recalls. "I was eight and I lived on a little island with only two families. I had never seen a motor boat. I looked at that engine with great enthusiasm. Captain Schmitt was a great sailor and he liked to use sail very much, but I would always prefer an engine. He took me from West Point to Carcass, the neighbouring island an hour's sailing away."

Around that time the Islands' government rented the boat to undertake a pioneering study of the sea lion population. Napier remembers that a little before the outbreak of the Second World War, Schmitt, a German who had fought in the First, decided to leave the British Colony and moved to Chile, where he opened a business. "I don't remember if we saw him here, after the war."

The war paralysed the *Penélope*, which didn't leave Weddell till the end of the forties. They couldn't get spare parts for the German engine. However, John Hamilton couldn't be without a boat, and in 1941 he travelled to Punta Arenas to buy another one. In Puerto Natales, on the Chilean coast, he acquired a boat which was a little bigger, but made of inferior wood. In honour of his island and in memory of another old ship, he called it *Weddell*. From then the managers and foremen of Hamilton's islands only used the new vessel. On the 6th September 1945, at the age of 35, John Hamilton died at his Merlo estancia. With him was his daughter Penélope, who inherited his islands in the Falklands, but never visited them.

* * *

There is something that immediately attracts your attention in the archives of the Islands that Jane Cameron runs: many of the texts (and on some subjects, the only ones available) were written by authors aged between 9 and 14 years.

They are the entrants in the Alistair Cameron History Competition. This prize was instituted by Jane in memory of her brother, the Islands' first Director of Fisheries and community leader, who died in a car accident at a young age. "My principal allies are the very old and the very young" says Jane. "After the war we became aware that our history, the history of the people, the hard history of this small community, was important, and that due to changes and the disappearance of old people we faced the danger that it would be lost.

"Really before the declaration of the fishing zone and the beginning of a certain prosperity in the Islands, life was so difficult that the study of our history was a luxury we could not allow ourselves." The historian, with the hesitant manner of speech of a school teacher in *Harry Potter,* sketches a tenuous smile as she finds the words for what she wanted to say some time back, "You have to have achieved certain comforts and to accept the present with some enjoyment, to start investigating the past with pleasure."

So it is that every year the Islands' school pupils (there are two schools in Stanley and a boarding house for those who live away from the town in what is known as the Camp) are encouraged to interview their parents, grandparents and neighbours to rescue stories from the Islands' past. "When they get to adolescence the boys tend to be enthusiastic about military exploits and sometimes, like the whole world, rely too much on the internet. Curiously, in general the best histories are those from the primary school children. They write about life in the Camp in the old days, the shops that no longer exist and the ships which meant so much to us in the pre-war era. We have some well-written histories, some of a surprising level for those age groups."

For example, some of the information about John Hamilton's life came to the archivist by means of the work, 'John Hamilton's Life Story' by eleven year-old Tanya Marsh. Tanya is the daughter of the owners of two of the four Passage Islands, which belonged to Hamilton.

Asking the older members of her family, Tanya was able to find out that Hamilton paid £325 for the Passage Islands, and also that in his indefatigable search for development, the pioneer tried planting trees on his islands, particularly on Weddell, bringing the seeds from Punta Arenas. Another of his ideas, which was much less sustainable ecologically, was to set up an industry killing sea lions to obtain oil. Hamilton abandoned the project after killing 384 sea lions and only obtaining eleven barrels of oil.

After the death of Hamilton in 1945, Penélope did not want to sell the islands. Perhaps she wanted to maintain the link that had united her father so strongly to them. In 1987, a little after the daughter's death, her islands were finally sold to the government of the Islands.

From the 1980s onwards a policy based on a report written in 1980 by the economist and politician Sir Edward Shackleton (son of the explorer) favoured the partition of the great estates and the sale of the land belonging to owners who did not live in the Islands. The government was buying up land and was selling it on easy credit terms to local families, in many cases the same people who had lived and raised sheep on the same land for decades. So it was that Hamilton's islands came into the hands of local families, like that of Tanya Marsh, who work them now.

* * *

And what happened to the *Penélope* meanwhile? After the end of the Second World War, the managers of Hamilton's islands could have obtained German spares for the ketch's engine, but with the war's ending came also the owner's death and the boat continued languishing in Weddell for four more years.

It was as late as 1949 that the British Antarctic exploration service (Falkland Islands Dependencies Survey) bought it to take to the White Continent. With this in mind they took out the original German motor and installed in its place a gigantic British machine, which, as those who remember it recall, did no honour to its size, being less powerful and less reliable than its German ancestor.

Roddy Napier recalls that after the costly conversion to transform it into an Antarctic vessel, the new Captain, Smith by name, was ordered to make a test voyage around the Islands. "He met with a big storm outside Smylie's Channel and took on some water. That was because they hadn't sealed around the deck correctly. When they got back to Stanley it was decided that the *Penelope* was not ready to go to the South." The owner of West Point continues to think that the boat was fine and that the problem was with those who had wrongly calculated its potential. "It was fine for many things as is shown by the fact that it kept sailing, but not to the Antarctic."

Until its sale in 1952 the ketch was used for transporting building materials between islands and those who remembered it from the thirties, like Gerald Roberts, were happy to see it again. Amongst other missions, it carried all the materials that were used for the construction of a freezing plant at Ajax Bay, near San Carlos. That was the plant where Lieutenant Horacio González Llanos was held prisoner for two weeks, thirty years later.

The vessel was also used in the installation of the first radio telephones on the most distant farms and islands. There was no communication system until the fifties and people had to wait for the arrival of boats like the *Penélope,* which could take several months before making an appearance. Until the middle of the century, when someone fell ill, or an accident or other emergency occurred, the Islanders went up the highest available hill and lit a number of simultaneous fires to give the alarm signal.

The radio telephones changed the lives of the people in the Camp. Neighbours could now talk to the authorities in Port Stanley, to the doctor and amongst themselves. However they could not exchange secrets nor have confidential chats, because everybody could listen to everything they said.

In 1952 the Falkland Islands Dependencies Survey sold the vessel to Jim Lee, the owner of Sea Lion Island. His captain was a German by the name of Chris Bundes, who had bought land in the Islands and, according to some Islanders, became Jim Lee's business partner. Bundes took as his engineer George Betts, a young Islander with a calling to be a sailor.

George Betts is the earliest crew member of the *Penélope* that I could interview in the Islands.

With regard to his role as engineer the first thing that Betts remembers about the boat is the immense engine that it had. "It was British: a five cylinder Rustin Hornsby. It could sail at eight knots, like a lot of others, but that was going to cost you down below." George keeps an acid sense of humour about his sailing days.

A few years previously, as an apprentice, he had his first contact with the *Penélope.* "In '63 I worked on putting together and placing some beams which kept in place the false keel, which had been damaged. I put my initials on one of the beams and I know that they are still there."

Betts is a weather-beaten and wrinkled old sailor and I found it hard to know when he was being serious. He received me in his office at the fishing company Consolidated Fisheries Limited, where he is employed as operations manager. "I miss the sea a lot" he confesses, "but only when it is calm like today."

"I don't recall us using the sails. We went a lot to Weddell and to Speedwell Island at the south of East Falklands. We never went far from the coast. We had a crew of four, three of us permanent and the fourth any lad that wanted to make a few pounds for a week's work"

George Betts remembers his boss as a silent and seaworn sailor, who had passed the greater part of the forties and fifties working in South Georgia in the Norwegian whaling stations.

The old sea dog wrinkles his brow, lifts his hand to his beard, and turns his vision inwards remembering some stories from the *Penélope*. At the end of the interview he digs up a day in Punta Arenas when he visited the family of 'Joe' Schmitt, the second captain of the Hamilton era and the last person related to the ketch's original history. "They had some fabulous pieces from the boat's first period, like a sextant with pure silver used in the graduations of the arc and a precision German chronometer. They were lying about in the kitchen, like any old thing. I remember looking at them and wondering, 'do they know what they've got here?'"

From George Betts' office I return to the centre of Stanley and on the way I enter a small book and souvenir store, The Pink Shop. On the wall in front of the cash desk a picture of at least one metre

CAPTAIN JOSEPH ('Joe') Schmitt on board the Penelope in the 1930's. Falkland Islands Archives, courtesy of Jane Cameron.

in length hits my eye. It is entitled: *The Penelope from the Charles Cooper.* It is an oil painting of minute naturalistic detail which shows Stanley's shore line near where the Anglican cathedral stands. Raised up on a wooden platform, at the water's edge, rests the ketch in her red and white version (during her lifetime the Islanders recall having seen her blue and even green. The owners either had distinct colour preferences or, perhaps, when it came time to paint her, they used any old pot which came to hand).

The picture is clearly a nostalgic image of the past painted many years later. The *Charles Cooper* is a semi-sunken ship, which can be seen from the port. It is famous for being the last vessel to leave the old South Street Seaport in New York in November 1856. With the due permission of the port authorities, the artist climbed the blackened wooden skeleton and from there was able to enjoy a privileged view of the whole of the town of Stanley.

In his picture, the *Penélope,* with her square wheelhouse and rounded stern in the foreground, dominates the scene. It was the centre of the Stanley of yesteryear. The painter is John Smith. "I took a year to paint that picture. I'm glad that it has impressed you," Smith told me. "That was the *Penelope* when I arrived in the Islands from England. It seemed to be on show, waiting for a new owner." Surely that was the time when Jim Lee was trying to sell her.

In 1967 the *Penélope* found a buyer, the very powerful Falkland Islands Company, owner of a large part of the Islands' farming land. For this reason, during this period she worked around half of the islands.

For 19 years from 1967 to 1986 the Islanders could see the *Penélope* carrying building materials, loading and unloading sheep, cows and horses, and transporting bales of wool. In the small islands her arrival was like a party, in Port Stanley a sign that soon they would have fresh greens on the table. And her image all this time was joined to that of her captain, the man with the cap and the ironic sideways smile.

Now it is night and I confess that I am nervous. We have just talked on the phone and he is about to come by to pick me up at Celia Stewart's house. He says he remembers me and wants to meet me again. I go up and down the recently painted stairs. I forget my scarf and afterwards I remember that I haven't got my notebook. Now I have everything and the door bell rings.

I go to open it. On the other side of the opaque glass is drawn the compact silhouette of Captain Finlay Ferguson. But I have just remembered that my camera is still on my bed and I run back up the stairs one more time.

CHAPTER 3

Snow in the palm of the hand

I open the door and there he is. He doesn't look any older than 24 years ago, but perhaps a little more fatigued, with his blue cap shading his small bright eyes. He smiles. I take his hand. I tell him about my trip and say that I saw the *Penélope* in Hamburg. He asks me if I have a family. We are both standing a little awkwardly in the entrance. Luckily, Finlay Ferguson soon comes out with the magic words, "Shall we go for a drink?"

We walk arm in arm over the dangerous ice to the Rose, his favourite pub. I buy him a whisky and they serve it as he likes it, more than half a glass of pure whisky, without ice. I keep him company with a beer. By the second drink – another whisky and another beer, that he buys – we are already remembering the nights in Fox Bay, the big waves in Falkland Sound when we were looking for the *Isla de los Estados* and 'Uncle' Luna's anthological stew.

The Lieutenant had asked me to ask if he still had the submariners' pin, which he had given him when they disembarked at Egg Harbour. I ask if he remembers the pin. "Of course, but they took it from me. When we got to Egg Harbour we walked to Darwin, leaving the bags there in the house near the harbour. The pin was in my bag. When I went back some weeks after the war, I found everything turned over and the pin wasn't there."

He asks me about my old companions. He particularly remembers the Lieutenant and 'Uncle' Luna. A young couple approaches the solid wooden table. It is his daughter Marie and her brand-new husband. Between the three of them they explain that the wedding was on Saturday, that Finlay had worn an elegant suit with a flower in his buttonhole and that the couple were the first to use a form of transport which had just arrived in the Islands: a white stretched limousine.

"We thought that nobody was going to want to use this in Stanley's narrow streets, and now we can't cope," the boss of the local taxi service explains to me a few days later. The article which came out in the *Penguin News* which was on sale in the West Store during the week of my visit must have contributed in some way. It was about the wedding and the journalist highlighted the curiosity of the use of the limousine.

The couple hardly took any days off to celebrate. Marie soon returned to her job as cashier at the Co-operative (Co-op). Her husband also rejoined the local air service (FIGAS), where he works as a mechanic.

Finlay's son-in-law goes to play darts with his friends and Marie buys us another drink. The old captain is already on his fourth whisky and I am being shipwrecked on my third beer, but it's a special occasion and an invitation in a pub is never refused, especially in the oldest and most traditional one in the Falklands.

Every now and then, Finlay takes a deep pull on his cigarette and shakes the ash into the ashtray on the table. "One of my companions in the crew reminded me that on the *Penélope* you collected the ash in the palm of your hand and then threw it into the sea," I tell him.

"But that was only because there wasn't an ashtray" is his commonsense reply.

The bell rings at ten to eleven and the owner announces the last round before closing time at eleven on the dot. Finlay does not waste his last opportunity and stocks up with another glass of golden whisky. I cannot follow in his wake. We arrange to begin the interview the following morning.

The four of us leave the pub and the night is silent and full of stars. The air is diaphanous and through the befuddlement of my own dizziness I feel each footstep crunching in the soft snow. Luckily everything is near in this town and we are only two blocks away from my bed and breakfast. I collapse onto my bed, but I cannot sleep. An insistent draught creeps through the windows and I have to sleep with two pairs of socks on to combat the cold.

Finlay Ferguson has a better method for combating the infernal weather. The following morning, before beginning to tell me about his life, he confesses that from the Rose he went to his club, where he stayed till three in the morning, rounding off his night with four more whiskies.

* * *

New Island is the most remote of the inhabited islands of the archipelago. It is situated at the extreme north-west of the Islands and is a treasure house of wild animals like penguins, fur seals and an endemic and threatened bird of prey called 'Johnny Rook' by the locals and 'striated caracara' by the ornithologists. The only whaling station that there was on the Islands existed there from 1906 to 1916.

In the spring of 1935 the Scottish immigrant John Ferguson and his family came to live in the house at New Island – a stone cottage constructed in the 1870s.

John Ferguson was born in Harris, in the Hebrides to the north of Scotland, in 1913. He came to New Island to look after the sheep and shear their wool. John and his English wife brought up five children on this remote island: three girls and two boys.

This is how Bob, the oldest of these children, recalls their childhood. The story is extracted from the scholarly work of his granddaughter, Sian Ferguson, aged nine: "In those days there was no electric light, so you had to get light with candles and lanterns. If they needed to call the doctor, they had to go in the boat to the big islands to find out where he was. When they found that out, they had to go and look for him. The doctors travelled around on horseback. The only means of transportation in those days were horses and boats. Grandfather Bob had a travelling teacher, but he didn't come very often, so he went to live in Stanley for two and a half years to be educated."

Bob was born in 1926. Nine years later the youngest of the Ferguson boys was born, and baptised with the sonorous name, Finlay.

"I had a younger sister, but she died, so now I can say I am the youngest," he says with his sideways smile. "I was born in Stanley, but we moved to New Island when I was six weeks old and I lived there till I was thirteen. We were only two families. Apart from ourselves and the four members of the other family, we only saw other people when the *Weddell* came three or four times a year. The travelling teacher came in the boat. "He stayed six weeks living with us, then left us homework and went. The truth is that I was not a very good student."

If there was sickness or an accident, they had to light several fires in the hills and hope that the boat would come. "One time my sister broke her arm. We knew that the *Weddell* was nearby because we had heard it on the radio, but we couldn't send messages."

That wild life ("natural," Finlay calls it) ended when his father got a job in Stanley. John Ferguson died a little time after arriving in the capital and the situation of the widow and her five children became difficult. Finlay began work when he was 14.

His first job was as errand boy for the Globe Store, the most traditional general store in Stanley. Between April and November of 1949 it was a common sight to see this puny adolescent pedalling his bike loaded with clothing recently arrived on the ships or bags of vegetables, or heavy metal tools. "A lot of snow fell during that period and the Globe was almost at sea level. A lot of times I had to get off my bike and push it uphill."

His next job was in a station where they extracted and processed seal oil. "They tried to go and build a new station where there was absolutely nothing. We had to take it all there on the boat, the *Protector*. There were 36 men and I was the youngest, but they all looked after me. In those days, everybody knew everybody else. We were there for 14 months and when the seal killing season ended, we left."

"Killing seals at fifteen? It sounds terrible." I let this slip and regretted it almost before the words were out of my mouth.

"It was the way of life in those days, what we were going to do," he says smiling. "We put them in big containers and got the oil out of them. From there I went to Weddell where I worked for three and a half years and afterwards to Stanley. I was eleven months in Fox bay and afterwards worked on road construction for a German. When I reached twenty-one I was already in Stanley driving a lorry, but what really attracted me was the sea, the life on the boats.

In September of 1952, he finally boarded his first boat, the *Gambler*. She was a little longer than the *Penélope*. "It was a steady job which I needed because that was the year I got married. A little bit later, the Falkland Islands Company bought the *Gambler* and I stayed working for them. In August of '58, they named me captain. We carried sheep, cattle and building materials."

But in 1962, those in charge of deciding whether boats could continue sailing sentenced the *Gambler*. The verdict, which allowed no appeal, was "condemned."

Finlay Ferguson was the first person during my visit who talked to me about this act of "condemning" a vessel. During the whole of my interviews in the Islands, I came across other accounts in which the dramatic moment arrived when a ship was declared "condemned" and it always caused a commotion.

The nautical cemetery where these condemned vessels generally ended up was the "Canache" a beach at the extreme east of the harbour. But there are also condemned ships, abandoned or semi-submerged, the whole length of the harbour. Those with most luck, like the *Egeria*, on one of whose beams someone wrote "Long live me", are used as warehouses and come to form part of the jetty. The book, *Condemned at Stanley*, with text and line drawings by John Smith (the painter of *The Penelope from the Charles Cooper*) is a valuable record of these abandoned ships.

"The *Gambler* was a good boat; them condemning her hurt me a lot." says Finlay Ferguson. "She was built in Puerto Natales in Chile. The construction was good, but the quality of the wood wasn't great. When she began to give problems, they asked a carpenter to repair her, but the carpenter wanted too much money and they realised that it was going to cost more to repair her than to buy a new one."

Finlay returned to Goose Green, where he had lived for a number of years and went on to captain a smaller boat, the *Black Swan*. But that did not last long. She was already a vessel at the end of her useful life. They tried to improve her with bits from the *Gambler*, but in a few years they condemned her as well.

That was the point at which the Falkland Islands Company bought Jim Lee's old boat and asked Finlay Ferguson to be her captain.

"And weren't you afraid that they might condemn this old boat as well?" I ask.

For the first time in a long morning's interview, while the sun's rays melt the snow in Celia Stewart's garden and we take our umpteenth cup of coffee, Ferguson smiles. "Of course not! Everybody knew that she was a very strong boat. The *Penelope* had already made a name for herself in the Islands. This one they weren't going to condemn."

* * *

The first time that Finlay Ferguson saw the vessel to which he would dedicate the two central decades of his life, she was stranded at Weddell Island. "I would have been about 11 or 12 and I had gone to Weddell with my travelling teacher. I remember asking, 'what is such a nice boat doing tied up here?' They said that she had been there for many years and that nobody knew what to do with her. It seemed crazy to me."

And there he was, twenty years later, captain of an historic ship. When he went down to look at the engine, it almost gave him an attack. "It was much bigger than the engines I had dealt with before. It was full of cables, pipes and tubes everywhere. It was a nightmare. I thought, 'How am I going to learn all this?' Fortunately, the ship's former engineer stayed on to share the first voyage with the new captain.

Down the years more sailors have passed through the ship than Finlay can remember. "The young ones thought they were on some sort of holiday, but it was nothing like that. It was hard work and long hours lifting heavy things and enduring the cold. Some stayed one or two years and then went. Now I meet some of them and they say that they had a good time and learned a lot. There was a good side too."

I ask him if any had stayed longer or left their mark on the *Penélope*. "Of course, Brian Jaffray, the engineer. He stayed with me for five years and afterwards still came to help me when he had free time. When he began he was very young, 18 or 20. It was his first boat. Brian was very shy, but absolutely trustworthy and a great worker."

The normal tasks during those years were to carry sheep from one island to another, shear the wool, press it and transport it. "But we transported many more sheep than wool, an average of 7 000 per year," Finlay makes clear.

"In the bigger islands where there is a jetty, the job is relatively easy; we get the sheep onto the jetty and from there we lift them onto the ship, but in the little islands we have to get the sheep onto the beach, put them in the dinghy, row to the *Penelope* and lift them on board."

"How many sheep can you get in the rowing boat?" I ask.

"About twenty."

"You are telling me that twenty sheep at a time can travel in that little dinghy we had when we were using the ship?" Suddenly the disembarkation in Fox Bay comes to mind. The said dinghy was a little wooden scallop into which you could hardly fit seven Argentines.

"Of course, twenty sheep and two of us. And when we got alongside the ship, we lifted them up with the two oars. We had to stay sitting down in the dinghy or we would have tipped over."

I calculate that in 19 years at 7,000 sheep per year, that makes 133,000 sheep. "And they behaved themselves?, I ask him, imagining the scene of Ferguson and Jaffray making sheep sit down so as to row cleanly.

"Some yes and some no. But we didn't only carry sheep; cows too and sometimes horses, but not many, because it was dangerous. In a boat of that size it was easy for them to break a leg."

When Jeff was there he took charge of the motor. "He was very skillful." If not, it was Finlay himself, who besides steering was responsible for seeing that the engine functioned without contretemps.

The *Penélope* carried people back and forth, letters and supplies. "Many people came to my mother's house in Stanley and left packages and letters with her that I would pick up when I was next passing through. She got annoyed, but never reproached me for it," says Finlay.

One of the passengers who would not forget his voyages in the ketch is the English teacher, John Fowler. At that time, Fowler was headmaster of the school for farmers' children in Darwin. The children of the "Camp" (a very Falkland Islands word, derived from the Spanish, which is used to refer to anywhere in the Islands outside Stanley) spent the winter as pupils at the school and returned to their parents in the summer. Fowler often went on excursions in the *Penélope.*

"They were very enjoyable trips." Fowler recalls, "I remember that it was on the *Penelope* that I saw my first boiled penguin eggs. They were having breakfast and they had an egg in the pan, quite a bit bigger than a hen egg. The problem is that the white doesn't go opaque, but stays transparent. The yolk looks like a fluorescent pink eye floating in gelatine. I thanked them for the offer, but refused politely."

The tourist guide, Tony Smith, is another of the many who have stories to tell about the *Penélope.* In 1977 the boat was sent to take down an old sealing station in a far distant part of the

West Falklands. "It was my first job; I was fifteen years old and very keen. There was an older man and me. We had to take off all the corrugated iron, put it on the *Penelope* and take it somewhere else. We made something like five voyages. Everything was lifted by hand and very rusty, because the station had to be 50 or 60 years old."

Tony remembers the life on board especially. "We lived on the *Penelope* for over a week and every night Finlay would tell us stories about the old days, about hunts or about storms. The stories about storms were endless. He was a hard guy, very firm, but I liked him, because at bottom he had a sense of humour and also because he always went to the point."

A little before '82, the Falkland Islands Company appointed Finlay Ferguson manager of all its islands. He had to go round them all and besides being involved in the movements of sheep and wool, he had to concern himself with provisioning, maintenance and the management of workers. This, he says is why he found himself at Speedwell Island, at the southern end of Falkland Sound, on April 2nd 1982.

"I was there with the family that lived on the island, when on the evening of April 1st we heard on the radio the Governor's announcement that an Argentine fleet was approaching to take the Islands."

* * *

On April 4th, two days after the Argentine landing, Ferguson received an urgent message from the manager of the Falkland Islands Company, Brook Hardcastle. For the first time, he wasn't asking him to carry sheep, but children.

The parents of the children boarding in Stanley were keen to have them home. Permission was granted by the Argentine authorities. A caravan of Land Rovers was hastily put together, led by the Superintendent of Education, John Fowler, which took the children towards Fitzroy.

Some miles from Fitzroy, this caravan was met by another one from that settlement, where some of the children lived, which then carried all the children onwards. Fowler and the majority of the adults then returned to Stanley, though some people carried on, hoping – fruitlessly as it turned out for many of them – to escape the Argentine presence.

Eventually after many hours of driving over grass tracks and including some 'boggings' of vehicles in the soft peaty ground of East Falklands, the several children who lived there and the others who lived on the West Falklands reached Darwin and Goose Green.

The children from the farms on East Falkland were picked up by their parents, but those from West Falkland and some from the outer islands, had to be carried across the Falkland Sound. "This was where the little ship *Penelope* and its skipper, Finlay Ferguson, came in," writes Graham Bound in *Falkland Islanders at War.* That same evening, those children and also some returning adults – like the owner of Carcass Island, Lorraine McGill – embarked on the *Penélope* at Egg Harbour.

"The *Penelope* was perfumed with diesel, sheep manure and whatever the cook, Ivan Fairlay, happened to be frying in the galley; probably penguin eggs," writes Bound. "For the children this voyage was an adventure, but Lorraine recalled being nervous: 'We were half way across the Sound, when we realized there were aircraft coming towards us – and we weren't flying a white flag. One of the children, Susie Nightingale, had some of her things stuffed into a white pillowcase, so we emptied them out and Finlay hoisted Susie's pillowcase up the mast. The planes obviously saw us and flew off, but it made us very aware of our vulnerability'" Lorraine's testimony concludes.

Ferguson remembers that day very well. "It took us a few hours to get the kids across from Egg Harbour to Port Howard on the other island," he recounts. "Some of the parents were waiting at Howard, but not all. They were distributed among the farms in another caravan of Land Rovers."

The captain says that from then, until the arrival of the helicopter with the naval commandos on May 7th, he remained at Speedwell Island. "It seemed as if they might have forgotten about us, but the peace and quiet ended on Friday May 7th, when the helicopter arrived with six or seven heavily armed soldiers on board." The head of the group communicated to him that they would search the boat. "In March, before the war began, the owner of

Lively Island had given me a box to take to his island," he explains to me.

"I always carry boxes from here and there. The officer opened the box, and inside were 5,000 cartridges. He was very annoyed and made signs like, 'What is this?' I tried to explain, but the man didn't understand a word of English. In the end I think he believed me, but, by sign language, he asked Brian and me to stay, because the following day a crew was coming to take charge of the ship."

Finlay says that Brian did not want to stay. "I told him not to make any problems, because they could force us." That morning a big helicopter landed near the house on the island and seven Argentine sailors got off. Finlay Ferguson was standing on the jetty wearing the blue cap which always protected him from the wind, when two of the new arrivals approached him. One was the officer in command and the other was a young sailor who said he would be the interpreter.

* * *

Ferguson assures me that it wasn't difficult explaining the workings of the vessel to the Lieutenant. "That can't have been due to the quality of my translations," I say, as an aside.

"We left quite late that same May 8th, a Saturday. It was already night and the weather was worsening. We went to spend the night at Bull Cove, which is a good place, very good, a very safe refuge in bad weather, if you know it. If you don't, there's no way of finding it, it's quite shallow" the veteran captain adds.

"Next day we sailed between North Arm and Bleaker Island. That was where we met up with the *Buen Suceso* and the order was changed. The Lieutenant wanted us to go along with the ship towards Fox Bay, but there was a lot of wind getting up and it was dangerous. I recommended anchoring in the lee of a little island. The second night we arrived in Fox Bay following the green ship, the *Monsunen*."

He stops himself for a moment, looks at me fixedly and tells me: "That was the worst night that I spent on the *Penelope*."

I ask him if he means that was the worst experience of all the week that we were aboard. "No" he clarifies, "the worst night of the 19 years I've had the boat. I had never seen such a storm and never saw one like it again. The waves were enormous and the wind blew more and more strongly. Everything was falling. We were berthed alongside the *Monsunen* and I said to the Lieutenant that if we stayed there we were going to sink in a couple of hours. The timbers were creaking every time the waves made our hull crash against *Monsunen's* steel sides."

That was when we separated from *Monsunen*'s steel hull and went to anchor in the middle of the bay, where the wind continued to blow and the ketch bounced about crashing against the waves all night.

"On Thursday, we left Fox Bay to look for the *Isla de los Estados*, but they didn't send us to where the ship was sunk, but to Port King. There was nothing there and when we were returning we met with the big cargo ship *Carcarañá*. That was when the Sea Harriers flew over us, wasn't it?"

Yes, that is how I remember it.

"My family and Jeff's were prisoners in Darwin, which was why I asked the Lieutenant to let us off at Egg Harbour. You all knew how to manage the boat by then." They off-loaded their kitbags and those of the other three onto the wooden jetty. "There's a big house where anyone that is passing can spend the night, but nobody lives there. It was quarter past seven when we disembarked at Egg Harbour. We said goodbye, the Lieutenant gave me his submariners' pin as a souvenir and you went off. The first thing we did was to go into the house and have a good bath."

They began their march in mid-morning. As he had already told me in the pub, they left the kitbags in the house because two days of walking over swampy ground without tracks awaited them before their arrival at Darwin. They walked for some six hours before arriving at another house on the track, Paragon House. "The second day we walked to Goose Green and the Argentine soldiers who saw us got nervous. They didn't know who we were or where we had come from. Once again there was no one who could speak English so that we could make ourselves understood.

"They searched us twice and took us to a store shed in Goose Green which was very cold. By day we hadn't felt the cold, because walking kept us warm, but when it was night we froze. I don't think I slept at all that night. The next day they took us to the Goose Green Social Club hall, where many people from Goose Green and Darwin were held prisoner, along with some from Stanley who had turned up there. There I met a niece of mine who spoke Spanish and she could explain that I was her uncle."

When Finlay Ferguson and his neighbours got out of the Social Club hall, the battle for Goose Green had already ended and the

Parachute Regiment was in charge. "I could go back home and from there I heard the news of the final battles and the surrender. A week later, the authorities said that I had to go to Stanley to look for the *Penelope.* Jeff and I went in the *Monsunen* and when I saw her, she was unrecognisable, all painted black. When did they paint her black?"

"When we got to the port in the first days of June," I tell him." It was to use her for nocturnal harbour patrols."

To Finlay it seemed that the black version of his ketch had a macabre appearance. "We quickly asked for tins of red and white paint and painted her proper colours again."

* * *

The expression, "her proper colours" catches my attention, as if it was to do with the 'natural' skin of an animal or a person. I comment that the ship's original colours, when she was called *Feuerland,* had been white almost to the flotation line and a thin stripe of red and another of black, and that when Bernd Buchner bought her and went back to calling her *Feuerland,* he went back to painting her that way. "Yes, I know that she is white now, but I can't help thinking that the colours that suit her best are those that we liked most here, that is red up to deck level, and above a white band."

Afterwards a helicopter took Ferguson and Jaffray to Egg Harbour to look for their things. They went into the house escorted by two Ghurkhas. "Everything was turned over; the house was upside down, but almost all our things were there. The pin was gone. I should have taken it with me to Darwin."

Like many other Falkland Islanders, Ferguson and his crew soon put themselves to work on reconstruction. In a few weeks they were again lifting sheep up with oars and sitting them on the ketch's deck as if nothing had happened. The only marks which reminded him of the past war were, "the damage made by bullets and shrapnel in the mast, on the deck and in the hull's bow."

In 1984, he gave up being the manager of all the islands and took charge of one in particular, Bleaker. Bleaker, known to us as Isla María, was the island where stopped during our return to Stanley, the island where we dreamed of remaining till the end of the war, the island where Ni Coló, Contreras and Peralta could not kill a sheep.

For seven years Finlay struggled to advance the economy of that island, despite depressed wool prices. He used the *Penélope* only for coming and going, moving sheep and taking wool. Sometimes he got a visit from his friend and former engineer, Brian Jaffray, but most of the time there was just him and his wife and the farm work was becoming more and more of an uphill struggle. His knee hurt and the years of hard work were taking their toll. "They were very hard years" he tells me. He thinks for a bit, takes more coffee, then his face clouds over and he repeats "very hard."

In 1989 the Falkland Islands Company decided to sell the *Penélope.*

Thanks to the policy of selling the farms of absentee land owners to locals, Finlay's older brother, Bob Ferguson and his son John were able to get enough credit to buy Weddell Island. Two years before, John Hamilton's descendents had sold his islands and now in one of those many surprising twists to this story, the Fergusons bought the *Penélope* from the FIC to take her back to Weddell.

Two years later the FIC also sold Bleaker Island. In 1991, Finlay Ferguson returned to Stanley, where he first worked as manager of the Land Rover agency and finally as FIC's warehouse manager, until 1997.

"You retired that year?"

"No, they made me redundant", he declares with the most acid smile of his repertoire. In Spanish, the word 'redundant' is not used to refer to a worker that a company does not want anymore. We use the euphemism that they 'decided to dispense with his services.' 'Redundant' is, I believe, clearer but more brutal. Finlay Ferguson had worked thirty years for the company.

Finlay continued working in the Co-op until February 2006. When I meet him, he's been retired for six months, but still keeps going to the Co-op nearly every day and is available whenever his friends need him.

Tomorrow, for example, he is going to Bleaker Island. He'll be there for a couple of weeks looking after the island, because its present owner, Mike Rendell, is a member of the Islands' Legislative Council and has to be present for the arrival of the new Governor, this week.

Twelve hours have gone by and once again the night is full of stars as we get in Finlay Ferguson's Land Rover to have dinner at the Malvina House Hotel. During dinner, Finlay tells me about his trips outside the Islands.

The first time he left was in 1980, when he was already 45 years old. As part of their contracts, the FIC gave its employees passages to Great Britain every few years. He spent two days in Buenos Aires and three months in the British Isles. "Buenos Aires is a big city, but you can walk about in it. London is demented," he says and shakes his head as we finish our roast lamb.

He went back to Great Britain in 2001 and this time decided to take his wife to visit Harris, the island in the Hebrides, where his father came from. "It was the worst possible day, a Sunday. They are very religious people and they don't go out or do anything on Sunday. We didn't have an address so we walked about, looked at the village and left. The truth is that it is very similar to how it is here. Seeing what the north of Scotland is like, I can understand why the majority of the Scots who arrived in the Falklands stayed."

Three years later, he travelled again, but this time for an operation on his knee, which would not leave him in peace. "They took almost all the pain away, but now I can't bend the knee like before," he tells me and sticks his leg out from under the table so that I can see how far he can bend it. "It doesn't go any further, but then I don't have to crouch down much, do I?" he says, finishing off the last of his wine.

Back on the street and although we both have to get up early the next day to catch planes going in different directions, Finlay invites me to take a last few drinks at his club, the Falklands Club. "It's the oldest and most exclusive" he tells me. "We serve ourselves. Each member has a key and can go in when he likes, but there are very strict rules."

One of the rules, of course, is that women cannot be members. Only members and their guests are allowed in, but so that it doesn't get too crowded and lose the sense of belonging to the members, non members who are resident in the Islands can only go in once a week. Non-resident guests can be taken in whenever. Finlay gets the key from his pocket and we leave our coats and hats in the entrance. Almost a third of the space is occupied by a large wooden bar counter. On the wall at the back hang the precious bottles of whisky, head down, ready to be used. On the wall there are photos of the members, their boats and their festive moments.

In front of the bar are the ten commandments or laws of the club and the list of its honourable members, among which figures – I hardly need to look for it – the name of Finlay Ferguson.

Four regulars have already got ahead of us with the whisky, so Finlay quickly puts his hand to the task. This time I accept the whisky he offers me, but I ask to have it with ice. Finlay introduces me to the members. It is obvious that they respect him and perhaps this may have made him feel safe in inviting me to this temple of Kelper pride without knowing who else was going to be there.

When I say that I am an Argentine veteran, the most talkative of the group asks me a question which I feel sure he has asked on other occasions, "Did you come here to bury some ghosts?"

They give me a cordial reception. I tell them that tomorrow I am flying to the distant island of West Point to see Michael Clarke, the *Penélope's* last owner. They tell a few stories amongst themselves about Clarke, who is a friend of a couple of those present. "Don't fight with him; he's got the biggest and strongest hands in the Islands," they advise me.

Just as in the Rose, when others are talking, old Finlay retreats prudently into the background; he listens, smiles, and pays attention to his whisky. He leaves me at my boarding house. We don't spend much time on farewells, because tomorrow our flights are programmed to take off at the same time and from the same place.

* * *

As on every morning, Celia Stewart serves me a breakfast fit for someone who will spend the day driving sheep or cutting peat. Is this an excess of kindness, or is she trying to kill me? On the table are two slices of toast, butter, several different jams, scrambled eggs with fried bread, yoghurt, granola, cornflakes, honey, sugar, a couple of apples, orange juice and coffee with milk. I eat what I can because at half-past seven, Derek, the pilot cousin of Michael Clarke, is coming by and has offered to take me to the airport, which is now only used by the little planes which travel round the islands.

It's raining. Derek Clarke shows me the pre-fabricated houses of the suburbs to the east of Stanley, the houses which give shelter to the population 'boom' since the war. The population has risen from 1,000 to almost 2,000 inhabitants, more than half the total population of the Islands, excluding the military at Mount Pleasant. We go by the 'Canache', the graveyard of condemned vessels and by various fields which have been fenced off because they still contain Argentine mines from the time of the war.

The Falkland Islands Government Air Service (FIGAS) has four passenger aircraft, two more for doing fishery patrols and five pilots. Tourism increases the number of flights in summer and they bring in an extra pilot.

CAPTAIN FINLAY Ferguson at the figas office, just before boarding for Bleaker Island.

Finlay Ferguson has already arrived and is sitting in his Land Rover, driven by his wife, waiting for his plane to Bleaker Island. He is wearing a blue boiler suit, the eternal blue chequered jacket, brown boots and his peaked captain's cap. We put our bags on a long table. Each one has to have a string attached with a piece of paper which indicates its destination. Mine says, "Carcass Island", which is the neighbouring island to West Point, where Michael Clarke will come to get me in his new boat, the *Condor.*

On the luggage counter there are boxes and messages. My attention is caught by a packet of books from Amazon.com that is going to one of the islands in the south. During Finlay Ferguson's childhood they had to communicate with bonfires and now from any island they connect to the Internet to buy a book from New York, which arrives a couple of weeks later.

Finlay Ferguson gets into one of the eight-passenger planes which runs to take off and then gains altitude as easily as a bird. It is already lost in the clouds.

My turn arrives. There are only three of us passengers on this flight. The pilot is called Tom Chater. Tom is tall, thin and angular and is thirty, but when he turns serious, looks even younger. He offers to let me sit next to him in the co-pilot's seat. He explains that the plane is a modern *Islander BN-2B*, capable of landing and taking off from the undulating grass strips which serve as runways on the farms and out-lying islands. "The secret is keeping the tyres only half-inflated, so that they don't burst on such uneven ground. Many pilots of much bigger aircraft are amazed at the places where we dare to land," he tells me with pride.

The flight will make a stop at Douglas, where Michael Clarke's farm is and another at Port Howard, the port on the West Falklands where the children that the *Penélope* carried arrived on April 4th 1982. We fly low and the new roads that cross the East Falklands can be seen, the sheep and the cows grazing, the mountains and lakes, the low areas of bushes.

Tom Chater tells me that I am the first Argentine veteran that he has met.

"How old were you during the war?" I ask him.

"Six years old. For me the war was like a game. My first toys were planes and boats that I made out of wood and other things I found. I had an aircraft carrier *Invincible*, from which planes went out to bombard Argentine positions. It was during the war that I decided I wanted to be a pilot, a Sea Harrier pilot."

On April 2nd 1982 a platoon of Argentines who had taken part in the landing arrived at the house of Tom and his parents. "I remember that one of them asked us why we were listening to the BBC and why we were not happy that our fellow citizens had come to liberate us from the British occupiers. They had no idea about who we were, what we thought or what we wanted."

We fly over Douglas and Tom makes sure that there are people on the strip, that there's at least one vehicle there and that the shed where the fire-fighting apparatus is kept is open. There are two Land Rovers and five little figures which wave their hands at us over the grass. The landing is bouncy like that of a toy plane, but I don't feel afraid at any time. Tom Chater seems to have it all under control.

At the end of the runway a robust young man is waiting for us, who is introduced as Michael Clarke's younger son. Michael Clarke is the owner of Kings Ridge farm at Douglas, but now spends the best part of the year at West Point Island, where tourism brings him more profit than the wool from his sheep.

The well-built young man greets Tom effusively. He has a girl of about six years by the hand.

"How are we?" Tom Chater asks the girl.

"Freezing" she says. All her interest is placed on a parcel she is waiting for. Tom opens the plane's door, gets out the parcel and deposits it in the open hands of the girl, who runs off skipping across the porous ground.

Another take-off. We reach the Falkland Sound. I am flying over the scene of so many stories, of so much history. Everything seems so natural, so peaceful, so far from the world. Little drops of drizzle are pinging against the windscreen and the soft rain carries on falling on the land and on the sea.

The last stop before 'my' airport is Howard. The two ladies who were in the back and the better part of the packets and boxes get off here.

Tom and I continue the flight alone. When he reached adolescence, Tom decided that he didn't want to be a military pilot any more. He saw the war in Bosnia on the television and knew that he did not want either to kill or be killed in a war. "But I kept the desire for the epic adventure of flying and I am achieving it in these planes which land miraculously on little patches of pasture."

During the last leg of the flight, we fly across the West Falklands, which appear a little more rocky and rugged than the East Falklands. It stops raining and great flocks of birds keep us company, flying almost at the same height as us.

"Do you know what I've just remembered," says Tom, "the two Argentine girls who came here; it would be about five years ago, when the 1999 Agreement allowed Argentine citizens to come. They were the first Argentines I had ever spoken to and I didn't know how they would react to me or me to them". They were the daughters of a Pucará pilot who went down on Pebble Island and wanted to be taken to the place where their father had died.

"They were more or less my age and were very pretty, especially one of them and that was the one who asked to sit next to me." Tom anticipates what he thinks I am thinking and points out, "I was still single then." Later he tells me that he is married to a helicopter pilot who works at the military base and that they are expecting a baby sometime in the next two weeks.

The thing is that the Argentine girls "didn't know anything about the Islands nor about us. We began to talk and they had a

TOM CHATER'S plane and the Carcass Island Land Rover which Michael Clarke used to fetch me in the most desolate airfield in the world.

lot of questions. After the flight we met in Stanley and went for a few beers together."

"And?"

"And what? Nothing; nothing happened, but the fact is that talking to them made me change my perspective. I could see the Argentines differently and understand that these girls were very moved to see the place where their father died. They admired him and said that he was a great pilot."

We are arriving at Carcass. We fly over the bay where the *Condor* is anchored. From this height she looks very like the *Penélope*, an elongated Coca Cola bottle, red down below and white above. Instead of two, she has only one mast, thin like a sewing needle. There are a couple of buildings in the inlet, maybe a house and a store, but we go on, because the landing strip is on the other side of the island. We begin to descend and the grazing Upland Geese, so common in the Islands, move off under protest.

Tom banks over the sea and turns decidedly to face the imaginary runway. On one side of the strip I see a sleeve of orange plastic for measuring the wind, a dilapidated Land Rover and a big, solid-looking man in a red jacket. The sleeve, the man and the vehicle get bigger and bigger and with the departure of the last goose, the half-inflated wheels of the Islander caress the grassy surface of the most desolate airport in the world.

CHAPTER 4

The last years of the *Penelope*

On touching down on Carcass Island, the plane reverts to coming to a stop in a series of little hops. Tom Chater completes the landing manoeuvre with same calm as on the previous occasions and parks his Islander at the side of the Land Rover, which has the fire-fighting equipment attached behind it like a trailer. This time the pilot does not leave his seat. I say goodbye, wish him good luck with his imminent paternity and get out my suitcase with the wheels, which in these parts are as useful as those on the fifteen year old Finlay Ferguson's pushbike in the snowy hills of Port Stanley.

Michael Clarke gives me his hand and I can't help but remember the comments of the Falklands Club regulars. If they hadn't made them, I wouldn't have noticed his hands, but now I see them: powerful, tanned by the cold and vigorous, with big knuckles. More than working hands they appear to be hands that have been worked.

Michael stays talking a while with Tom, and I cast my eyes over this part of one of the most distant islands in the archipelago. Away on one side is only the sea, and even more sea till the horizon; on the other the prairie with sparse grass which rises up until it loses itself in a rocky mountain. Above is the leaden sky with a flock of distant birds. All that can be heard is the gentle murmur of the waves washing over the stones on the shore and the faint honking of geese.

When the little plane disappears amongst the clouds I get in the Land Rover. Michael is engaged in the task of dismantling the airport. He lowers the pole where the orange windsock was and puts it in a bag. He leaves the bag and the fire engine trailer in a shed and secures everything with a padlock, although I can't imagine the possibility of thieves ransacking this airport.

The Rover advances slowly due to Carcass Island's lack of roads. Three times I get out to open and close the gates, which separate different areas of pasture for cows and sheep. Passing over streams and some boggy bits, we cross the island and stop in front of a shed with tin-clad wooden walls. The colours are typical of the Islands: muddy cream and pale green.

This island belongs to Rob McGill's family. His wife Lorraine had embarked on the *Penélope* for that perilous crossing with the children returning to their parents on April 4th, 1982. This week the McGills are not here, but their friend and neighbour Michael has taken the opportunity of coming to get me to go in the store shed to sort out a generator, which isn't working. Michael's big hands take only a couple of hours to fix the problem.

We are in the McGills' house which reveals the passions of a naturalist. In the corridor there's an entire library with books of landscapes, birds, marine mammals, voyages and sailors' tales and on the walls there are frames with photos of eagles, penguins and albatross. Each summer for over a decade this island has been welcoming armies of wildlife lovers. The twenty or more mugs for tea and coffee show that the island is not always so empty and the mundane pleasures of its occupants are evident in the big roundel of cork that hangs in front of the window. Both the roundel and the wooden board – which they stuck behind it as a precaution – are full of dart holes.

THE *CONDOR* behind the *Penelope*, both moored at West Point in 2005. Photo by Jeannette Clarke.

On the sofa lies an open newspaper. It is the *Daily Record*, an English paper, dated the 23rd December, some five months back. It's open at a page where a couple tell the story of how the mother, when about to give birth in Lanarkshire, was taken to hospital in Dundee, 75 miles away. While I am reading the paper a fat black bird with a sharp beak comes trotting in through the door and starts running about the dining room looking for crumbs to peck at.

When Michael has finished fixing the generator, we get in the Land Rover and head for the raised access point to the jetty. Michael lowers his rubber Zodiac into the water and we cover the two hundred metres across the water to the *Condor*, the steel vessel with which he replaced the *Penélope*.

I am about to live one of the most exciting moments of my visit to the Falklands; I am going to sail again in a place to which for more than twenty years I never imagined I would return.

This sea voyage is, in fact, a happy result of the bad weather. West Point has a short landing strip that goes up and down a hill, but is impracticable in days with strong wind, like today. If the weather had been better, Tom Chater would have dropped me at my destination and Michael Clarke would not have had to come to the neighbouring island to get me in his boat. Now we are already ploughing the waters of the passage between the two islands.

Michael is at the wheel with his brow furrowed. I go on deck and catch a face full of cold drizzle mixed with the salt water that the risen wind lifts from the crests of the waves. I walk, staggering from the battering of the waves, to the bow rails. I get a lump in my throat. I am sailing in the Falklands once again in a vessel like the *Penélope*.

Michael shows me the changes he has introduced on deck; he has roofed it and converted it into a dining room and enclosure where the passengers may enjoy the trip sitting down, without getting wet. All it lacks at the moment is the furniture. The wheelhouse is much bigger than that of the old ketch, but the ship itself is a couple of metres shorter. Riding over the waves it seems solid and comfortable to me and its space is well distributed. It rolls less from side to side than its predecessor, but pitches from bow to stern like a seesaw.

Perhaps I am not allowing myself the possibility of being seduced by it, but it seems to me that this metal ship lacks the enchantment, the magic and the elegance that the *Penélope* had. Sailing, touching its cold rough skin makes me miss even more the experience that probably I shall never be able to repeat: sailing through these waters in that ketch.

* * *

Sailing from Carcass to West Point is like being seized by a flock of migratory birds and flying from one planet of *The Little Prince* to another. Instead of one family, in this island there live two: Michael and Jeanette Clarke and the legendary owners of the island, Roddy and Lily Napier.

Roddy and Lily were brought up on these islands and don't think that living in such isolation is anything out of the ordinary. The first owner of West Point was Arthur Felton, Roddy's great uncle. His mother bought it from him and practically since his birth in 1928 Roddy Napier has lived in this house of stone and wood. It has a roof of green zinc and the walls are horizontal wooden planks, painted white the same colour as the fence which surrounds the carefully tended garden. In the thirties they received visits from a few sailing boats. "The only one with a motor was the *Penelope*. I loved sailing in the ketch, because she had the best cabin. There was nothing else like the *Penelope* in the Falklands of that period."

This quiet life and the raising of sheep began to be interrupted by the first tourists, who came to remote West Point in 1968 on the cruise ship *Navarino*. "Lars Erik Lindblad was the visionary Swede that brought the first tourists" Roddy Napier tells me in his Victorian accent. He takes me to the wall opposite the front window of his living room, where there hangs a large framed photo of the cruise ship which Lindblad bought and with which he made the majority of his voyages: the *Explorer*. "A hundred lovers of nature and exotic places came on that ship. The majority were English. They got on in Buenos Aires or in Ushuaia. It was a marvellous ship, but Lindblad sold it in 1984."

The impresario died fifteen years ago, "though he was the same age as me" and the arrival of tourists was only re-established in 1992 with the coming of the *Ocean Princess*. "This one could carry up to four hundred and we were asked how we were going to deal with so many tourists. But we managed them." It is certain that at first they took some outlandish decisions like buying what looks like a yellow school bus from the USA. It seemed to them that they would need it to carry so many people from the house to the other end of the island, where the colonies of penguins are and the nests of the majestic black-browed albatross. The bus is now abandoned like a curious relic on the track that runs from the Napiers' house to that of the Clarkes.

Now the crossing is done on foot or in Land Rovers, but the age and fragile health of the Napiers made them realise some years ago that they needed help with the hordes of summer tourists. Michael and his wife Jeanette, who already have their own sheep farm, which survives with the help of their grown up sons, started coming to West Point in 1993, when they bought the *Penélope*. Besides being glad to see the ketch of his childhood again, Roddy offered them the manager's house a few hundred metres uphill from his own and asked them to help with the maintenance of the tracks and looking after the tourists.

West Point is one of the smallest inhabited islands of the archipelago, with a surface area of 1255 hectares and, according to the census, just two inhabitants: Roddy and Lily Napier (the Clarkes are listed on the census at their Douglas farm).

The text which accompanies a collection of stamps dedicated to this island points out that Roddy Napier, great grand-nephew of West Point's first inhabitant and his wife Lily are "representatives of a traditional and independent form of life which is rapidly disappearing from the archipelago. They cultivate their own vegetables, raise hens and milk cows every morning." The leaflet also says that from the arrival of the first cruise ship in 1968, thousands of tourists come each year, not only to see the great colonies of yellow crested or rockhopper penguins and black-browed albatross. "They also come to find out what it really means to live on your own island."

It's the morning of my arrival and while I take coffee and listen to stories of the *Penélope's* old days with Roddy, Jeanette is cooking up some pasta resembling little shells, much liked in the Islands, with a finger-licking meat and tomato sauce. The five of us have lunch in the Clarkes' house. When I arrive with Roddy and his wife Lily, a little old lady with white hair, knock-you-flat energy, and a razor-sharp tongue, the dining room table is already covered with photos of the red and white ketch.

During lunch – principally, I suppose, because of my insistent questions – the *Penélope* is spoken of as one might of a family member who has just left on a long journey. Each time that someone lifts their plate for another serving from the enormous and succulent pan of pasta, it reveals another of the place mats which have on them big photos of the *Penélope* sailing in a calm sea which reflects her two colours. A few brilliant fenders on either side give her a festive appearance.

This is not the only souvenir of the ketch in Jeanette and Michael's dining room. There's a little life buoy, maybe big enough for a chihuahua, hanging on the wall, with the words 'Penelope' and 'Kings Ridge' in the white half.

One of the stories that they tell when we are already at the dessert stage happened at Christmas in 2001. Robin Woods, a scientist friend who made many investigative trips around the islands with the *Penélop*e, had told them the long story of the ketch during the time when she was called *Feuerland,* but had got her launch date wrong by one year. He told them that it had been in 1926.

In 2001, Michael and Jeanette thought that the *Penélope* was turning 75 and because of this decided to celebrate her birthday, together with Christmas. "I made a cake in the shape of the *Penelope*" says Jeanette with pride and nostalgia. "We ate it with gusto and drank toasts to our ship."

"There's no more wooden boats like that left in the Islands" growled Roddy Napier.

"I would say that there are three: one is a little bigger and another a little smaller, but you don't see them everywhere like the *Penelope*" says Michael. "The Falkland Islands Company has two launches in Stanley and that's it; with all the vessels they had before."

"That's because before there were lots more people on the small islands and you couldn't go by plane," Lily interjects.

As if at a wake, we eat our delicious chocolate cake, made to Lily's recipe, without talking.

Michael finally breaks the silence. "Thirty or forty years ago there were at least four boats of *Penelope's* size and a lot of smaller ones. Now the majority are lying on the scrap heap at the bottom of Stanley's jetty."

"Condemned" I add, happy to use my new word.

"Yes" says Roddy, moving his head with difficulty, "when the *Penelope* went I would say that marked the end of an era in the Falklands."

* * *

Michael Clarke can't explain what attracted him to the sea and ships. "It was an impulse, an urge." From childhood he liked to go aboard the wooden boats that ploughed around the islands. "The *Penelope* was one of those boats, but she didn't stand out. She didn't mean much to me." Michael made a voyage in the ketch in 1965, in the time when Chris Bundes was captain. "She was pretty well looked-after."

For Jeanette, on the other hand, a life at sea holds no attraction. For her the only life worth living is that of the Camp, with firm ground underfoot, open spaces and lungs filled with fresh air. She spent a while in Port Stanley "and hated every minute." Despite not sharing her husband's passion for boats, she does have a special relationship with the *Penélope,* which was born on the long-ago day when her school group went on a nautical trip.

Her family lived at Teal Inlet in the north of the East Falklands. Jeanette was at the Darwin Boarding School when she got to go with her companions to a little island nearby. They went in Captain Finlay Ferguson's *Penélope.* "It's one of the best memories of my school days."

When he reached adolescence, Michael Clarke began to study mechanics, but he didn't finish and afterwards went to work for the British Antarctic Survey (BAS), going south in 1970. "We went to Ushuaia, Punta Arenas and the Antarctic bases and in May the ship returned to England for re-provisioning. I was 18 and didn't get as much benefit out of the experience as I would have today." Michael's mother was already living in England and he stayed with her during those months. At the end of the following Antarctic campaign he stayed in Stanley and married Jeanette.

"Jeanette and I already wanted to start a family. When our first son was born, we moved to the Camp and my life has been a rural one since that time, although we did live in Stanley for some periods." Michael turned into a respected "contract shearer" and began to travel all over the islands stripping sheep of their wool with speed and precision.

"Perhaps if I hadn't started a family so young I might have spent more time at sea, but things just turned out that way," he reflects today philosophically. In 1973 they moved near to his in-laws in Teal Inlet. Afterwards they lived on the large farm at Douglas, but from there they moved to San Carlos where they stayed five years, before moving back to Douglas at the end of the seventies.

The war didn't affect them like some other Islanders. "Only in the last four days they put us all in one building. The soldier who was guarding us seemed about fifteen; he didn't look old enough to carry a gun. When the British troops were getting near, a helicopter came and very quickly took all the soldiers away. The next morning a detachment of 1,300 Royal Marines was already there. We guided them to Teal Inlet which was on their way to Stanley." Suddenly Michael gives funny grin and says, "It seems strange telling these things to an Argentine..."

The Clarkes say that they lived peacefully till the eighties, "but we didn't have anything, we didn't own any land." Then came the new post-war policy, obliging the absentee landowners to sell, and the sub-division of the big tracts of land into smaller farms. In 1988, the 100,000 acre Douglas Farm was divided into four parts. The Clarkes bought one of 28,000 acres (some 11,600 hectares). Taking the name of a hill in the middle of their property, they called their farm Kings Ridge.

"But still there's no profit," Michael throws out this remark with a smile.

"Since we bought the farm 18 years ago, inflation's gone up, materials have gone up, fuel's gone up, and the price of wool hasn't moved. At first we were living well. We are now, but we wouldn't be living well if we only had the wool."

In order to buy Kings Ridge they had to sell everything they owned of any value and still they are paying off the debt to the bank. They sold the house they had in Port Stanley, the Land Rover and the boat that Michael had at that time.

"Whenever I could I used to buy little boats for the pleasure of sailing. In 1977 I had bought a 22-footer (6.82m), the *Queen Mary*. In '83 I changed it for one slightly bigger, 36 ft. (a little more that 11m). It was old, from 1900. Now it's one of the scrapped vessels lying in the canache in Stanley".

Jeanette listens to her husband, sitting on the sofa while she knits a sweater. Her face shows that she has heard this story many times before. She has already told me that "I didn't like those little boats that he had at the beginning."

Despite Jeanette's lack of enthusiasm Michael didn't give up dreaming about a new boat. "I felt the urge to sail."

* * *

When in 1993 he began to hear on the radio an announcement by his friend John Ferguson that the *Penélope* was for sale on Weddell, he didn't give it much importance.

John and his father, Bob, Finlay's older brother, had also taken advantage of the sale of the properties of absentee landowners to acquire Weddell from John Hamilton's heirs. They needed a means of transportation for their new island. When the Falkland Islands Company had sold the *Penélope* in 1987, leaving Finlay Ferguson without a boat, the buyers were his brother and his nephew. This is how the ketch returned to the place that had been its home in its first two decades in the Islands.

After a few years the Fergusons saw that they needed a new boat and began to look for a buyer for their old wooden vessel. "But there were no buyers," says Michael. "Months went by and the radio advertisement kept on being repeated. I remembered how good the *Penelope* was and decided to give them a call."

The Clarkes flew to Weddell to have a look at it in August 1993, but Michael had already made up his mind. "John put the boat on the beach so that we could also have a look at her undersides when the tide went out. Really I didn't need to have a boat, but it was the realisation of a dream."

Without more ado, they took the boat north from Weddell. It was his first voyage as owner and captain and Michael was exultant. He went to show his acquisition to Roddy and Lily Napier. Roddy was delighted to see the ketch, which brought him so many nice childhood memories, once more.

"But at that time I didn't imagine that I was going to come here so often," Michael says, "or that finally the *Penelope* would spend her last years in the Islands anchored out there, in this harbour at West Point."

* * *

"If you want to make a tour of the island you better hurry up, because the sun is going down," Jeanette recommends.

We get in the Land Rover and make our way to the cliffs on the other side of the island, going through three gates and along tracks barely visible in the hard yellowed winter grass. We arrive at the imposing albatross nests, walking between grassy areas. "They'll be back in two or three weeks" says Michael. "In summer, tourists come cruising half way round the world to see them." By the size of the nests – constructions of mud and twigs, the size of the old wooden bowls for grinding corn – you can guess the size of these white oceanic birds, which in winter sleep on the sea's waves.

In the eighteenth and nineteenth centuries this place was known by the seal hunters as 'Albatross Island.' Seventy-five per cent of the world population of this, the most common species of albatross, nests in the Falklands. Each year, 15,000 pairs build their nests on these cliffs at West Point. I go near to the cliff edge and my guide shows me the rocks where the penguins will come ashore when the spring is a little more advanced. The experience is a bit like arriving at the theatre some hours before the show begins.

THE ALBATROSS cliff at West Point Island.

However, even without the protagonists, I'm deeply impressed by the spectacle of the rough sea, the mist covering the island's highest mountain and the grass lands punctuated by little groups of sheep and cows.

One of the wild animal that doesn't leave the island in winter is the Johnny Rook (*Striated Caracara*) When I return to the Land Rover, a Johnny Rook follows me, bouncing along on its short powerful legs. It has the sharp, curved beak and fierce insistent look of all the raptors. I don't know why it is following me, but judging by its attitude I am glad that I am much bigger than it.

At our next stop, I walk to the promontory from which there is a view over the bay and the nearby coast of West Falklands. Michael explains to me that the Johnny Rooks are used to people throwing them scraps of meat and that my Johnny Rook with the aggressive face was waiting for me to feed it. The *Condor* rocks in the middle of the bay, and the island's three houses rise up on the hill which dominates the jetty where the dinghies are moored.

Back in the house with a steaming coffee to shake off the cold, Michael continues telling me stories about his voyages in the *Penélope*, which have a lot to do with the growing interest in ecological tourism and the environment in the Islands.

After a year in which they were pretty much limited to using the ketch for carrying stores from Stanley to Douglas and back, at the end of 1994, a scientist who was working for Falklands Conservation, a non-governmental body which concerns itself with the protection of wildlife, advised Michael Clarke that his organisation was designing a study of the sea lion population in the small islands. "They needed a vessel that could get into all the small islands and also carry a three metre Zodiac inflatable. I put in that bid and they accepted it. There was no other bidder. There was only one other boat that met the requirements in the islands, but it was not available".

Roddy Napier is surprised by the curious twists this story takes, because he remembers that the first sea lion census was carried out in the 'thirties, also using the *Penélope.*

"I was the captain and navigator and Jeanette the cook, and we carried three English scientists from the marine mammal department of the British Antarctic Survey. For thirty days in January and February we went round all the little islands, leaving from

Stanley towards the north, passing San Carlos and stopping at some islands so small that they aren't on the maps," Michael explains, while marking his passage in pencil on the map in my book: a guide to ecologically interesting sites produced by Falklands Conservation.

"Nobody had ever been to some of these islands and they aren't places which are often seen, especially the more distant islands to the north-west: the Jasons. These animals look for places where no one will bother them," Michael tells me. "We had pretty bad weather that month, with lots of windy days."

"I wanted to get off at first," Jeanette intervenes, "but I stuck it out to the end. There's something that gets to you on those voyages. Afterwards I went as cook on some others."

"From Steeple Jason" Michael continues, tracing the route in pencil on the map, "we continued to Weddell, went down to Speedwell and Sea Lion and then returned to Stanley after exactly one month. On the last leg we could see whales swimming under the keel. They looked really fine in the calm, quiet water. For the study they were counting the pups. In their report they said that they had seen 165."

Michael enjoyed travelling around the islands in his ketch and, besides, they were paying him by the day, which made it very profitable. Because of this he didn't hesitate the following year when they asked him to put in for a study of rockhopper and gentoo penguins. "We went all round again that year and once again it lasted for a month."

In 1997 it was the turn of another study, this time of the carancho's first cousin, the southern caracara, which in the Falklands goes by the formal name 'striated caracara' although the people call it 'Johnny Rook.' "This tour was much more difficult. Johnny Rooks were in serious danger of extinction and we didn't finish the count in the month that we had available. Because of this they contracted me to complete the study the following year." It was on that trip that the scientist in charge was Robin Woods, who first spoke to them about the German origins of their ketch.

In that year's report detailing the worrying decline of the population of the Johnny Rook, which sheep farmers considered a pest and took pot shots at, Falklands Conservation concluded the document with a special thank you: "This study could not have been carried out without the local knowledge, wise seamanship and great support given by Michael and Jeanette Clarke, owners of the auxiliary ketch *Penelope*."

During the year, the Clarkes looked after their farm at Douglas and used the *Penélope* for other jobs commissioned by the government, like anchoring over the submarine pipe through which the fuel for the Mount Pleasant complex passes. "Every three years they used the *Penelope* as a platform so that divers could inspect the condition of the oil duct. Every day three divers went down and the controller remained in the wheelhouse with me looking at the images they were sending up from a camera."

And when the summer arrived Michael Clarke knew that there would probably be another study of the Islands' wildlife. In 1999 they went to Beauchêne Island, the most isolated of the islands archipelago in the direction of the Antarctic. "Steeple Jason in the north and Beauchene in the south are the most extreme points of the Falklands. Having been more than once to both those uninhabited islands you could say that the *Penelope* is the boat that has been round them the most" states Michael, who may have sold the vessel but still keeps the pride.

The little ship continued carrying scientists to count animals and plants and in 2003 the *Penélope* did her last job of this kind:

MICHAEL CLARKE on the turf of West Point.

a study of sea lions, just like Michael's first eight years previously. This time the scientists proved that the population had risen slightly.

By then Michael was getting worried by the fact that the insurers were declining to offer policies for such an old wooden boat. If he was going to continue working with Falklands Conservation and above all getting involved in the lucrative tourist business that Roddy Napier was proposing to him, he had to change the ketch for a more modern vessel. But, if John Ferguson couldn't find buyers for the *Penélope* in 1993, a decade later the mission had become almost impossible.

At that moment an unexpected letter arrived at Michael Clarke's house. It was sent to him by a German merchant seaman called Bernd Buchner. To Michael this name didn't sound at all familiar.

* * *

In the letter Buchner told him that the previous summer he had been to the Falklands as Second Officer on the cruise ship *World Discoverer* which had stopped some hours at West Point so that the tourists could get off to see the albatross nests and the penguins. A few metres from where the cruise ship was anchored Bernd saw the *Penélope* and knew immediately that this was the vessel on which the German explorer Gunther Plüschow travelled round Tierra del Fuego at the end of the twenties.

During the few hours of the stay, Bernd was on watch so couldn't get close to the ketch or go ashore, but he wanted to know if Michael would be on West Point at the time of his next arrival with the *World Discoverer* and expressed a wish to meet him and to look at the vessel more closely.

The meeting took place in January 2003. "That was when Bernd told me that he wanted to buy the boat from me. I told him that I needed the boat for my work and therefore couldn't sell it, unless I could get another one suitable for what I was doing with it. That's when the long negotiation started."

Bernd Buchner made a tentative offer to show the seriousness of his wager. In the summer of 2004 when Michael was thinking about going to England to visit his mother, Bernd invited him to go over to Germany to have a look round boatyards. Buchner thought that a vessel made for fishing in the harsh waters of the North Atlantic might fit the bill for sailing in the Falklands.

While pondering this suggestion, Michael Clarke did his last job with the ketch. In February 2004 he went to East Cove, to allow the petrol company divers to go down to check the state of the oil duct again. The search for *Penélope's* successor began three months later and would end after many adventures with the purchase of the *Condor.*

"My life has changed so much since I decided to buy the *Penelope* thirteen years ago, that now I can't be without a boat," Michael ponders.

A little while later the sun goes down on my second day at West Point. I slept two nights as a guest of the Clarkes, who had offered to put me up, when they learned how important it was for my search to talk to them. "Come to West Point and we will take care of everything," they told me. With these few words and the generosity of the good people of the Camp that goes beyond understanding, they hadn't even said that they were inviting me to stay with them.

And in the same spirit of neither expecting nor giving thanks, next day they gave me two treasures that they knew I would value: one of the place mats with the *Penélope's* photo and a grey cotton tee-shirt with the shape of the ketch embroidered in white, red and black on the chest and the words, "Kings Ridge." This is the 'official' farm tee-shirt, made by Jeanette.

I grab my notebook, the recorder and my camera and we put on coats, hats and scarves to go out into the night. The stars shine here even more than in Port Stanley. The only signs of life are the lights of the house we have just left and that of the Napiers, whose chimney smoke promises a tasty dinner.

In this cold and rugged corner, on this island swept by the winds of the South Atlantic, which it takes less than an hour to go round, I am enjoying a marvellous dinner washed down with good red wine. Roddy tells a lot of anecdotes about his frequent visits to Argentina and how much he likes the country and the people there. All four only participate when the conversation turns to stories about some Islander that they all know. And that's easy because they know practically everybody.

At eleven next morning, the dot which is the plane that will take me back to Stanley appears on the horizon, piloted this time by Derek Clarke. The morning is sunny and almost windless and the Islander can land at West Point without any problem. It is the doctor's plane. Every two or three weeks one of the hospital's doctors travels in the plane around the far away farms or to places where there are old folk like Roddy and Lily.

While the doctor checks his patients, Michael gives me a job to do: to take a bag of raw meat down to the beach and give it to the Johnny Rooks to eat. I go down the esplanade to the old 19th Century shed where the island's sheep are traditionally shorn. Over the door of rough wooden planks, which were once painted red, rests an already mouldy skull of what appears to be some sort of seal or maybe a pig.

I continue walking across the stones on the beach, taking care not to slip on the sticky seaweed called kelp, which gives its name to the Islanders and in this harbour is encountered frequently in the spaces between the stones. Listing to one side and rotting on the beach lies Roddy's old boat, the *Redwing*, a yacht a little smaller than the *Penélope*. A terrible storm left the vessel dying on the beach and from then on the Napiers have not had a boat of their own.

I take a turn round the bay, always followed by the Johnny Rooks who know that I have something for them. The *Condor* meanwhile continues dozing peacefully in the middle of the harbour. Finally I decide to open the bag and throw the meat on the beach. The Johnny Rooks mill about ferociously around the carrion. As soon as one succeeds in getting a bit of meat in its curved beak, it flies off, pursued by two or three others, which hope, not always in vain, that it will let something drop. In a few minutes the meat is gone, the spectacle is over and I go back to the house for the goodbyes and the departure.

In the plane, Derek sits me at the back, next to the doctor. The machine makes its short run across the grass and I see the figures of Michael, Jeanette, Roddy and Lily getting more and more distant. The four of them stand waving by one of the Land Rovers. The plane lifts in flight and leaves behind little West Point Island with its whole world of stories.

CHAPTER 5

The colour-washed postage stamp

The little plane's shadow continues to stroke the yellow hills and the cliffs of the West Falklands. Shouting above the engines' roar I tell the doctor who I am and what I am doing here. He tells me that he is called Barry Elsby, that he is married to another English doctor and that they both worked in a hospital in England before they decided to come to the bottom of the map. "We have never regretted coming here," he says.

Doctor Barry assures me that here they feel much more useful and have challenges and surprises every day. Their profession is so much a part of them that even the couple's joint email address is a simple variation of "Doctors 1 & 2" rather than a combination of their names.

"And which of you is one and which is two?" I ask.

I'm sure that they have been asked this question a thousand times, but "she is number one, of course" replies Doctor Barry without ever losing his smile.

"In England a doctor has to become a specialist, but here you do everything and the relationship with the people is much more personal" shouts Barry. His daughter is 17 and also wants to be a doctor. "I hope that she changes her mind," the doctor gesticulates.

We descend into Hill Cove, a settlement on the west coast of the island. Ray Hanson comes to get the doctor and everyone with him in the plane to take us to his house. Dene, his wife for the last 52 years, has cooked a stew and it simmers on the hob while the doctor holds surgery in the living room.

There are five people from the neighbourhood waiting to tell Doctor Barry about their aches and pains. While they are passing by Ray tells me that he came here more than half a century ago as a tractor driver, rose to be manager and that after retiring in 1987, bought the settlement store.

After hearing an abbreviated version of my history, they ask me to sign their visitors' book. I look through the earlier pages and the majority of names include their military rank. One officer writing in December 1982 says that, the house is "the first dry place I have been in for 35 days."

I continue looking through the pages. On January 10th 1983 there appears a photo and a famous signature, that of Margaret Thatcher. Above the signature there is a eulogy to her hosts which in two words totally embodies the Iron Lady: "Very British!" One of those present, a humble lad, who hasn't opened his mouth till that moment, approaches and points out an adolescent smiling timidly at the edge of the photo. It is him.

On another page, members of 23 Squadron, Royal Air Force have stuck their coat of arms: a brown eagle with a bird in its talons. The Squadron's motto is beneath it and does not need much Latin to understand: *"Semper agressus."* There are the signatures of some thirty or so members of the Squadron around the coat of arms.

Dene gets the first consultation with the doctor, because she has to leave rapidly to continue preparing lunch. The young man from the photo and other neighbours go in, come out, say goodbye, get wrapped up and go on their way. Finally only Ray, Dene, Barry, Derek and I remain. Between us we give our attention to a big dish of pasta with mince and another of mashed potato. For dessert there's a cake full of strawberry jam. Dene, a cheerful and active old lady, says that the doctor's visit is always a special occasion.

They ask me questions about Argentina. Dene says that I am the first Argentine she has spoken to. Just as in Roddy and Lily's house, the conversation quickly turns to local news: who is pregnant, who are separating, and who is going to London. A heated debate begins about how the councillors are doing. Following legal changes in the wake of the war, all decisions which affect life in the Islands are taken by a Legislative Council elected every four years by direct popular vote. "Now we discuss everything, we feel that decisions are taken here and we scrutinise everything through a magnifying glass," Ray says.

Doctor Barry's second stop is at Port Howard. Three people are going to board the plane there to go to San Carlos. During that second leg of the flight I ask the doctor about the young people of the Islands. Barry Elsby is especially worried about under-age and promiscuous sex. He published an article in this week's *Penguin News* warning that adults who approach under age girls to "use them and then forget them" should not be taken lightly. Thanks to the enclosed nature of the community the doctor says that the hospital hasn't had to deal with any cases of AIDS or drug abuse. "Compared to big cities it's an isolated and idyllic place, but fragile."

There are two elements which put the community's insulation in danger: there are many soldiers from elsewhere and every year more tourists. There are about 2,000 people from elsewhere in the military base at Mount Pleasant, who mix with the local population now and again and some 45,000 tourists came ashore from cruise ships in 2005. Admittedly the average age of these visitors is 78 (with an old man of 103, holding the absolute record) but younger ones are starting to arrive, particularly from the USA.

While I am listening to Barry Elsby detailing his worries I look out at the landscape. What I can see through the window doesn't show much sign of over population and doesn't appear to harbour any danger: only rocky hills, meadows with sheep and cows grazing, the rugged coast line and, in the distance, a road with a Land Rover going lethargically along it.

There's only one patient at Port Howard, so we don't get out of the Islander. The three new passengers come and I move into the front seat, alongside Derek. Michael's cousin has a commanding voice and lofty bearing. He tells me with pride that he is a captain in the Islands' defence force (FIDF) and that in a few days he will be decking himself out for the ceremonial signing in of the new Governor. He is one of the most experienced pilots in the Islands' internal air service, FIGAS.

The chat with him through the cabin's microphones and earphones is as interesting as the one I had with Tom Chater on the way out, but the topics are different.

Derek is showing me places connected with the war in the middle of what we are flying over. The low altitude of the flight makes everything appear with disturbing and terrifying clarity. We cross the Falkland Sound and arrive at the beach where the British troops disembarked. In the distance an enormous transport plane is making its way to Mount Pleasant.

There is no one waiting at San Carlos for the three passengers from Port Howard. There's no windsock, no Land Rover and no fire-fighting equipment. Derek talks to his base in Stanley, does a couple of circuits and decides to carry on towards the capital. The passengers will have to go by land or wait for a flight the next day. I am distant and distressed, anchored in 1982, because I know what we are going to fly over; I have seen it on the map.

"That mountain down there is Mount Longdon and that one further away is Mount Harriet," Derek says in his baritone voice and my heart constricts. We are passing over the scene of the bloodiest battles of the war. Hundreds of Argentine and British soldiers died down there on the fateful nights of the 12th to the 13th of June. From there on almost to the entrance to Port Stanley all was death and desolation. A white cross stands out over Mount Harriet, with an earthen track snaking its way up to it.

The terrible mountains have not yet disappeared when suddenly without warning the houses of the town come into view. "That's my house" says Doctor Barry, reaching from behind to touch my shoulder. I am not surprised that he likes this more than the London suburbs. The house, which is big and surrounded by a well-kept flower garden, seems from the air like the most beautiful in the Islands, in the middle of the countryside, bordered by a stream, but just a few minutes from the hospital.

We fly over Port Stanley and just like 24 years ago make for the old airfield. The runway, seen from the cabin of the little plane when it comes in to land, looks just as I remember it: grey and smudgy, like a line carelessly drawn on the spongy earth.

"Where were you before you joined the *Penelope*?" Derek asks me, while he presses the last buttons and takes off his earphones. I tell him about the house at 10 John Street. "But that's where my boss lives," the pilot exclaims. "If he's there, as soon as we get out of the plane and I finish with the formalities, I'll take you there."

* * *

How was I going to recognise it if there was nothing left of the original house? We arrive in Derek's Land Rover and I realise immediately that I have walked past this house several times in the last few days. But this one isn't my house. Instead of the front lawn, there's a gravel entry for two cars. Instead of the porch with square windows and plants there's a studio-room with a bay window to the outside. In place of the white paint work there's varnished Nordic wood; it's new from the roof down.

Derek rings the bell and Frazer Wallace, the manager of FIGAS, comes out. Frazer, who a second before was reading a book, listening to music and stroking a big dog, has the look of an intellectual. He is tall with tousled hair, black beard, thin framed spectacles and a grey pullover. The dog is black, hairy and almost as big as its master. Through the open door I see it stretched out in the middle of the living room, taking things easy. Frazer is interested in my story, but we don't have much time. The real visit will be the next day.

I return the following day to take coffee with Frazer and his wife Helen who works as a clerk in the local police station.

On this second visit I notice that the house has a name. It is called, 'The Shackleton.' "I put the name up when I discovered that Sir Edward Shackleton had lived here," Frazer tells me. The house was built in 1957 and in 1976, being owned by the government, it housed the Labour politician, expert economist and son of the famous Antarctic explorer.

During the two months of his stay, Shackleton completed the study of the Islands' economy that bears his name. His recommendations, which were presented at the end of the seventies, included among other things that the government should buy up the lands owned by absentee landowners, divide them up and sell them, on credit, to Islanders to increase productivity and reduce emigration. While it is a fact that the *Shackleton Report* was not put into effect up to the conflict in 1982, after 1984 it provided the basis for the Falklands own agrarian reform.

In 1982 the house still belonged to the Falkland Islands government. That was why the person who lived there then was the colonial civil servant Michael Growcott, the owner of the clothes I put on when they disguised me as a Kelper.

"My mother bought it in 1989. Would you like to have a look round?" Frazer asks me. He, I and the dog begin a tour through the place which was the naval headquarters during the war and where I spent the last weeks of the conflict. "There were two bedrooms here, but we joined them together to make one big one" he says, opening the door to the room. In the centre is a square bed with a deep mattress. The floor is of light-coloured wood and to one side a large mirror makes the bedroom look even bigger.

Everything is so changed that it is impossible for me to compare what I am seeing with what I remember.

"Where's the little room that was next to the bathroom?" I ask him. I want to see the conscripts' garret. He takes me into a bathroom almost as big as the bedroom. Where once there was an old porcelain wash basin, now there is a stone worktop of modern design. "There" I say "What's over there?"

He opens a door and in the place where we slept with our uniforms on and a rifle under the camp bed, there is now a Norwegian sauna, with light wooden walls and a place in the middle for the hot stones that will make the house's owners sweat healthily.

"We changed everything; we took down all the front part and all the bathroom and kitchen are new," says Helen, bringing an album of photos of the demolition – by a bulldozer – of the old part and the construction of the new. If anything remains of the furniture from that time, it would be the desk." The desk she shows me is old, it has a worked edge and the wood shows scratches and marks. I stroke it hoping that it will reveal some secret to me or that it will awake some memory, but in vain.

Then I go into the kitchen – shiny, metallic and functional – and there, at last, the past hits me like a sledge hammer, not in the kitchen, but in what I can see through the window. There is the garden, the fence and the pub, The Rose. There is the view that I saw while I was peeling potatoes and the army boys were scaring us with stories about the Ghurkhas.

I go out into the garden on my own. The greenhouse is no longer there, much less our pathetic anti-air raid shelter. But there's something in the lawn, the partition wall and more than anything in the pub's peeling roof on the other side of the street. I breathe deeply. The drizzle falls softly and the dog looks curiously at me from the kitchen door.

The feeling is curious. I have changed so much in all these years and now, however, I have come to 10 John Street and find that the house has changed even more than me.

In the living room Helen and Frazer are waiting for me with a big cup of coffee. All around are rows of books, all neatly arranged. There are many books about history and about the war, the biographies of Rex Hunt – the Governor in 1982 – and Margaret Thatcher, the impressive and enlightening project of the historian Martin Middlebrook: *Operation Corporate* the war told from the British side and the *Fight for the Malvinas*, the same war told by the Argentines. There's also one very unexpected little book: the English version of Daniel Kon's *Los Chicos de la Guerra.*

"You don't by any chance have *The Heart of the Matter* by Graham Greene?" I ask them. No, that would be just too much.

"I'm from Portsmouth" says Helen, "the port the fleet sailed from to recapture the Islands."

"I was nineteen and I offered to go as a volunteer nurse on the hospital ship, but they didn't accept me. I saw how the fleet left. We went to the beach and saw the lights of the ships going by. We were also in the crowd when the *Invincible* returned. We were three girls who were shouting like crazy when the officers began to come off. The first one off was Prince Andrew. The Queen and her husband Philip were there. When the second one came off he walked straight towards where we were. The three of us surrounded him and kissed him."

She takes a sip of coffee, smiles as if to poke fun at her own memory and says in a low voice: "You can do stupid things when you are nineteen."

Afterwards Helen had a Falkland Islands boyfriend who brought her to the Islands. "My first impression was horrible; it was December, but the weather was dreadful, very cold. In the airport was that officer who stands on the luggage carousel and gives us a sermon about land mines. Luckily they don't do that now. But I cheered up when I got to Stanley and in three weeks I had a job."

The boyfriend didn't find things to his liking, but she did and when they separated, she decided to stay. "I was on the radio for three years, putting on music that I like: folk, sixties and seventies rock, the Rolling Stones, Bob Dylan, and the Beatles." Helen has now left the radio, but still misses the microphone and the contact with the people.

By contrast, Frazer Wallace is proud to tell me that his family is one of the oldest in the archipelago. "One of my ancestors was part of the group that moved the capital from Port Louis to Port Stanley. I grew up running in these streets. We used to make the six hour trip to go fishing in the Malo River; now you can get there in an hour."

Frazer worked in the Customs Department at the airport and also as a policeman. At the end of April 1982, he left the Islands in the last plane to take civilians. "They took us to Buenos Aires. There was a crush of journalists at the door of the hotel. The police took us to Ezeiza from where we flew Swissair to Switzerland." In July, just after the end of hostilities, he was back in the Islands. He worked in FIGAS, in the Customs, in a shipping agency and finally returned to FIGAS again.

I say goodbye to the Wallaces and to their house, which for some hallucinatory days was my refuge and life raft in the war's sea. I walk hurriedly to the Malvina House Hotel, where I have a date with a seventeen year-old girl.

I arrive at the hotel and the girl is there, sitting at a round table with her mother and her grandmother.

Megan Middleton was eleven when she wrote a text full of child-like tenacity and capacity for describing the amazing and curious. With these weapons this girl began the story that she had chosen to write for the Alistair Cameron Prize. Of the twenty or so youthful works that I read in Jane Cameron's archives and in the complete collection of the annual *Falklands Journal* magazine, Megan's seemed to me to be by far the most promising and I don't think I am showing favouritism just because her subject was, '*The Penelope.*'

I had read Megan's work in a version edited by Jane Cameron which appeared in the 2002 *Journal.* Jane had helped her photocopy documents, Roddy Napier had sent her a fax with his memories and Finlay Ferguson had granted her a long interview. It was he who told me that the girl, who was now seventeen and was working as a cashier in the Islands' only bank, was the great-niece of the *Penélope's* old engineer, Brian Jaffray. "You could meet her in the bank in the morning."

I went to the bank on my return from West Point and there she was behind the glass with her round and freckly face. When I said that I had read her work and wanted to interview her, she had an attack of the giggles. We arranged to meet in the hotel and she asked if she could bring along her mum and her grandma.

Sitting around the Malvina House Hotel coffee table are Megan, her mother Caroline and her grandmother, Shirley Richards. Shirley is Brian's older sister. She tells me that the quiet engineer was the youngest of eight children. He died suddenly, some years ago, without anyone having suspected that he was ill. "He was working as a lorry driver when they made the new roads. He had a devastating heart attack and the lorry kept on going, hit a fence and ended up in a field. That's how his work mate found him," says Shirley.

Meanwhile, Megan is twisting about in her chair with a folder in her hands. She is dying to show what she has brought. It is her original work: the longest and most complete that may have ever been done on the *Penélope* till now.

"There were 32 in our class and the majority entered the competition" she tells me. "Some made models. One was really good of a sunken ship in the harbour with coral and everything. I wanted to do something different, something that hadn't been done before."

Her mother smiles and shows her approval with energetic nods of her head.

"It took me two months. The first thing I did was to ask Finlay Ferguson if he would come to our house. Then I spoke with my four great uncles. It was difficult getting all the pieces of the story together, but I enjoyed what I was doing and the things they were telling me seemed very interesting."

I open the folder and the first things that appear are the words, '*The Penelope*' big and bright, like on the psychedelic covers of rock albums in the seventies. Beneath the name are two intertwined flags. "One is the German one, because that's where the boat came from," she explains, "and the other is our Union Jack."

The word 'Penelope' appears written vertically in the margin of each page and each time the colours of the background and those of the letters are different. The first page tells the story of how "Dr Gunther Plüschow" ordered the ketch *Feuerland* to be constructed in Büsum "from carefully selected oak and extra thick glass" so that he could sail in turbulent seas. "Dr Plüschow had with him five men, 1.5 nautical miles of unexposed cine film, a tiny rapid-assembly Heinkel float plane and his wife."

The text tells of Plüschow's death when he falls from the plane and the sale of the *Feuerland* to John Hamilton, "who owned farms in Patagonia and the Falklands, including Weddell Island, where she was to be based." On the second page Megan stuck two maps, one of Argentina and the Falklands, where Patagonia and Tierra del Fuego are marked in brilliant colours and the other of Germany. An arrow shows the mouth of the Elbe and the port of Büsum.

The second page tells how Hamilton brought Patagonian animals to the Falklands. In the bottom part are two very nice drawings representing a guanaco and a Patagonian fox. They both look at the reader very seriously. "In 1938," writes Megan in her clear round hand, "*Penelope* made her last trip across to South America."

"This is my favourite drawing," the author tells me when we come to the next page. It shows two smiling youngsters with an enormous basket full of eggs. The text reads "*Penelope* was used to carry all the sand and shingle needed to build a freezing plant at Ajax Bay, San Carlos. My Great Uncle Bill Middleton was skipper of the *Penelope* at around this time. My granddad (Len Middleton) can remember when he was about my age (11) or maybe younger he had to help his mother carry dozens and dozens of hen eggs to a point which was quite a long way from Brenton Loch House, where they lived, to be picked up. Between them they carried an old tin bath full of eggs and in their spare hand they had a bucket of eggs."

"They were penguin eggs" the grandmother puts in. "Everybody ate penguin eggs in those days; they were very nutritious."

"Pooh!" complains Megan. "I am vegetarian."

The pages that follow are devoted to the very many stories about the *Penelope* under the command of Captain Ferguson: the adventure of towing the *Black Swan* (Ferguson's earlier boat) to Bleaker Island to use it as part of the new jetty and another occasion in 1971, when the ketch was sent to Port William to transport sheep that came on the cargo vessel, *Tasmania Star.*

The chapter devoted to Finlay Ferguson begins with these words: "Finlay came to my house to talk to me and to my Mum about the *Penelope.* He had a lot of interesting stories. He told me that over 19 years of shifting sheep on the *Penélope* he averaged 7,000 sheep a year."

"*Penelope* was painted white when she came to the Falklands. Since then she has been blue, grey, black and red. Mum and Finlay both agreed she is best red."

The episode of the children's' crossing in the first days of the war is told in detail and a whole page is given over to the list of the names of those children. "Apologies to anyone not listed."

"After *Penelope's trip* across to Port Howard with the Stanley House children etc. in 1982, she went to Speedwell Island to shift sheep. Jeff and Finlay were ordered to leave Speedwell Island. Seven Argentines went with them. They set off for Stanley, but the weather was too bad so they were told to turn around and head for ´Bay Fox` (Fox Bay)."

From her long chats with Finlay, Megan tells of the frustrating search for the *Isla de los Estados* survivors, the tying up to the *Carcarañá* and the disembarkation of the two Kelpers at Egg Harbour: "Jeff and Fin spent the first night at Egg Harbour House, the second night they spent at Paragon House and walked into Goose Green the next day. They were captured by dozens of Argentines in the Cart Horse Park and marched into the Galley at Goose Green. Later that day they were taken to the Hall where one hundred people were being kept (including my mum)."

"After the liberation of Stanley, Fin and Jeff came to Stanley and took *Penelope* back out where she belonged. The Argentines had painted her black, but she didn't stay this colour for long."

Megan Middleton made a list of 32 people who had worked on the *Penélope* over the years. Ferguson and Jaffray are 1 & 2. George Betts is number 19. There's half a page devoted to the 17p stamp that the Philatelic Bureau brought out in 1998. The artist was Jane Cameron's partner, the Dutch mechanical genius, painter and designer, Robbie Yssel.

Another section deals with the engines. Megan lists the German motor with which the vessel arrived in the Islands, the enormous five cylinder Hornsby that the Antarctic service put in her, the four cylinder Calven "which was taken out of *Cleo*" and the six-cylinder Ford that they installed in 1978, "which is still in her today" (in 2002, a year after Megan's study, Michael Clarke changed the Ford for a Caterpillar from a lorry).

One of the photos that Megan presented with the work shows the ship exactly as I remember it. It's from Christmas 1985 and the photo is taken from the wheelhouse. Finlay Ferguson in a red and black chequered shirt-coat and his ever-present captain's cap is in the middle of the deck, talking to two other men. Around them are three restless horses and at the bottom the square shaped white wooden construction through which one descended to the galley and the cabin. In front of the bow, there is only the endless calm sea.

The final pages are dedicated to the voyages to study sea lions, penguins, Johnny Rooks and albatross that Michael made with

Falklands Conservation. "Recently (August and September) the *Penelope* took building materials to West Point Island for the jetty which is being built out there."

"When Michael bought *Penelope* she was blue and white; he has since painted her red."

Once she had presented her work, Megan began to chew her nails. "I had finished in good time, because I didn't want to rush, but I was sure that someone else would win" she told me. "Days went by and still the winner was not announced. One day I was in my grandmother's kitchen when they called my mother to make sure she would be there when the medals were given out. Suddenly in the big school hall they called out my name. The only thing that occurred to me to do was to turn round and say to my mum, 'Why didn't you warn me?'"

Megan proudly gets out her medal, the diameter of a glass. "Jane Cameron presented the prize to me." Her mum and her grandma pass it around. They have already seen it many times, but never cease to admire it.

"Today at noon we were looking for it to bring and we couldn't find it!" Megan exclaims melodramatically.

"It was exactly where I told you it would be" her mother retorts calmly.

* * *

That morning *Penguin News*, the Islands' weekly newspaper had interviewed me. The interview was conducted by Jenny Cockwell, the young editor. I asked her about the origin of her surname and she told me she was married to Adam, the son of Richard Cockwell. I already knew that Cockwell was a well-known personality with a certain amount of power because he was one of the eight councillors who decided the internal affairs of the Islands. "Tonight at Malvina House the family and some friends are getting together to say farewell to Richard's son who is going back to London tomorrow to start his second year at university. Come along, if you would like to."

Will Richard Cockwell remember me? Will I recognise him? After Finlay Ferguson and Brian Jaffray, he is the only local who I remember well, but for some reason I feel that those conversations under the hanging washing happened centuries ago.

The interview with Jenny Cockwell goes backwards and forwards. I tell her the story of my search for the *Penélope* and my impressions of my stay in the Islands and she tells me that she was born in Auckland in New Zealand, that she came on holiday to the Islands in 1996 when she was nineteen and stayed for ever. She began to work for the Islands' weekly in 2000 and has been editor for the past three years.

"It is such a small community so everyone knows you and everyone tells you what they do and don't like about your articles," she complains with a smile. There is a lot of local news in the paper, like the activities of the school choir, weddings, obituaries and what the councillors are doing, but its topics are not all so mundane. "People are getting more and more encouraged to criticize and to offer solutions. Besides, of course, they want to know what's going on in Argentina, what the Argentines are thinking and how relations are between London and Buenos Aires."

I look beyond my interviewer's head. On a board by Jenny's chair someone has written with a marker the telephone numbers of President Néstor Kirchner's press office and the Argentine Foreign Ministry.

"There are only three of us to write, take photos, set up pages, place and sometimes design advertisements and distribute each edition," she says and then has no more time to tell me about the joys and the miseries of *Penguin News,* because already in the door are two Chilean entrepreneurs whose turn it is to be interviewed now.

It's the evening. I have hardly finished my interview with Megan Middleton, her mum and her grandmother before Jenny takes me over to a very tall man with a loud deep voice and a few strands of hair crossing his cranium from ear to ear. He is talking to the group of people around him. The man looks at me, half-closing his eyes, as if he wants to see beyond what's in front of him.

"Are you the soldier who came up to talk to me in Fox Bay?" Richard Cockwell asks me.

"That's me, or perhaps that was me." I tell him. Cockwell asks the Saint Helenian waiter, who obviously knows his tastes well, to bring some beers. We can only talk a little because already the other guests to this family party are arriving, but Richard is interested to know about some of the things that I did in those years and tells me about the difficulties in running the farm at Fox Bay, then with the Argentine Army, later with the wool market and finally with high politics. Despite his ironically charged complaints he seems to be a man who is full of vitality and sure of himself.

"I remember this chap," he tells his children and his friends while clapping me on the shoulder with his big hand until he almost makes me spit up my beer. "He used to come and talk to me while I was hanging out the clothes. I have sometimes wondered about what might have happened to him and here he is." He lets out a sonorous burst of laughter which echoes around the bar.

John Fowler, former teacher and superintendent of education and now manager of the Islands' tourist board, is also at the party. John appears in all the books about the war, because it was in his house, almost at the western end of Ross Road, where the only deaths of Islanders occurred during the conflict. A misaimed British shell exploded over his kitchen, killing as it did three ladies who had taken refuge there, trusting in the house's solid construction.

"The officer who gave the coordinates for the firing of the missiles from an observation point on land came to see me some years back" John tells me. His name is Hugh McManners.

McManners is a celebrity today. He has a television programme about survival in extreme circumstances and has written several books. "When he came here he appeared devastated by what had happened and asked my forgiveness. I told him that these things happen, that he was not to blame and that he shouldn't punish himself any more. He was the one who wasn't forgiving himself."

Later, McManners was asked by the Imperial War Museum in London to compile a book of interviews with people on both sides of the conflict, for the museum's *Forgotten Voices* series. In his own well-written account of his experiences during the war, *Falklands Commando,* it is clear that the shelling of Fowler's house was as the result of a previously unnoticed fault in the computer system which guided one of a British destroyer's big guns.

John and his wife also figure in a recent Argentine book. In August 1999, Edgardo Esteban travelled on the first flight on which Argentines were allowed back into the Islands. In his book *Iluminados por el fuego,* he relates that had his last dinner in the Islands in the Fowlers' house. In the middle of the conversation, Edgardo notices that the song '*Cambia, todo cambia*' is coming from the CD player sung by the unmistakeable voice of Mercedes Sosa. "At that moment I had the feeling that many things were changing in my life. If it hadn't been for the language, I would have felt that I was having dinner at the house of some friends in whatever part of Argentina, and really that's how it was."

My conversation with John, sitting on armchairs in the bar of the Malvina House hotel, gave me the same feeling of a long-lasting previous friendship that Esteban describes. We talked a little about the *Penélope* and he told me his story about the penguin eggs. Then, almost at the end of our conversation, I told him that I had spent the last part of the war in the house at 10 John Street.

"The milanesas were very good." John Fowler comes out with this as if it were the most natural thing in the world.

I am confused. "What milanesas are you talking about?"

"The ones that they left in the freezer, of course. We moved in there just after the end of the war as my house had been destroyed by the shell. I thought that Menéndez had been sleeping there."

"No" I tell him, "they were naval officers."

"And whose were the silk pyjamas that we found?"

This conversation was turning surreal. John described the living room as we had left it, with maps drawing-pinned to the walls and piled up on the big dining room table. "But the best thing was the milanesas. Nobody makes milanesas like the Argentines!"

We laugh and drink a toast to the milanesas. After 24 years, I am glad to find that someone had enjoyed them.

Adam, Richard Cockwell's son and Jenny's husband, perhaps the blonde boy that Guillermo Ni Coló saw in the act of letting someone cut his hair, told me a war story in the course of a couple of beers. During April and May all the people who lived in Fox Bay East or round about moved into the Cockwell's house. It was a bit uncomfortable, but at least they were all together to confront whatever might happen. One day a group asked Richard if he would ask the commander of the regiment stationed at Fox Bay, if they could leave this area and go away from the troops and the possibility of combat.

"No sooner had my father come back with the news that anyone could leave who wanted to, they all began to pack their bags." They were all going to go and leave only the four members of the Cockwell family. "I was with mum in the kitchen, when in came George, a very shy, silent farm worker, who always looked at the ground when he addressed my mother."

This time, however, George looked her in the eyes and said that it seemed wrong to him that everybody was going and he was going to stay. "We had hardly exchanged words with him before, but that gesture ... it's what I remember most about the war."

I'm not sure why Adam wanted to tell me that story during his brother's farewell party, but I thanked him for George's story, which I understood to be a gift. It is a precious memory and a lesson that Adam learned during a difficult time for him and his family. It's also another of the big and small stories that I am encountering on this long return path, which bring something of meaning and a tiny pinch of comfort to the demented experience of war.

On my last morning in the Islands I had breakfast with Jane Cameron. Jane had helped me a lot with my investigations during my stay, putting me in contact with people in the islands – I have the impression that she knows everybody – and, without being grandiloquent, had impressed me with her practical sense of the importance of knowing and appreciating the past. In her archives I found particularly memorable her patient series of interviews with old people, in whose ebbing memory live so many things that are on the point of being lost with modernity, and her history prize for children, which wakes their curiosity and pride and relates them to the stories of their elders.

In answer to my questions, during my visits to her office she was bringing treasures out of boxes and, like the shipping register with the notice of *Penélope's* first arrival, old news sheets where the voyages of Hamilton and his daughters were mentioned and a series of historic sepia photographs.

While there are still people who might have stories to tell, Jane Cameron is working feverishly to record those stories. "With the boom in massive cruise ships" she comments in her low, somewhat hesitant voice, "we run the danger of converting ourselves into a little tourist town, a southern Disneyland where the penguins, the seals and ourselves may end up like nice cartoon characters."

On my last visit I leave her working for a while in the archives and visit the museum which is next door.

My guide is called Sian Davies. She had been in the job for two months and in the first part of the exhibition recites the texts of the pamphlets almost from memory. There are many objects from the daily life of the 19th Century, portraits of governors and important men, models, paintings and artefacts taken from old ships, along with a representation of a typical 'camp' house. As the displays approach the present day, my guide becomes more animated. She tells me that she likes the work a lot because here she is learning things and can use several of her skills. The natural history section houses stuffed penguins and other birds, together with drawings and photos of the islands' very rich wildlife, and shows the apparatus used by the scientists who study them. Sian tells me stories about herself or her family with each animal.

The section on the war, in a room apart from the others, has newspapers, weapons, uniforms and equipment. There is a ration pack, like the ones we used to eat when we were got off the *Buen Suceso* and, behind glass, a complete foxhole and a radio like a big green box. There's a waterproof poncho too and, in the middle of the fox hole, a letter from a mother to her son in the trenches. "Dear Leo" the letter begins. The display is done with respect and didactic intentions, but the sight of this fox hole and the letter can't help but give me a shudder.

Suddenly Sian tells me "I am an authentic 'war baby.' I was born on the 11th of May in the middle of the war." On May 11th we were returning to Fox Bay after our frustrating search for the *Isla de los Estados*. Now the war babies are twenty four years old! Sian tells me that there were five young Islanders born during the conflict, who went to the same school and felt themselves to be a little bit different. "Everybody gets very excited about that time, but us especially."

Sian assures me that there is some material about the *Penélope* in a file and I go with her to her office, where she has made her own sanctuary. On the door of a steel cupboard she has stuck up three posters of footballers: Cristiano Ronaldo ("my favourite"), David Beckham and Ashley Cole.

"I'm an Arsenal fan," she confesses.

Next to this very modern and personal exhibition hangs an enormous map of the landholdings in the Falklands as they were distributed in 1883. Weddell, Passage and other small islands are coloured dark green. These are John Hamilton's. At that time, West Point was already in the possession of Roddy Napier's family.

When I come out of the museum Jane has already finished working and takes me for coffee at her house in one of those old Citroëns with the thin tin doors. Sometimes she seems like the feminine version of the nutty professor, lost in her own world of encyclopaedic knowledge and profound ideas, but just when she is in danger of getting stuck hanging on her own cloud, she brings herself down with dry humour and a few words of the old English variety.

Her house is called "The Old Bakery" Jane tells me, because it was the workplace and home of an Irish baker, who made hundreds of Christmas cakes each year for people who lived far away and sent them off by boat in August or September. "The table is more than two metres long and was upstairs; we had to wait till the house was being remodelled to break the floor and bring it down."

I tell her that I have also ordered a cake to take a long way. After so long spent watching Celia work and smelling from the little dining room the delicious sweet things that she was preparing while Dennis Bolt was chatting to her, I decided to ask my landlady if she would make me a big cake to share with my companions from the *Penélope.* "Next Sunday we are having a barbecue at the house of one of them" I tell Jane. "I want to take them a cake made here from one of Celia's traditional recipes."

While she is making coffee on the stove with a metal Italian coffee maker, she shows me her partner Robbie Yssel's design table. "It must be here somewhere," she says turning over the plentiful work stacked under the table. From a folder of stamp designs she extracts the original design for the postage stamp showing the *Penélope.* It is one of four, all designed by Robbie.

The other stamps show the *Ilen* (also an 'auxiliary ketch' constructed a year before in Ireland), the *Weddell* (the one that John Hamilton bought in Chile to replace the *Penélope,* which ended up being condemned, and the *Lively* (constructed in Punta Arenas in 1940 for a Norwegian company). This last, the smallest of the four boats, is the only one which continues sailing in Falklands waters.

THE DESIGN of the the *Penelope* stamp, part of a series of four small historical vessels by Dutch artist Robbie Yssel.

Each stamp has a fine wash of gentle colour. The *Penélope* and its background are a sandy brown, the *Ilen* violet, the *Weddell* green and the *Lively* turquoise. Each one also has a small flag which represents its place of construction or the nationality its first owner: German, Irish, Chilean and Norwegian.

"He worked for a long time, almost a year, on the design for these four little historic vessels" says Jane.

The drawing is the size of an old long-playing record. The outline is traced in black ink on a transparent paper. I lift the paper and the colour remains without distinct form, an earth-coloured wash with big white spaces in the middle where the sails are drawn. In one corner is the black red and gold of the flag of Germany, the ketch's country of origin. I play for a while with the strange effect of seeing only the lines without colour or only the background, the yellow stain without a silhouette.

When the transparency is not on top, the ochre spreads out over the page and only the three colours of the German flag remain defined. It's a thick mist where only the country, the ownership and the collective identity are seen. When I hold the paper above to the light, there are only black lines, which precisely draw the outline of the boat and the lines of the wooden planks. It is obviously a boat, but lacks, depth, movement, warmth. When I put the two sheets together the *Penélope* comes to life on the table.

Jane Cameron approaches the table with two mugs of steaming coffee and I am still raising and lowering the transparent paper, trying one way or another to bring everything together, to complete the image and the memory of the ketch.

THIRD PART

Feuerland's return

CHAPTER 1
From Tsingtau to Wonderland

The agreed meeting place is in the Hipopótamo cafeteria across from Parque Lezama in San Telmo, the old quarter in the centre of Buenos Aires. I sit down by one of the square wooden tables, full of stains, scratches and letters carved over the years. Over the marble counter an enormous mirror framed by wooden spirals reflects the large windows which give on to the park and the faces, also carved by the years, of the few regulars who are taking coffee, smoking and chatting as if the twentieth century had never ended.

Suddenly the door opens and my namesake appears like a gale of wind. He is beside himself with joy.

Roberto Litvachkes, the principal Argentine expert on the life and work of Gunther Plüschow, has a mane of white hair which appears to be swept by the Patagonian wind, even though we are inside the cafeteria. At first sight he looks like a cross between Albert Einstein and an ageing rock guitarist. Before telling me where he has come from, he places on the table the two treasures he has brought: one to show me and the other, a present.

What he wants to show me is an old photographic camera from the twenties, a black box hanging from a strap on the point of disintegration.

"This is exactly the same model of camera that Plüschow used," Litvachkes tells me, as if he had found the Holy Grail.

He opens the camera, turns it round and shows me its wheels and cogs. It isn't even the explorer's camera, but it doesn't matter. The fact that it might be the same model makes Roberto Litvachkes feel just a little closer to the man to whom, with pauses, but without interruptions, he has dedicated the last thirteen years as documentary maker and writer.

The other object that he brings is much more modern. It's a book and comes fresh from the oven. It is the first edition in

Spanish of Plüschow's first book, *The Adventures of the Tsingtau Aviator.* Plüschow wrote it in 1917 and now Roberto has got it published in Spanish with a good translation by Ilona Selmeczi and an enthusiastic and informative introduction by Litvachkes himself.

After his collaboration on the re-publication of *Silberkondor über Feuerland (Silver Condor over Tierra del Fuego)* including writing the text for the cover's flyleaf, and his publication of a synthesised biography of the aviator and navigator, this book is the culmination of his work to restore the name of Plüschow.

But for Litvachkes there is still a long way to go. Already he has placed a full size cardboard Plüschow, with camera, tripod, flying jacket and helmet, in the airport at El Calafate alongside other heroes of Patagonian exploration like Francisco P. Moreno, Florentino Ameghino and Charles Darwin. However, he still dreams of making a model of Plüschow's tragic seaplane, the *Silver Condor,* of finding the lost film from his final voyages and, who knows, perhaps one day being able to put together all the pieces still missing from the fascinating biography of the first man to fly over the peaks at the world's end.

Like many of the members of the small but proud confraternity of Plüschow, Roberto Litvachkes first fell under the spell of Patagonia, but little by little the German's obsession with this still mysterious land was ensnaring him, until it became the main theme of his efforts.

"In the beginning I didn't go south looking for Plüschow, or for the landscape," Litvachkes says. "What I really liked was skiing."

His brother, a doctor, used to live in Río Gallegos with his family and invited him to visit them. The brother suggested he should get to know the Perito Moreno glacier. Roberto went to El Calafate with Susana, his girlfriend, in a battered Citroën. They were stopped by the military en route – it was during the middle of the military dictatorship – and when they arrived, at first sight the town seemed rather primitive and depressing.

Everything changed the moment they saw the glacier. "I was in such ecstasy looking at that marvel that I spent two hours without moving," he remembers.

The love of skiing and the discovery of the Patagonian landscape were taking him in the direction of becoming a documentary maker specialising in recording mountain descents. "I loved to watch people skiing in Bariloche, so I learned to ski and afterwards to film skiing or to ski filming, however you want to put it."

"Skiing is like riding a bicycle or making love," Roberto explains, "once you've learned it well, you will never forget it. I learned to ski with my girlfriend and we used to get up at five in the morning and ski for six hours. By the third day, I couldn't get up." Each day the atmosphere of the area and the possibility of sharing it with his partner pleased him more.

"I was looking at it as a tourist and concentrating on touristic things, but Susana was very excited by history. She made me look at all the history there is in Patagonia. Since then I can guess when a celebrity has an interesting history and I follow it. I love to track down the information that others didn't find," he says, while we drink another coffee in the Hipopótamo and the winter sun begins to sink behind the tall gum trees of the Parque Lezama.

Roberto is describing an adventurous and cheerful past to me, filming, skiing and searching for stories all at the same time. Although they went on living in Buenos Aires, they travelled to the south often and she was insisting that they should move there.

The story of Gunther Plüschow came into his hands quite accidently in the middle of this Patagonian fervour.

"My work colleagues went to Ushuaia and as I had wanted to go but had to stay in the capital, as a consolation they brought me a very big book on the history of Tierra del Fuego." There was an article in the book about Gunther Plüschow's voyages, written by Jorge Enríquez. "It was talking about how the first airplane to fly over Ushuaia took a photo and the story grabbed me. I was very taken not only by the fact that someone had flown at that time, but also that they had taken photos. However when I really began to think that there might be a documentary in all of this was when I learned that besides photos, they had made a film."

Roberto's work at this time was making promotional tourism videos. This was the first time he had conceived a biographical and historical project which would need a lot of research and the acquisition of a lot of graphic material. "At that time I knew nothing about his life. I didn't know if he was married, if he was single, if he had children or how and when he died." Bit by bit he was getting together with descendants of Germans who maintained a memory of the aviator, he found articles of the time, like those in the *La Prensa* newspaper which told about his exploits and interviewed him.

It was a difficult time for Litvachkes. In the mid-nineties his company was having financial problems, which afflicted him with personal anxieties. One day, travelling on the underground and deep in thought about what he should do about the Plüschow business, he missed his stop and finally emerged on Corrientes Avenue, four blocks from his destination. "Suddenly, in the middle of the street, somebody put his hand on my shoulder. It was an old friend who had gone to live in Germany fifteen years ago. We had a coffee together and he offered to help me with letters in German."

Roberto emphasises the accident of having missed his stop and says that the hand on his shoulder was a sign of fate, a help at a difficult time. Little by little the project was taking shape with the help of his old friend, his wife Susana and from other unexpected places. The representatives of several German companies with branches in Argentina joined in, pleased to help out of affection for the memory of the German explorer.

The grandfather of one manager had studied with Plüschow in Germany; the father of another had seen him when he passed through Buenos Aires in 1928. The documentary maker went to Germany and retrieved material from the Ullstein publishing house, which had largely financed the *Feuerland's* voyage, from Deutz, the makers of the ketch's engine and from Heinkel, who made Plüschow's seaplane.

In the middle of getting his documentary together, Roberto was overcome by personal tragedy. His wife Susana died and he entered into a state of depression. His partners initiated a legal action, kept the material and finished the documentary without him. It would take him years to get over it and to recover the material that he had collected, along with the enthusiasm and the drive to continue the search for Patagonia's almost forgotten explorer.

I get the impression from the way in which he is telling me all this in San Telmo's Hipopótamo cafeteria, combining Gunther Plüschow's story with his own in a narrative full of drama, colour and humour, that for Roberto the old sailor is much more than a subject for research and the production of documentaries and books. I feel that for him Plüschow is an example, a mirror, a source of inspiration and a permanent reminder that life is a struggle, but that dreams can be realised.

I met Roberto Litvachkes on the afternoon of August 10th 2006, the day following my arrival in Buenos Aires to tie together the three legs of the *Penélope's* story. "Tomorrow I am presenting a documentary on Plüschow's life," he told me. "Come to the National General Archive at the junction of Leandro N. Alem and Sarmiento at 6 pm."

There were six of us: a pair of Plüschow fans who had come from El Palomar, a librarian who had heard about it through the librarians' network, Adriana, Roberto's current girlfriend and me. I sat by him and he gave me a commentary which clarified various aspects of the documentary and then we went to eat pizza.

Since that time, whenever I've had a free moment in my week in Buenos Aires, I have taken the opportunity to read Plüschow's books and to watch the documentary of the *Feuerland's* voyage and the flights over Tierra del Fuego. I have met Roberto several times to talk about Plüschow, but as always happens when someone talks about something that excites him, in helping me to trace the profile of the German explorer, he is also drawing the silhouette of his Argentine admirer.

* * *

"Plüschow is born in Munich on a fine day, the 8th February, 1886" This is how Litvachkes's book begins. The book is entitled: *Gunther Plüschow, a life of dreams, adventures and challenges in pursuit of an impossible love: Patagonia* and is the only one in Spanish which brings together all the facets of the aviator's story.

Almost the only source of information on Plüschow's childhood is the biography that his widow, Isot, published in 1935. What is known comes, for good or bad, filtered through what he told his wife in conversations and letters since they met in 1912 and through what she remembers and chooses to include in her biography. This account by his wife is Litvachke's primary source for the adventurer's first years.

Plüschow was a descendant of the Duke of Mecklenburg, the feudal lord of that state. The aviator's grandfather was the nobleman's illegitimate son and although he did not give his surname to his lover's family, he did bestow upon them the castle that overlooks one of his properties and the name of that place. The building is called Schloss Plüschow and is now a cultural and social centre near Schwerin on the coast of the Baltic Sea.

His father, Amandus Plüschow, gave him the name of one of the characters in *Der Ring des Nibelungen* at the height of the German fever for Richard Wagner's operas. Roberto Litvachkes points out that the name Gunther also evokes "stories of Vikings with their epic and romantic songs, who cross the seas and arrive at distant Nordic places. This is a symbol which would mark his life from the beginning."

However Gunther did not spend his childhood either in his ancestors' state of Mecklenburg in the north of Germany, or in his native Munich in the south. A short time after his birth, the family moved to Rome where his father had found employment. Litvachkes, who crisscrossed the Italian capital looking for facts and places for his documentary, tells it like this in his book: "For the little Gunther, Rome meant the possibility of enjoying the sun and the freedom of the streets to commit mischief. Soon the neighbours would give him the name of the "little blonde devil."

One day his mother found him wandering through the streets of Rome shouting at the top of his voice, "Buy something from the poor boy!" Shortly afterwards this wild child was enrolled in a strict school run by French Jesuits. In the documentary based on Litvachke's original script, we are told that the Jesuits instilled in Plüschow the interest in voyages to distant lands and geographical discoveries which would have such an influence on his whole life.

In 1894, when he was eight, another move took him away from Rome for ever. His father accepted a position in the museum of the small city of Schwerin. "They occupied a beautiful old house near woods and lakes and Gunther lost no time in making a new friend," Litvachkes tells us. The friend was an old sailor who taught him the rudiments of navigation. "It thus became very common to see this dissimilar pair out in the sailor's little yawl. Gunther soon becomes a skilful sailor, who would even surprise his teacher."

In 1897, at the age of 11, he enters the military cadet academy at Ploen. He was following a family tradition, as his father and his older brother were both cadets. After a character-building four years in the military boarding school, Plüschow, who has already decided to be a sailor, entered the Imperial German Navy's school at Gross Lichterfelde. From Lichterfelde, in 1905 he emerged as a nineteen-year old Sea Cadet. In pictures of this era he appears martial, haughty and dashing: a fine young man with a carefully disciplined attitude, who years later would wreak havoc among the ladies.

Roberto rescues a significant anecdote from his passage through officers' school. In a geography book Plüschow found a picture of a ship in a marvellous landscape, surrounded by mountains, woods and glaciers. It was the first time that Gunther came across the magic name of Tierra del Fuego. "Gunther contemplates this embellished landscape of mountains, hills, sea, glaciers and woods. 'How can all this be together in the natural world?' he asks repeatedly: 'Is this our earth or is it the end of the world?"

Almost without thinking young Gunther ripped out the page and hid it among his clothes. He said many years later that this was the start of his passion for that then almost inaccessible zone at the end of the world.

Plüschow completed his training in the ship *Stotch*. Litvachkes writes that "when they gave out lockers (to the new Sea Cadets) it occurred to him to stick on the door the photo of Tierra del Fuego, which he had torn out of the geography book. Finally, his first ship as an officer was the torpedo boat *S87*, in which he completed a long voyage to England, the Dutch Indies, the Malay Straits and Hong Kong.

Later he travelled to the port of Tsingtau, a German enclave in the middle of the Chinese coast, to board his next posting, the steamer *Bismark*. This will be a short stay, but during the First World War Tsingtau will have a vital place in Plüschow's story and the name of this Chinese port will be linked with his forever.

During his two years in the *Fürst Bismark*, Plüschow had to comply with strict naval orders and even more strict rules of etiquette. Roberto Litvachkes summarises in this sentence the whirlpool nature and climate of those years. In the short period of one month, Plüschow amused himself with a marchioness at a party in the house of a French colony's governor, helped to put out a fire on the ship, participated in the Cherry Blossom Festival in the port of Myatsu, lived through a "frustrated" encounter with a woman called Molly and ended up helping "an English steam ship called *Port Maria* by diving in the water and managing to fix a hole in its hull and thus prevent it sinking."

His parents died in 1911. Gunther was already pursuing his naval career, but his restless spirit made him interested in aviation, an activity, which was just taking its first steps at that time.

Imagining that his desire for liberty and adventure would be better served in the solitude of the air than in the confined world of a war ship, he requested a transfer to the Navy's newly created air service and while waiting for an answer made a visit to the city of his carefree youth.

In Rome he met up again with Isot, a friend from Berlin. According to Isot, during their walks through Rome Gunther told her of his dreams of travelling the world and asked her to be the woman who would wait for him in Berlin at the end of all his voyages.

It was now the summer of 1913 and as there was still no answer from the Navy, Plüschow visited London. It is that precise and strange moment that the sailor chooses to begin to tell his story in his first autobiographical work, *The Adventures of the Tsingtau Aviator*. Because of this, from the time that he returns to Schwerin from London and asks his uncle if there is any news of his next naval posting, we do not have to rely on Isot. Here begins the adventure as narrated by himself and this is the time when the legend of the hero of Tsingtau begins.

* * *

A good part of the mysterious fascination that Gunther Plüschow still awakes in us has to do with the way in which he wrote his books.

It seems as if we are sitting with him in a ship's dining room during a long after dinner period and while we are savouring liqueurs, the orchestra is playing agreeable waltzes and the sea is lulling us, the captain is spinning his yarns. He doesn't draw any grand conclusions or look for stylish effects and brilliant metaphors in his accounts, but his strength is that he keeps the story moving on and trusts that it will entrap us and that we will want to know more.

The Adventures of the Tsingtau Aviator sold 600,000 copies in the final months of the First World War and in the first post-war years, in great part because it was a book of propaganda for the Germans of that period. However the energy and ingenuity of the protagonist and the narrator's delight in his story remain infectious for some readers from other countries and other times.

At the beginning of the book, Plüschow talks about his enthusiasm at having been chosen by the Navy's aviation section and hearing that they were going to send him as a reconnaissance pilot to Tsingtau, the Chinese colony of which he had good memories.

First, however, he had to learn to fly. He assures us that he soon learned all the secrets of the job. He had still not finished learning to fly the aircraft when, with his instructor, he made an attempt on the German altitude record.

On one of his flights, he met up with the Zeppelin dirigible somewhere above the clouds. "What an incredible moment at an altitude of 3,000 m! Far away from the noise of the world, above all daily worries and problems, two flying machines seem to have agreed to meet like an emblematic example of the capacity and talent of Germany. We fly around our big brother waving our hands as if giving a 'Good luck' salute."

This brief paragraph shows the constant features of nearly every page of Plüschow: the almost adolescent excitation demonstrated by the permanent signs of admiration, the mania for waving at all the people, vehicles and flags that he meets and the wearisome reiteration that each exploit, each leg of his voyages, each job well done, he does as a German with the end of demonstrating "the capacity and talent of the Germans."

The moment for his departure to the Far East arrived, where he met up with his new Taube aircraft which had wings of wood and paper. The name of his chapter about his stay in the German colony is significant: *"Marvellous Days in Tsingtau."* He had a big house there with a sea view, efficient Chinese servants and society parties.

But the First World War exploded in mid-party.

Some days before the beginning of the war, Plüschow notes a football match "between the German sailors and their British comrades from HMS *Good Hope.* The *Good Hope* was anchored in Tsingtau on a visit. The match turned into a brilliant game and ended one all."

Later on Plüschow comments on the dramatic corollary to this scene. "Hardly six months later the same opponents faced each other in a much more serious and terrible game, where the only options were to win or die. It was the naval battle of Coronel in which the German blue jackets sent HMS *Good Hope* to the deepest part of the Pacific Ocean in just 27 minutes."

In the First World War, Japan was not allied to Germany and an enemy of Great Britain as in the Second, but an enemy of Germany and a British ally. In Plüschow's story, Tsingtau was a distant port, beyond easy communication, which was waiting for the Kaiser's orders to know whom they had to kill.

With the enclave besieged by the Japanese, the aviator carried out dangerous reconnaissance missions. In one accident the wings were destroyed and the propeller damaged. The author describes the repairs in minute detail and calls the return to flight epic, another marvel of the willingness and ingenuity of the Germans.

He was once again observing the enemy's movements from the air. "They were the most beautiful flights of my life; the air was so clear and transparent, the sky so marvellously blue and beautiful and the sun shone with such love on the spectacular land, over the wild peaks of the mountains and the deep blue ocean which framed everything."

But below the bucolic blue the Japanese were closing the blockade around Tsingtau. Plüschow came back from a reconnaissance flight with ten bullet holes in the fuselage. The city was bombarded, the civilians had fled and when the fall was imminent, the commander ordered the airman to abandon Tsingtau before he and his aircraft fell into enemy hands. "The 6th of November 1914, early in the morning when the moon was still shining in the sky, my aircraft was ready to go, with its propeller cheerfully humming a morning song. There was no more time to lose. The place had been turned into an uncomfortable hell by the endless Japanese grenades and shrapnel."

Plüschow managed to evade the blockade, flew for 250 kilometres and landed in a muddy rice field which destroyed his undercarriage and made his propeller fly off. The airplane did a somersault and stopped. A great number of people came out to see the spectacle. When at last he managed to start the motor they ran away terrified. Plüschow gave them some coins. "When the rest saw this they came in such numbers that I thought they would crush my Taube. The amazement of the Chinese! Their sense of touch and feeling! The chatter and laughter! Only

AIRMAN NAVY Lieutenant Gunther Plüschow "the Dragon-master of Tsingtau" in his a craft Rumpler Taube (dove). Source: Gerhard H. Ehlers, Odenthal, Germany.

someone who knows the Chinese and knows how childish they can be will appreciate the delicacy of my situation."

The Mandarin of Daschou gave a party in honour of the German airman and a passport with which he was able to cross a good part of China and arrive in Nanking. "In this city he feels that his own allies are watching him so he evades custody right in the street, hops on a rickshaw and goes to the railway station, where – concealing himself and bribing a guard – he takes a train to Shanghai," Roberto Litvachkes tells us.

In Shanghai Plüschow begins his flight over land and sea, with disguises and assumed names, miraculous escapes, captures and chases that will last nine months and keep the police and the newspapers of half the world on tenterhooks. More than half of *The Adventures of the Tsingtau Aviator* deals with this escape and his ingenuity.

It was in the great Chinese port that Plüschow began his disguises. He adopted the personalities of three North Americans, Messrs. Scout, Meyer and Brown, but when the time came to board a passenger ship heading for San Francisco, his disguise had to be more elaborate. "Suddenly I transformed myself into a wealthy and distinguished Englishman, with the beautiful name of McGarvin. This gentleman was the representative of the Singer Sewing Machine Company and was travelling from Shanghai to their factories in California. What could be more natural than that Mr McGarvin should take the next North American mail steamer?"

The ship made a stop in Nagasaki, which was enemy territory. Before the inspection by the Japanese authorities, Mr McGarvin turned into a sick man. He had to maintain this posture for five days and when the ship at last heads out to sea the reader breathes more easily with the German officer. Plüschow got into an agitated discussion on board with an American millionaire. The man announced: "in a few months Germany will be destroyed and then you will have no work opportunities." He also said that the Kaiser would be deposed by his own people and that the country would remain divided.

The author assures his readers that his reply was energetic. "This was too much for me. I immediately gave a very forceful answer to this man and taught him what a German officer is like and what the German reality is, to the point where the good man himself began to be enthusiastic about my country." Time, of course, would prove the American right, but in 1917 a great part of the book's German readers would have wanted to hear Plüschow's patriotic bravado.

The disguised fugitive crossed the continent by train and found to his surprise that the newspapers were supporting Great Britain in the war. At that time the United States had still not joined the war and was officially neutral.

He went to the opera to see a performance of Engelbert Humperdink's *Hansel and Gretel* ("German music, words and song in German,") which filled him with emotion and nostalgia, but on coming out, he met with an enflamed mob who were celebrating the triumphs of the English, French and Russians in the Great War. "Later they projected some pictures of battles: first of all of some English and French war ships and then, suddenly, the German cruiser *Goeben*. The mob went mad with hisses, whistles and coarse shouts that seemed to have no end. These were the neutrals, the defenders of human rights and equality, the preoccupied Americans!"

A 'man with a hectic life,' a specialist in making false passports, helped him to assume a new identity so as to board a ship bound for Europe. Now he was Ernst Suse, a Swiss lock maker. On the 30th of January 1915 with his new disguise he boarded the Italian steam ship *Duca degli Abruzzi*. His plan was to get off in Italy and take the first train to Germany.

The ship made an unscheduled stop in Gibraltar. Denounced by "traitors" he was submitted to a test of his knowledge of Swiss language and culture by the British authorities. He failed and was imprisoned. A lady among the many who were always disposed to helping him agreed to carry a note to his family in Germany. When he was convinced there was no longer any point in continuing with his Swiss fraud, Plüschow finally gave his British captors his true name and rank, demanding that from then on he should be treated as an official prisoner of war.

Together with some others in the same state he was transported to England by ship. "We were more than a thousand prisoners on board the steamer. The accommodation was the most shameful that I have ever seen. We sat squashed together without light or air in the internal areas of the ship and the only chance of exercise was to walk back and forth on the poop deck and the bow."

Plüschow describes in minute detail his protests at being transported with German soldiers and not with other officers, but when they arrive at their destination, the small port of Dorchester, he doesn't miss the opportunity to remind his readers that over and beyond military rank, the flame of patriotism remained alive in German prisoners. "When we went through the pleasant little town, suddenly from behind us were heard loud and clear, bright and enthusiastic, the beautiful soldiers' songs *The Guard of the Rhine'* and later, '*O Germany in your honour*.'"

"We believed we were dreaming," continues the aviator, "and then we noticed with surprise that behind us was a troop of fifty thin German soldiers who had been sent to the station in the town centre to look for our baggage. Oh, how our hearts swelled! In the middle of enemy territory, despite wounds and prison, this brilliant enthusiasm, this reviving song!"

Plüschow dedicates long pages to describe the conditions of his captivity and his letters to achieve his goal of being sent to a prison for officers only. Finally they send him to Donington Hall, an old 17th Century castle, where there were "three very good tennis courts" and they scrupulously paid each of the 129 officers his due wage as a prisoner of war.

I remember the moment when I was reading these pages and I suddenly stopped, surprised by a memory. Where had I read or heard the story of a prisoner of war of the British who had received his wage and signed a receipt? Suddenly I remembered. In the ship where he was a prisoner in July 1982, seventy-seven years after the events that the German officer Plüschow describes, the Argentine Lieutenant Horacio González Llanos received his wage as a prisoner of war of the British and remembered the event in almost the same words.

From the moment that he arrived at Donington Hall, Plüschow began to plot his escape. One dark stormy night, he and his friend Trefftz passed themselves off as sick and while other colleagues answered their names in the night time inspection in the block, the two officers crossed the electrified wire and walked to the city of Derby where they separated.

Plüschow travelled to London by train, where he learned through the newspapers of Trefftz's capture and discovered that the last 'extra' editions off the presses were announcing the frenetic search for "the escaped German prisoner."

One of the photos of the collage which forms the cover of the Spanish edition of *The Adventures of the Tsingtau Aviator* reproduces an article which announces the hunt for the fugitive. Curiously, among the details that the police gave so that people could recognise him was that the timbre of his voice was very sharp and that on his arm he had a dragon tattoo, a souvenir of his years in China.

But neither the articles nor the posters in the street produced any effect. Disguised as an English workman, Plüschow roamed the streets of London. In this, he was well served by the knowledge of the city that he had gained during his visit of scarcely two years before, when he was awaiting the approval of his requested transfer to naval aviation.

He went into the British Museum and, as Roberto Litvachkes points out in his biography, while in there "he took the opportunity to read books about Patagonia."

After many ups and downs and nights spent rowing between hawsers trying to stow away on a ship bound for the 'continent' the fugitive finally managed to board the *Princess Juliana* and hide under the drum of the anchor chain. Once in Holland he boarded a train and when got to the German border they thought he was a spy. Finally all was resolved because the officer in charge turned out to be an old comrade of Plüschow's. So he arrived in Berlin where "two marvellous blue pupils" were waiting for him. (This seems to be a cryptic reference to Isot, though in the book he never mentions having a girlfriend).

In the last lines of the officer's book he recounts that he ordered new clothes to be made, because he had left his old ones in Tsingtau. "Soon I was able once again to present myself in my beloved blue uniform of a naval officer and my heart beat very fast when I received the Iron Cross (1st Class). The real prize came later; I was going to be a pilot again. I could return to the front together with my comrades in the struggle and help them fight for the fatherland. I was named commandant of a large naval flying base on the Eastern Front.

* * *

The historical personality of Gunther Plüschow planted many questions and doubts in me. The more I read, the greater became my need to make another voyage to Germany to seek out the German counterpart of Roberto Litvachkes.

The questions were piling up for me. What significance did this First World War hero have in the Germany of today? Who was this man who reinvented himself as an explorer in Tierra del Fuego and, in passing, had a boat built which turned into the *Penélope*?

So it was that in November 2006, after my return from the meetings and interviews in Argentina and from the journey to the Islands, I put myself in contact with Gerhard Ehlers and Ingrid Gaa, the organisers of the first exhibition about Plüschow to be mounted in Germany.

Ingrid Gaa, a graphic designer and television producer, whom I visited at her home, near Mainz, had also made the first documentary about Plüschow to be shown on public television in Germany.

"What first attracted me to Plüschow is his way of appreciating the unknown," Ingrid explained. "He sought out the unusual and that immediately appealed to me. I was very surprised that a German of those days had achieved such fame in a place so far away. I liked the fact that he was an adventurer, a man who went towards new things with positive energy, with a real love for what he was discovering and never gave up following his own goal."

"And how was it you decided to make a documentary about him?" I asked her.

"Because I thought he was a person who would interest the public. I didn't want such a person from Germany's past to be forgotten, when there are so many terrible ones who still remain in our memory."

I already knew Gerhard Ehlers. He had approached me after the press conference in Hamburg on the day of the *Feuerland's* arrival. With his appearance of a friendly bear from the forest, his shaggy beard, tousled hair and the glasses of a compulsive reader, I had liked him from the beginning. We spoke for only fifteen minutes before Christian Bauer invited me to take a turn round the boat in his skiff, but what he said left me thinking, opened my mind to new subjects and gave me the feeling that he was a person with whom I would have to speak much more.

"You have to remember that Plüschow began his military career when he was eleven years old" he told me then. "He was a patriotic

German, but I believe he lived his patriotism in a natural way. It wasn't like a political plan," he stressed putting his hand to his chest, "but more like a feeling."

"He's a difficult person to take today, but perhaps that has to do with what you see in the streets these days: all these people with German flags because of the World Cup."

In those few minutes, Ehlers explained to me that since the rise of the Nazis in 1933 and, above all, since the incontestable evidence of their crimes, "German pride became a suspect and reprehensible attitude. This flag fever makes me feel very old. I don't like it."

I asked him what he felt for his country. "I am a lover of the German language and of many things in my culture, but 'being Germans' continues seeming to me something that can't fill us with pride. They did too many horrible things in the name of love for this country."

"And isn't Plüschow an example of a German patriot?"

"Yes, but for better or worse he died in 1931. Perhaps he is the last 'white' or stainless patriot that we Germans have. For me at least what captivated me about him is his adventure in Tierra del Fuego, not his escape and even less his military career."

Five months have gone by and here I am once again in Germany, in a train which is taking me from Cologne airport to Ehlers' house in a delightful little village in the mountains, which is now a suburb for those who work in this ancient Bavarian city. It is not summer now, like it was when I came to Hamburg to see the *Penélope's* return. Now it is the dead of winter, the carriage is freezing, a group of young people are chatting animatedly in a language I don't understand, and in one corner a poor old man is sleeping clasping a bottle of beer.

The train crosses suburbs and industrial estates. Dead from the cold, with my cap on my head and my scarf wound round my neck, I am bent over my railway map, mentally ticking off stations with very long names as dozens of Germans get on and off. The only one who doesn't move is the old man with the bottle.

Finally Gerhard's station arrives. There he is, smiling like a happy bear in the middle of the platform, with a bag of bread that he has just bought for tomorrow's breakfast. We still have to wait half an hour till the bus arrives to take us on a route between little two-storey houses with trees in their gardens.

"You know that I was banned from this part of Germany for almost twenty years?" he tells me as we wait for the bus.

Several generations will have to come and go before the differences between the two Germanies are erased. After talking with many people I notice that those who were born and brought up in what was Federal or West Germany say simply that they are 'German', but those from the East, will remain 'East German' for many years. Many years will go by and the men and women of the former Democratic German Republic will continue to carry the mark of the East inside themselves, like emigrants who never were, like citizens of a country which disappeared from under their feet.

Gerhard Ehlers was born in Rostock in the same state of Mecklenburg from which Gunther Plüschow's family came. He was born in 1954, almost a decade after the end of the war. When it was still possible to go from the East to the West, he remembers excursions to West Berlin with his mother when he stuffed himself with the sweets that you could buy on the capitalist side.

In 1961, when Gerhard was seven, the Red Army built the wall and going to the West became a crime. In his adolescence he fed his liking for travel, rucksack on back, by trekking through the countries of the Eastern Block with his then girlfriend, now his wife, Gabriella. "We made our first trip in 1972, to Prague. From then on we went to Poland, Russia, Bulgaria, Czechoslovakia and Hungary."

Gerhard and Gabriella, friends from secondary school, married at 22. They had two children. They had good jobs – he in a shipping company – and everything was going well. "So well, it was frightening. I imagined living like that for the rest of my life." The idea of fleeing to the other side of the wall didn't occur to him, he explained, because it would be seeking a paradise which he well knew did not exist in the capitalist world. "I was looking for freedom, not as a grand concept, but as something concrete and practical, which gave you the opportunity to decide, to choose. It's something that makes you feel you are drowning when you don't have it. There everything was grey, everything was prescribed, everything controlled."

We get off the bus in a residential district with a lot of greenery. There is not a soul to be seen. Gerhard and Gabriella have a chalet with a small garden behind. Peaceful coloured fish swim in the pond. We take off our shoes to cross the thick carpet of the living-dining room, where we continue chatting. As he had promised me on the phone, Gerhard gets out a bottle of good Mendoza red to spark up the conversation and warm us after the cold outdoors.

The whole long wall of the living room is occupied by a library in which the classics of German literature stand out, along with many history books and novels in English. On a tall shelf among other English authors I discover Graham Greene's, *The Heart of the Matter.* The German translation is *'The Heart of the Horror.'* Another title change, another interpretation of the book's unsettling plot, this time towards the dramatic and dark. Like the *Penélope*, like Plüschow, with each new language and each new cultural world, Greene's novel becomes different.

There is nothing in this library about Gunther Plüschow or Tierra del Fuego, which are Ehlers' two parallel passions. The books, the maps, the wooden masks of the Yahgan Indians, the Fuegian relics and his prized certificate for having sailed around Cape Horn, are kept in his work room in the cellar.

Before going down to the cellar and while the wine is still working its health-giving effect, Gerhard tells me about his flight to the West. In mid 1989, without knowing how they were going to survive in the West, the Ehlers locked up their house in Rostock, crossed the frontier into Hungary and a few days later were in Nuremberg as political refugees under the protection of the Red Cross. Gerhard wants to emphasise that he did not expect that the Wall would come down. As soon as he saw a chink of possibility of escaping without risking the life of his family, he fled to a very imperfect, but at least liveable world.

Seventeen years later, Gerhard Ehlers now works in the agrochemical division of the multinational Bayer Corporation. He travels all over the world and proudly shows me his three storey house and his multitude of artistic and anthropological objects from three continents. He seems to be a man who has found peace and equilibrium.

Now his dream, his hobby and his ambition take him in another direction. It all began in 1999, when having accumulated a lot of air miles and having a limited time in which to use them he decided to fly to Chilean Patagonia and Tierra del Fuego. "I always loved sailors' stories, Magellan's voyage and the novels of

Jules Verne. I went into the museum in Ushuaia and what I wasn't expecting was to meet a German explorer that I had never heard spoken of. The first thing that caught my eye was that the motor of his seaplane had been made by Heinkel, a company from my city of Rostock.

The End of the World Museum in Ushuaia has a section dedicated to Gunther Plüschow's memory. Besides copies of his books and photos of the explorer they exhibit the compass from *Silberkondor's* cabin and the crankshaft of the Heinkel motor. There's also a shortened version of Plüschow's film which the visitor can ask them to show.

When Gerhard returned to Germany he asked his mother if the name was familiar. "She told me that of course it was; she knew all about his exploits and that besides he had been a neighbour of ours. But why was this fellow so forgotten? Certainly he didn't fit into any of the stories that circulated about the Nazis. He hadn't been either an anti-Nazi hero or one of the genocidal monsters of that period. During the struggle that followed what had happened in Germany, it appeared that no one was interested in a member of the German military who had gone off to explore the ends of the earth, but his story captured me immediately."

To help me review Plüschow's life, Gerhard gave me the Power Point projection that he uses at conferences about the aviator. In the first part of his life, the facts are similar to those that Roberto Litvachkes presents: Munich, Rome, Schwerin, military academy, naval college, the *Bismark*, romance with Isot, Tsingtau, and his triumphant return to Berlin as an escape artist and master of disguises.

"When he returns he says in the book that they gave him a relevant post, but for a man of action like him, directing a flying centre is a bureaucratic job" Ehlers thinks. "Surely they would not want him to be captured by the enemy. He had been – and still is – the only prisoner of war to escape from England. I believe that in the months that followed his return the high command understood that they had to give him the time and the peace to quickly write his book. That book was going to be a tremendous propaganda tool in raising the morale of the whole population."

In the midst of bad news from all the war fronts, and with Great Britain wiping out the Kaiser's fleet on the high seas, Gunther Plüschow's successful escape was the story that the optimists in

Berlin wanted him to tell: how a German officer tricks his enemies and arrives home safe and sound armed only with his determination and intelligence.

After showing me a reproduction of the book's cover, the next image that Ehlers projects surprises me: it's one of the drawings of the acid cartoonist Georg Grosz, which shows a Berlin street full of haughty burghers and suffering beggars, chaos, ugliness and deliberately disagreeable factions. Grosz is the master of street scenes where social decomposition and offensive injustices leap out at the viewer, leaving the drawing of conclusions almost unnecessary.

"What are you explaining when you show this image?" I ask him.

"There I want to show the post-war Germany, the bitter, free and anarchic world that was being assembled, particularly in Berlin, at the beginning of the twenties."

The war ends towards the end of 1918; Germany emerges defeated and the Kaiser flees. The country is collapsed morally and the Treaty of Versailles which the allies impose obliges the country to pay enormous compensations for its role as the aggressor. Moral barriers fall and hyperinflation sharpens poverty and unemployment. The Weimar Republic keeps going with great difficulty hounded by the impositions of the allies, the well-organised workers' communist movement and the incipient but rapid advance of a new racist and demagogic group, the Nazis.

"In this new world without order or respect for tradition, Plüschow feels lost" says Ehlers. "In reality, like thousands of others, he is displaced. He's like a hero in a novel by Erich Maria Remarque, one of those broken heroes who return from the war mentally shattered. He leaves the Navy and begins to take strange jobs without reason or direction. He operates the film projector in a cinema, works in a steel foundry, sells used cars, opens a business selling bicycle parts and even spends 24 hours doing laps of a track on a motorbike to break the endurance record."

Plüschow was trying to promote himself as a hero of a lost war that everybody wanted to forget, but not all his ideas were crazy or pathetic. He took out a licence for civilian flights and opened a mail service between Weimar and Berlin. His company would be one of those that later fused into Lufthansa, however it never managed to take off.

Meanwhile he already had a family to be concerned with. He had married Isot in 1916 at the air base where he was the commander.

His son Guntolf was born in 1918. Finally, according to Isot, it was she who pushed him to go to sea again. She saw him as a viking who needed always to seek new horizons. Gunther Plüschow took another course to convert himself into a merchant seaman and left for the Mediterranean where he worked as an officer on board a cruise ship for rich tourists, whom he entertained with his stories of his exploits in Tsingtau and the adventure of his escape.

On one of these voyages he met the owner of the Laeisz cruise ship company, who offered him employment on one of his luxurious transatlantic liners, the *Parma*. Plüschow wrote to Isot asking her urgently to buy him a still camera and another one for cine, because he was going to explore the ends of the earth.

* * *

On the 15th September 1925, he embarked on the *Parma* in Hamburg. At last he was going to get to know Tierra del Fuego, the place in the photo which had set his imagination aflame when he was an apprentice sailor.

IN GERMANY Gerhard H. Ehlers has a huge collection of Plüschow memorabilia, one of the masterpieces is this 1:20 scale model of the *Feuerland*. Source: Christopher Arlinghaus, Germany.

The second of Plüschow's books, *Segelfahrt ins Wunderland* (Under sail to Wonderland), emerges from his voyage on the *Parma*. At the beginning of the story the voyager defines himself as a photographer, film camera man and the guide of an expedition "to explore unknown regions in South America." Next he lists his valuable "team": an old Remington typewriter, a Görz camera and the big box with a winding handle, that in Patagonia, the Pampas and forests were met with terror, because it was thought that they were "something magical."

After a couple of chapters in which he describes the changing temperament and appearance of the sea and pauses for some shark fishing, patriotic sentiment overcomes him when the ship passes close to the Falkland Islands, through the waters where the German fleet commanded by Count von Spee was sunk in the First World War.

"Down below us" he writes "is the cold tomb of Graf Spee, of his two sons and of so many valiant sailors who fought against the terrible supremacy of the English and sank with glory."

From his first contact with Tierra del Fuego he highlights the beauty of its landscape which reminds him of Norway and the hurricane-like winds of the Le Maire Strait. He dedicates the main part of his book to describing his journeys through Chile, Peru and Ecuador and always detects the fruitful German presence and the high virtues which adorn it.

"Valdivia, with its most faithful German appearance, with German strength and work, German hospitality, in happy union with Chilean hospitality and friendliness." He spends a few days of solace in the house of the Werkmeister family, "a German home, with a German housekeeper and, despite the fact that they were born in Chile, naturally only German is spoken."

He covers Chilean Patagonia on horseback, describes the customs and skills of the horsemen and goes into ecstasies in the contemplation of the Osorno volcano and the Tronador mountain, which marks the boundary between Argentina and Chile. On Richard Lauezzari's estancia, he is impressed by the ostriches and in Puerto Bories by the freezing plants of the English.

Roberto Litvachkes and Gerhard Ehlers both used almost the same words to tell me about an episode in his travels with Lauezzari. For both it is a key moment in Plüschow's life. Plüschow and

Lauezzari arrive at the foot of the impressive Torres del Paine and the aviator remains awestruck by the imposing snowy peaks.

"What's on the other side?" he asks.

"I don't know" says Lauezzari.

"And who does know?"

"Nobody. Nobody knows because nobody's been on the other side."

"I'm going to go," they claim Gunther Plüschow said at this moment. "I'm going to be the first."

That mixture of blind confidence and the romantic dream of discovering a marvellous and unexplored part of the world is an important element which captured those two followers of the explorer and many others.

However the general tone of *Segelfahrt ins Wunderland* isn't like that; it's more like a more conventional travel book. Everything is new to the discoverer and the little incidents on the ship or the horseback rides assume epic proportions. However, it's not the deeds that he narrates that engage the reader; as in *The Adventures of the Tsingtau Aviator*, it's more the contagious nature of the narrator's joy and astonishment.

Gerhard Ehlers points out two elements in Plüschow's story: on one hand his interest in ecology and the dangers that lie in wait for the natural world, and on the other his sense of social justice that makes him pay attention to the extreme poverty and inhumane conditions of South American workers. For example, referring to the nitrate workers he says, "These people work from sun up to sun down for the eight hour day is not known here. They live worse than animals and still are happy to be alive and to have work."

After travelling to the north of Chile, Peru and Ecuador in another ship, the *Planet*, Plüschow finishes this book, like his earlier one, with his return home and the joy of finding himself once more in his native land, amongst his own people.

This is the crucial moment in the life of the retired captain.

It was 1926, he was already forty with neither fortune nor work and his fame was tied to an uncomfortable war. However he had a dream and a plan, and the tenacity and ingenuity that pushed him to achieve what he was proposing still causes amazement and admiration among those who enter into his life through this, the heroic door.

After the success of his two books, Gunther Plüschow understood that his future lay in becoming a bold and adventurous personality, representing the best German virtues and at the same time being the constructor and narrator of his own adventures. He had to convince those who would finance his future expeditions that he was capable of holding the public's attention. More than living to tell the tale, he had to know how to tell the tale in order to live.

The plan forming in his head was audacious and difficult to accomplish. He had to have a boat built to lead an expedition of his own to the Tierra del Fuego of his dreams. The boat would have to be extremely strong to be able to survive the voyage from Germany and the harsh conditions of the southern winter.

But his principal aim wasn't to sail. The vessel would be only auxiliary, his operating base. His main desire and the most adventurous, was to fly where nobody had ever flown before. He had to do it in a seaplane, which would be the basic instrument in which to fly over the Cordillera and the snowy peaks, if he were to be the first person to see what lay behind the Torres del Paine and all the other marvels of the world's end.

And the team! He had to find at least three excellent crew members for the boat and an advanced mechanic for his plane.

This, however, was only the start. In order to tell the world about his voyages and discoveries he needed a good cameraman, cine and still cameras, kilometres of virgin film and his old Remington on which to write articles during the voyage and finally a great book. So that the world should learn of his exploits he needed to have a firm contract with a publisher who would place his constant articles in magazines and newspapers and would take charge of publishing his book and distributing his film. To do that he also needed funds, time and a modern editing suite in his ship.

He would be responsible for directing and putting the film together, although his only experience in this subject was as a technician working the film reel projectors in the Berlin cinemas, during his years of hardships.

The project as presented sounds crazy and so it seemed to the first people who listened to it. The fact that he would carry on to the end without losing heart is what continues to serve as an example and a source of inspiration to people like Roberto Litvachkes and Gerhard Ehlers.

"Plüschow travelled round Germany reading people paragraphs from his *Parma* book and saying to them, 'I was so close, why aren't you helping me to make the real voyage of my dreams?'," says Ehlers.

He approached dozens of firms asking for support for his voyage. By a lucky coincidence Ehlers was able to get hold of a copy of one of these letters. "A woman friend told me that her father remembered going to one of Plüschow's conferences in the Bayer factory as a boy," Gerhard continues. "I work for Bayer so I wrote to their archive and they sent me a copy of Plüschow's letter asking for money to go to Patagonia. I wanted to know what they had replied, but it was a bad time and they told him no, as I imagine many others would have done.

Litvachkes, always focusing on the positive, takes comfort in picturing the moment when his problems ended. Plüschow presented his project to the Ullstein publishing house, one of the most important in the world at that time.

"He brought an enormous map of Tierra del Fuego and put it up behind the chair where he sat to explain his plan. He went on showing the places that he thought he would explore which he had marked on the map with the word 'unexplored.' He showed them the photos and images of the places he wanted to record, and told them how important his voyage would be." They said they would call him and a little while later they announced that they would agree to finance his expedition, would pay part of the construction costs of the vessel, would undertake to publish his articles and his book and would produce his film.

"Plüschow was very convincing," smiles Roberto.

Little by little companies began to see the possible benefits in allying themselves to the lunatic who wanted to discover new lands at the world's end. Heinkel, the Rostock aircraft manufacturers, offered him the seaplane with wooden wings. BMW, at that time makers of aircraft engines, enabled him to get the 230 horse power engine and also sent their trusty mechanic Ernst Dreblow on the expedition. Deutz took care of the boat's engine, an HD 24. Agfa gave him forty kilometres of film.

Food, clothing, gasoline; the requirements were appearing as time went on. The recommendation of the companies that had already entered into an agreement reduced any lack of confidence in new ones. Ullstein took charge of the majority of the expedition's expenses on the understanding that Plüschow would feed the magazines of their publishing group with photos and stories of his fascinating adventures. The German Automobile Club offered him a good part of his nautical equipment and the Hamburg branch presented him with a nice mascot for the voyage, the dog *Schnauf,* some sort of fox terrier with the look of a picaresque nosy parker.

And that was the moment when into Plüschow's life, and into this story, appeared the ship of his southern adventure: the ketch *Feuerland,* the "ocean going clog" as Plüschow called her affectionately, the future *Penélope.*

* * *

"And why wasn't an existing boat bought for this expedition? Why did he have to get a new one built?" I ask Gerhard Ehlers.

"Like everything else, it was partly a question of money. The owners of the boat yard were war time friends and offered him a good deal. Besides, he needed a special boat, small enough to sail the Fuegian channels, but different from most boats of that size, much stronger so as to survive in those extreme conditions."

It is clearly modelled on the North German fishing boats of that period, but it had two characteristics which distinguish it nearly eight decades after its construction: it has a double hull made of oak from the German forests and it has something else which is unusual for a vessel of this size: two steel plates to separate the area below deck into three watertight compartments.

The Krämer, Vagt and Beckman shipyard constructed a variation of a North Sea fishing boat, following a design described as 'excellent' by numerous experts. The only problem was that the construction was delayed by at least four weeks more than was envisaged so that the expedition left at the beginning of the boreal winter.

The place where it was constructed and from which it left is the charming port of Büsum, where the Elbe flows into the North Sea. Büsum is situated about a couple of hours by train from Hamburg, has a famous lighthouse, a long tradition of deep-water fishing and is a favourite spot for summer holidaymakers, who stroll along its one kilometre stretch of muddy beach until they reach the sea. In Plüschow's time it was a respected port for the repair and construction of fishing boats.

It was also in Büsum where the captain met his helmsman and all-round man of the sea, Paul Christiansen. Christiansen had more maritime experience than Plüschow himself. He sailed his own boat and knew a lot about storms and this kind of vessel. Ehlers makes it clear that "in fact, during the navigation to Tierra del Fuego it was really Christiansen who had charge of the *Feuerland* while Plüschow busied himself writing his articles, coordinating the recording of the film and organising every step of the expedition."

The third member of the expedition was another experienced sailor, Josef Schmitt, who Plüschow refers to by his nickname, "Seppl."

At the end of his life Schmitt wrote his memoirs, primarily for his grandchildren. Mateo Martinic, a professor at the University of Magallanes and indefatigable student of the south of Chile published these valuable memories in Punta Arenas in the magazine *Magallania*. In the text, Schmitt recalls his hard childhood, his training as a cadet, sailor and pilot in sailing ships. In 1927 he was getting ready to enrol in the Navigation School, when the captain for whom he was working talked to him about a request from Gunther Plüschow, "who was looking for people to pilot his sailing ship." The personnel that Plüschow was looking for "had to have sailing experience."

Schmitt travelled to Büsum "to visit the yard where they were building the boat. It had 16 metres in length and 5 in the beam. Compared to SS *Passat* (the last ship in which he had sailed) with its four masts, 4,000 tons and 4,800 square metres of sail, it appeared a dwarf, which continued to scare me. At this time I knew the pilot, Paul Christiansen, who convinced me to take the boat to Tierra del Fuego. Paul only spoke the 'platt' dialect (from the north-west of Germany) and we became good friends. Paul Christiansen was a deep sea fisherman and owned his own boat so his economic position was rather better than mine."

The group was completed with three more crew members. They took on an adolescent cadet who had sailed to Tierra del Fuego. Plüschow only tells us that his name was Harry and pokes fun in a friendly way at his insatiable appetite and his idleness. A young cameraman, Kurt Neubert, also embarked, who appears in all the photos with a weather-beaten face, flattened like a boxer's and the wiry body of a marathon runner. The lad is almost always wrapped up in the same red shirt, which gives Plüschow the idea of giving him the nickname 'Garibaldi' like the Italian revolutionary.

And finally in the role of cook on board there is Isot, Plüschow's wife, who insisted on leaving their small son on land and joining the expedition. It is surprising not to encounter even one mention of his wife's name in the whole book that Plüschow writes about the voyage. Every time he refers to her he calls her 'smutje' an old sailor's term for a ship's cook. The Spanish translator renames her as 'Smutie,' probably because it is easier to pronounce.

The voyage was plagued with complications and dangers and Plüschow knew that he had to have every step clear in his head and convey his enthusiasm to the rest. It was his last chance and many things could go wrong. Two texts give some idea of Plüschow's worries during the months before the departure.

Gerhard Ehlers finds very revealing an article in which "the aviator of Tsingtau" salutes and congratulates his most successful colleague, the famous American pilot Charles Lindbergh. On May 20th 1927, Lindbergh, flying solo for 33 hours in his monoplane *Spirit of Saint Louis* had made the first flight across the Atlantic.

"Plüschow's article broke my heart," says Ehlers, "he is congratulating his great fellow aviator in a very gentlemanly way, but you can read between the lines that he would have given anything to be in his place. At the same time he reminds his German readers that he had also done something great. 'I know like you how hard it is to fall and have to get up again, to struggle against adversity and not give up' he tells Lindberg. He is encouraging himself. It is perhaps the most sincerely autobiographical thing he ever wrote."

During the same period, Ullstein brought out a new edition of *The Adventures of the Tsingtau Aviator*. In the new edition, the author adds a brief epilogue, in which he writes, "The years passed ... they passed struggling, fighting, full of hope, full of confidence in a good ending. My comrades were falling left and right, many good friends, and many family members. The fatherland fought with one. My own brother found a pilot's heroic death. Then, later, the finale came, the struggle had ceased ... was that the end?"

And then, immediately: "No, never! This was not the feeling of so many victims! To give up, to lose heart, to seek a destiny of one's own that peace was not capable of preparing? No, now less than ever! Now a man could show if he was capable of something ... and one fine day the ocean called me again and took me to far off worlds of wonder and everywhere I was received with respect and friendship for being German. The new era had begun!"

When Roberto Litvachkes made me a present of his book on Plüschow and a copy of the DVD with the original documentary of the voyage to Tierra del Fuego, I submitted my parents, my aunt, my sister and my nephews to a two hour session of black and white film.

The film begins in the November of 1927 and the scene shows a wooden slipway from which the *Feuerland* glides slowly towards her launching. The little blonde and smiling Guntolf, waves a handkerchief among the crowd. The vessel is decorated and garlanded and, aboard, Plüschow poses with his crew and the dog, *Schnauf*, who even has the luxury of a kennel on deck.

It is September 2006 and I am in my parents' house in Vicente López and we are all excited, milling around the television viewing the birth of the *Penélope* about which I have talked to them so much.

And the voyage begins. The 'ocean-going clog' is lost between gigantic waves in the labyrinth of the mist, while her tall masts trace a zigzagging and unsteady wake in the sea.

CHAPTER 2

Where no one had ever been

"With a crunch, the wide bow of the sailing ship rises slowly above the ice. A cracking noise echoes as the ice strives to hold itself together, before separating with a tearing sound, and piling up on both sides, leaving a free passage and allowing the dark grey sea water to rise to the surface laughing and gurgling." So begins Plüschow's book Over Tierra del Fuego. The title is in reality a shortened version of the original Silver Condor over Tierra del Fuego (Silberkondor über Feuerland).

Unlike his earlier books, this one gives the reader no chance to catch breath. From the first paragraph the nut shell is struggling boldly with dense blocks of ice which threaten to break the ship open. And still it hasn't left Büsum!

Plüschow has already completely developed a vigorous style full of descriptions with metaphors and surprising details, short, credible dialogues and a rhythm which does not slacken, despite half of the book being devoted to the schooner's very long voyage across half the world. One hundred and forty pages go by before the group finally arrives at Tierra del Fuego in October of 1928.

The beginning of the voyage was the hardest and most difficult part of the long sail south. They had to leave from the North Sea in mid-winter, fighting against storms and sea-sickness. In Plüschow's book it is Smutie who suffers the discomforts of the novice sailor the most.

During the first days of the voyage the boat began to take on water in the middle of the storm, the rain and the cold. Smutie was stretched out sick in the cabin with water up to her ankles.

"'Are we ship-wrecked? Are we going to the bottom, my dear?', Smutie asked me in a low voice, her eyes bright with fever.

"'No, Smutie, very much to the contrary. It's just that now we have to show that we are good sailors and worthy of this fine sailing ship. Excuse me but I can't spare even a minute more for you;

if you find anything of assistance to you, go up on deck and help with the pump!'."

"Quickly I grab *Schnauf* by the neck; he is dripping and stinks. I throw him – perhaps a little brutally – onto Smutie's bunk and, stumbling, hanging on, feeling buffeted at every step by the sail boat's diabolical motion, I arrive on deck once more.

"'Prow to port! Head for the coast! Keep an eye out for signals or the sight of land!' – I say to Seppl who is now on watch."

In the memoirs of Seppl Schmitt, it wasn't Isot who was the seasick one but Gunther himself.

"We sailed one November day, heading for the high seas. We had to shelter in Amsterdam due to bad weather. The boat was full of water and the pumps kept getting blocked.

Afterwards we steered for the Bay of Biscay, which was known for its storms. Gunther Plüschow remained seasick and we saw him on deck very little. He had a lot of trust in me and Paul Christiansen. Soon we got to the Atlantic and I must mention that little by little I was getting used to sailing in this 'nut shell'."

In Vigo after some devilish storms which never seemed to end, Isot put an end to her service on board. No more Smutie; she would go back to Germany. However when they got to the next port, which was Lisbon, just as they were about to leave Plüschow was surprised to see her waving her arms from the jetty.

"Smutie jumped on board and examined us all in silence for a few moments as if convinced of her guilt. Then she murmured in a low voice:

'I've been thinking ... Christmas is coming ... and which of you will decorate our little tree if I am not on board?'."

"She says this then disappears through the hatch. Half an hour later, our Smutie crosses the deck in her boots smiling and humming, before eclipsing again, going down below by way of the 'henhouse' ladder in the bow."

"'Thank God. We're going to have those tasty chips again!' Garibaldi sighs with satisfaction."

When Gunther was taking her to the cabin, Isot told him the truth within in everyone's hearing.

"'I have something to confess dear, I missed the train in Vigo. That's why I came back on board in such a rush!'"

However worrying news reaches them in Lisbon; Guntolf is ill.

Isot has to leave for Germany immediately. A year and a half will go by before she sees her husband again.

Before leaving Lisbon they come across a German transatlantic liner, Hamburg Sud's *Cap Arcona*, "one of the finest and most gigantic ships ploughing the seas at that time." In his permanent search for evidence of 'Germanity' in the world's oceans, Plüschow pauses to consider that 'our clog' appears by comparison, hardly bigger than one of its lifeboats.

"When we sail around our 'brother ship' (the biggest and the smallest of the ships which have sailed to South America from Germany to date!), our little siren sounds firmly and modestly three times and the flags of both vessels dip in mutual salute, under the rays of the splendid sun. When the *Cap Arcona* replies to our salute, the bellow of the powerful ship's siren, thunders in the air with imposing force as if coming from a tremendous organ.

"And this dream of beauty, this unforgettable memory," he concludes "carries Smutie with it to our country."

"That's the ship in which we came from Hamburg!" my father cries suddenly when the *Cap Arcona* appears in the film.

I knew that my grandfather had gone into permanent exile from Hamburg with his two children, aged 12 and 6. They were Jews fleeing from Hitler's Germany in 1937. The transatlantic liner which brought them to Buenos Aires was the *Cap Arcona*, the ship whose brilliant image in black and white, my Dad, my Aunt Marion and I were now seeing sailing serenely alongside the same boat in which I had spent the war in the Islands.

For a minute intense memories of two quite distinct eras crossed in us before we went back to the film and continued to accompany Captain Plüschow on his voyage to Tierra del Fuego.

During the Atlantic crossing the crew of the *Feuerland* entertained itself riding the enormous waves that the explorer poetically calls "Neptune's white horses." On another occasion they gave themselves over to annoying a shark to get the furious creature to show its great mouth out of the water.

When they crossed the Equator the captain organised an amusing ceremony. Plüschow disguised himself as Neptune with robe, trident and white beard. Seppl Schmitt was his wife, the Queen of the Seas. The crew members who were crossing to the other side of the world for the first time had to submit to a 'punishment,' which, given the circumstances, was reasonably benign.

PLÜSCHOW'S *FEUERLAND* in calm water near the equator. Source: Gerhard H. Ehlers, Odenthal, Germany.

Obviously everything that they were doing: the struggle with the shark, the *Feuerland* rising and falling on the backs of the white horses, was so that Garibaldi could record metres and yet more metres of film. This was especially so in the case of the unusual scene of the 'baptism' at the equator. In the film Paul Christiansen is the first victim. We see him docile, on his knees, in his underpants. Plüschow smears him with mud and between all of them they throw him in a mud bath, so that he ends up completely dirty. Even *Schnauf* doesn't escape the initiation or the skinny Garibaldi, who despite his protests also ends up in the mud bath.

"We were stuck at the level of the Equator for ten days, for lack of wind." Seppl Schmitt recalls in his memoirs. "We didn't use the motor because apart from being the ship's captain, Plüschow was also the writer and needed peace to concentrate."

Plüschow describes the long wait in his book. Nothing could be done until the wind should arrive to swell the sails. "We find ourselves lazily stretched out on deck, sweating through every pore. The little *Feuerland* rocks gently from side to side like an enormous cradle, rhythmically and pleasurably inclining before the beautiful, long and high undercurrent that arrives from a distance. Not a word, not a sound, nothing which interrupts the harmonious calm. The sea gives off reflections and glitters in such a way that our eyes hurt when we look at the water. But below our awnings, which project a mystical light, it is cool, that is to say something that we on board regard as 'cool' in comparison with the forty-five degrees Celsius which are regularly found below decks."

Finally the wind arrives and the vessel touches her first American port, San Salvador de Bahía. From there on, as Seppl Schmitt narrates, "we were following the coast of Brazil towards the south. We called in at various ports where he (Plüschow) used to give speeches with the object of defraying part of the expedition's costs."

In order to fulfil his obligations in terms of journalism and publicity, Plüschow had to prolong his voyage as much as possible. They took almost a year to complete a voyage which could have taken two months at most. In Brazil the captain and his photographer visited slaughter houses, cigar factories, coffee plantations, cattle stations and an Indian village – curiously and regrettably this last visit will cause this travel film to become a valuable ethnographic document today.

In Santa Catarina State some German colonists – Plüschow encounters German immigrants and clubs at every stop – take them to the interior of the forest where a war-like tribe live who dress in loin cloths and hunt with lances and arrows, just as in Neolithic times. They are the Botocudos. They reach where the Indians are after a long and risky march.

"In the blink of an eye we see Garibaldi and I surrounded by half a dozen totally naked savages with bestial faces and urchin-style black hair which they cut themselves using sharp pointed stones. After they have prodded us, smelled us and examined us as if we were beasts bound for the slaughter house, they inspect our bags and finding nothing in them, express their disappointment with a gesture which has nothing reassuring about it."

As those of us who already know something about Plüschow might suppose, the female Botocudos appeal to him more. "Here on the 'frontier' they still wear coverings and rags around the thighs. They have high waists and their bodies are in general well-formed, with fine firm breasts which remain uncovered, but further into the interior, in the virgin forest, they also, like the men, go completely naked. The faces of the women have nothing disagreeable about them. Surprisingly their lips are deliciously thin and their faces are identical to those of the Eskimo and brown like the rest of their bodies. They have lank hair, of a blue-black colour, which is cut with the sharpened stone and no hair on the body, or scarcely any."

The pictures show the Botocudos hunting a wild bull with their lances, cooking it and sharing large chunks of meat with their guests. They bite happily and laugh at the camera. This is the first filmic witness of the Botocudos and also the last. The tribe did not last long before it was engulfed and extinguished by civilisation. Today one of the main evidences remaining to science of the life, culture and world of gestures of the Botocudos, is Gunther Plüschow's film.

"'Onwards' is our motto; onwards, ever onwards" is the way in which Plüschow continues his story. But they had to do the following leg by sail, which took more time and needed much more sailing skill. On the Island of Fernando de Noronha, in the north of Brazil, the engine's crankshaft had broken.

Slowly they leave the Uruguayan coast, where Plüschow shows himself pleased by small, orderly and prosperous Montevideo and they cross the River Plate with all sail, a good wind and a horizon that makes them think they are on the high seas.

Finally they arrive at the 'little New York': "Buenos Aires, the city of 'good airs', the capital of the immense Argentine Republic, the country of great things, great beauty and great riches massed together. Here in this great city are concentrated the wealth and force of this powerful state with its gigantic future; also here the development acquired from the time of the war, (1914) which after the war reaches the limits of credibility. 'Poor Europe with all its preoccupations and feuds' I keep this thought to myself, but I think it is true."

The boat moors in the Buenos Aires Yacht Club, whose pennant flies at the mast head. Under that was "the Argentine flag; the Ullstein Publishing House's blue flag with the yellow owl hangs from the bowsprit and in the stern is my marine flag with its iron cross, deep red and gold on the black material. On the gaff the *Feuerland's* pennant flutters gleaming red in celebration of this great day."

According to Plüschow's ringing description of it, the entry into Buenos Aires was triumphal. When entering from the river along a channel, "on both sides a great crowd saluted us cordially from above, waving caps and hats, breaking out into deafening applause and calling out:

"'Long live Germany! Long live the little German schooner!'

"There's no doubt that they already know who we are here. Excited by that cordial reception, we shout in our turn:

"'Long live the Argentine Republic!' We are struck dumb by this magnificent welcome, although during our long crossing we have often been received with affectionate demonstrations of friendliness."

The crew spent several weeks enjoying the hospitality of Buenos Aires. Plüschow and his cameraman visited an estancia and continued accumulating images for the film, while the German magazines were filling with photos of the explorer's Argentine adventures.

Roberto Litvachkes gives much importance to an interview that Plüschow allowed the newspaper *La Nación* during his stay in Buenos Aires. The journalist asked him to define himself; was he an aviator, sailor, the leader of an expedition of discovery to the southern extremities, or a former military hero from the First World War? "And at that point, Plüschow says that he sees himself as a journalist more than anything: a man who tells stories for the people of his time."

The *Feuerland* continues its route to the south, but they still cannot use the engine and travelling under sail alone was becoming more difficult and dangerous as they were entering the Southern Ocean. The last stage of the voyage was quick, but the weather was getting worse by the day and tested the ship's robustness. The worst of many incidents happened before their arrival in Comodoro Rivadavia, when the boat ran a serious risk of hitting a reef.

"At my shout of 'Alert, all hands!' my comrades hurl themselves on deck giving proof of their exemplary willingness and energy, despite being dead with tiredness. The four boys find themselves at my side working like desperate men, but with an admirable calm, the calm of every good German sailor."

Plüschow describes them all so that we can picture the scene better: "Schmitt is at the helm, Garibaldi the cameraman-cook-crew is busy with the foresail yard, Christian and I take care of the mainsail and Harry manages the other foresails. *Schnauf* sticks his nose out of the hole in his '*Villa Schnauf*' in a strange manner, then turns and disappears into the interior at speed having smelled 'trouble.'

Finally, he concludes, the calm and diligence of everyone saved the situation. In Comodoro Rivadavia, Plüschow decided not to go on with the voyage till a spare part arrived. They had to wait a month for the arrival of the new crankshaft from Germany.

Schmitt recounts that "In general the voyage from Buenos Aires to Punta Arenas was very stormy." From Dungeness Point to the Chilean city they were delayed three days due to intense winds from the north-east. When they finally arrived in Punta Arenas on October 23rd 1928, "we anchor near the jetty and take refuge in our cabins to sleep."

* * *

In Plüschow's film a moving arrow marks on the map of Tierra del Fuego the fiords and coves that *Feuerland* passes through, and with white letters on a black background the captions that divide the scenes that are only found in silent films, indicate to the reader how he should be amazed before such scenes of prodigious nature.

One of the captions reads: "VOYAGE TO THE LAND OF MIRACLES, CLOUDS & WIND." Another: "THROUGH FIORDS AND CHANNELS, ENTRANCE TO A LONELY MAJESTY."

Gunther Plüschow was finally accomplishing his dream. The pages in which he narrates how he persuaded his dour and frugal sailors to share his enthusiasm have an infectious honesty. The explorer felt especially excited by the combination of green – trees, flowers, wind-blown grass, and twisted tree trunks – with the white walls of the snow drifts.

When he found the door to enter a sublime landscape, he prepared the

scene for his sailors. First he went ashore in the rowing boat. "As if I were entering a divine temple, I devoutly found a way into the green wood, feeling the moss beneath my feet, which sunk in it with every step. Thorny thickets and entwined dense branches made my progress difficult. An intoxicating perfume of flowers, dead leaves and spring flooded the atmosphere."

Although he was alone, he tells us that he shouted out at the top of his voice: "Almighty God, how wonderfully beautiful all this is! This is my Tierra del Fuego, the land of my eternal dreams!"

It is at this moment that the wall of ice split. "The glacier is 'giving birth'," he says. He went back to the ship to get his men. "During the crossing they had always laughed incredulously every time I talked to them about my enthusiasm for getting to Tierra del Fuego, believing no doubt that I was exaggerating like a maniac and now I am curious to see what effect the marvellous reality may produce in them."

The men advance cheerfully talking among themselves, and then suddenly they are all silent. "They come close to me very quietly and there I see them as if nailed under the limitless trees by the reverberant sun, struck dumb before the imposing spectacle, with eyes staring as if in ecstasy."

The first who managed to speak was Garibaldi: "Having seen so much as an old mountain climber, I was always sceptical about Tierra del Fuego," quotes Plüschow, no doubt putting his cameraman's thoughts into his own words, "but now I confess that what I am seeing here leaves far behind all the many things I have seen and anything the imagination of a painter could conceive."

After several weeks of sailing through the Tierra del Fuego labyrinth and after skillfully crossing the Strait of Magellan, the *Feuerland* entered Chilean waters and arrived at the city of Punta Arenas on the 23rd October 1928, eleven months after its departure from the distant port of Büsum.

In Punta Arenas the mechanic Ernst Dreblow was waiting for them. Dreblow had arrived almost a year ago in the transatlantic liner *Planet* with the unassembled pieces of the seaplane. From that time on, Plüschow's principal vehicle was the *Silberkondor*, which carried on its fuselage in enormous letters its official name: *Tsingtau D-1313*.

Why an 'official' name different from the one everyone knows? One of the first things that students of Plüschow learn is that 13 is his lucky number. He never tires of repeating this in his books and in his film. And *Tsingtau* may well be, amongst other things, a reminder to the German public that it is all about yet another adventure of the formerly much fêted hero of the First World War. The black letters on the side of the plane that Dreblow and Plüschow assembled on the jetty in Punta Arenas seemed to seize the spectator by the lapels. "It's me. Remember about Tsingtau, my flights in China, my famous escape!"

However, every time that Plüschow makes reference to the seaplane he mentions it by its other name, much more suited to the Patagonian skies through which it will slice. In the memory of the South it will always be remembered as the *Silver Condor*, the first airplane to fly over the uttermost end of the Americas.

From the moment when the aircraft was ready to begin its flights of discovery, the *Feuerland* was transformed, in the book as well as in the film, into a secondary presence, which slowly followed the aviators and waited for them at the end of their aerial evolutions or served simply as their base and lodging.

The accounts of his flights, full of descriptions, packed with amazed wonder at the magnificence and sudden beauty of the mountains which he is 'conquering' are also reminiscent of the style in which he wrote about his flights in *The Adventures of the Tsingtau Aviator*.

Ernst Dreblow, who was hired to be a mechanic, became in practice an aviator and photographer of high places. In the account, the two men always seemed to be either on the point of being swept away by a blow from a strong wind current, freezing cold, or at the limit of their fuel reserves.

There were some terrible moments like the eventful flight in which on their last litre of fuel they land in some open country on Dawson Island. Other moments had an almost childish joy, like one the film shows with Plüschow and Dreblow arriving on shore with water up to their chests. After they have tied the plane to some rocks they slide down a little mountain of snow, laughing like two children at play. In another cheerful scene the two men enjoy a traditional 'asado' (South American barbecue). A gaucho brings a kind of iron stake on which the pieces of meat are impaled and then with long knives they cut off chunks of meat as they are cooked and eat them in their hands. Poor *Schnauf* is at his master's feet looking longingly at the juicy meat and finally gets his reward.

Plüschow never misses an opportunity to stress that these flights in this zone are pioneering. In Punta Arenas he loads a bag of mail onto his *Silberkondor*, takes off and delivers the first air mail to the city of Ushuaia.

According to Roberto Litvachkes's investigation, the bag included a letter sent by his family to a prisoner in the Fuegian jail.

Nor does the aviator fail to assure the public that it was advanced technology and the heroic drive of Germany that opened the doors to these hitherto unexplored regions. When from the air the camera captures the *Feuerland* sailing near a German transatlantic liner, the scene's caption reads: "What an unexpected encounter! Three German vehicles at the world's end!"

With Plüschow and Dreblow almost always aloft in the *Silberkondor*, Christiansen becomes in effect the captain of the *Feuerland*, Seppl continues as helmsman and Harry as cadet. Kurt Neubert (Garibaldi) is in charge of taking shots of the aircraft from below which will be permanently combined in the film with the aerial shots taken from *Silberkondor*.

Always attentive to his men, Plüschow also allows his sailors to live the experience of flight. When Joseph Schmitt wrote his memoirs more than half a century later he still recounted with gratitude: "on one occasion I had the luck to fly over Monte Sarmiento with him; something that I never could forget."

Schmitt also tells a story which is both disquieting and revealing, when one considers the time in which it happened. He says that while Plüschow and Dreblow were flying over the extremities of Tierra del Fuego, "we sailors used to go at night to the German Club, a place where some of the members looked at us with a certain suspicion, due to the fact that the expedition was financed by the Ullstein publishing house, whose owners were of Jewish origin."

Mateo Martinic, the most important historian of the Magallanes region of Chile, points out in his notes to the sailor's memoirs that the influence of National-Socialist propaganda had again raised the lie that the Jews were to blame for the German defeat in the First World War. For Martinic this coldness with which they were received by their compatriots would explain "the absence of any mention of the Magallanes region's German community in his book *Silberkondor über Feuerland*."

Schmitt remained unmoved by the accusations of the German community and wrote: "As we were sailors, it was all the same to us who were paying our wages."

What is certain is that time was passing and Ullstein was not disposed to continue paying for its author's interminable voyages unless the expedition could start to bear some profitable fruit. "Telegrams from the Berlin publishers Ullstein demand my urgent return," writes Plüschow in his book. "If the works carried out during my long voyage are to have the value and success they deserve, I must be on my way immediately."

The voyage had been nearly two years long and the constant articles that Plüschow had been publishing in Ullstein's magazines had to be transformed into the book and film that the publisher was expecting. Besides, Schmitt points out another interesting fact: in 1929 talking films were just starting and causing a furore. As a silent documentary, Plüschow's film was going out of fashion, even before it had been sub-titled and exhibited.

Although his initial plan was to sail back to Germany in the *Feuerland,* time and money had run out. Plüschow had to take the irrevocable decision to sell his schooner. "The farewell to my valiant little white nutshell and to a part of my excellent expedition crew leaves a heart-breaking sadness in my soul," Plüschow laments.

The paragraph about the sale of the *Feuerland* is surprisingly frugal and frustrating. "A buyer soon appeared who acquired the vessel to take it to the Falkland Islands."

Showing good sense, the new owner asked if Paul Christiansen would stay on board as captain and Seppl Schmitt as pilot. "Harry went home." Plüschow writes, "Garibaldi and Dreblow continue the voyage with me. I still have a job to do! The direction this time is towards Patagonia!"

Seppl Schmitt says that before the sale, "when we were repairing the boat on land, a Scotsman, Mr John Hamilton, approached. In English he asked me: 'Young man, how many Scotsmen did you kill during the war?" Of course that, as Schmitt is quick to point out, "was meant to be a joke. When he introduced himself we knew that he was the *Feuerland's* new owner. The vessel was rebaptised afterwards as *Penelope*."

With Christiansen and Schmitt aboard, the *Penélope* arrived in Fox Bay on March 22nd, 1929. John Hamilton registered his vessel in the Port Stanley Registry Office on the 15th April. That was the document that appears on pages 78 and 79 of the gigantic tome that Jane Cameron photocopied for me in the Islands' archives.

On the Punta Arenas jetty Gunther Plüschow had bid farewell to the boat with his characteristic emotion. "The siren moans as if crying in pain. 'Farewell little ocean nutshell.' May fate be as propitious to you as it has been till now and may you make your new owner as happy under the command of the excellent Captain Christiansen as you have made us."

The fate of Captain Plüschow and his schooner were moving apart for ever.

* * *

Carlos Biscioni, the President of the Association of Friends of the Argentine Nautical Tradition (ATNA) is writing a book about the *Feuerland/Penélope*. When I call him on the day of my arrival in Buenos Aires, he invites me to go to the Tigre Naval Museum, along with another two notable members of ATNA, to work on the maintenance of a historic sailing vessel, the *Legh II,* in which the lone sailor Vito Dumas had made a solo circumnavigation of the world between 1942 and 1943.

With the work done, we eat a tasty barbecue by the Luján River. Through the window of the typical Tigre grill, the touristic zone of old houses stretches, unpopulated and peaceful on this winter week day. During lunch and on the journey back, Carlos Biscioni explains his vision of sailing as the school of life and his original approach to the story of the schooner and the person of Gunther Plüschow.

What attracted him to this story was not, as in the cases of Roberto and Gerhard, the incandescent figure of Plüschow. At one point in our interviews, he even confesses to me that the vessel attracted him almost "in spite of Plüschow." "He wasn't a bad captain, but the real nautical geniuses in this story are the designers and shipwrights. In my book I am going to explain each part, comparing them with other vessels of the same era and with nautical developments over the years."

Carlos Biscioni is a lover of German technological perfection and of the passion of the Germans for doing things well. This he explains comes to him from the times when he was "sitting on the knee of my paternal grandfather, Lelio, a self-taught Tuscan, who spoke four or five languages." His grandfather was a precision lathe operator. "He had many German friends and enjoyed doing things properly. He was a sailor once, but perhaps because of how he was – independent and not good at taking orders, a little like Plüschow – he was never promoted and left."

The grandfather, Carlos remembers, taught him "to want the German thing, the German spirit, although sometimes these values of making things well and doing things properly don't hold the same importance for the Argentines." He says that sometimes he sees the Germans as lacking in worldly wisdom; they laugh at any old thing, though the most profound thinkers of the 20th Century came out of Germany. In these chats with his grandson on his knee he talked to him about German ships and German sailors.

Just like Plüschow's father, Carlos Biscioni's grandfather is moved by the music of Wagner. "So that's how I came to love music and ships, just like him."

We stop at the traffic lights on Libertador Avenue. There's a Beethoven string quartet on the car radio, which is tuned to the Amadeus station.

"My grandfather was more fascinated by ships than by the sea," Biscioni says, "and the fact of being able to make them so that everything would work. He passed on to me his love for those parts and cables and sails and all the complex manoeuvres that they performed to make the ship go; the marvel of navigation."

Some days later we meet in his consulting room. Carlos is a renowned kinesiologist specialising – as he explained to me by raising his hand to the area that extends from the ear almost to the shoulder – in the temporal mandible joint and the neck, which he studied in the USA. In his consulting room he wears a white coat, appears more serious and his bald head gleams under the artificial lighting of the entrance.

No one would guess that the heart of a 'sailing fan' beats under his coat, although the decoration of the waiting room points to his great interest. Over the receptionist's desk an oil painting by the legendary marine artist and emeritus member of ATNA, Hernán Alvarez Forn, the *Hormiga Negra (Black Ant),* depicts the choppy sea spitting foam and a sailing ship ploughing through the waves. Above the speakers which waft the music of Radio Amadeus through the room rest two old ships' lamps.

"Plüschow was a good sailor" he admits when we sit down to continue the interview, "but, okay, there are lots of them. What was exceptional about his voyage was the boat, the *Feuerland*."

"The *Feuerland* could do all that it did – arrive in Tierra del Fuego, navigate through those channels, survive so many years in the Islands – because of the Germans," Carlos says. "I don't find in any other ethnic group this exactitude, this care for the well-crafted and for the detail. All the parts of this vessel were German and it is noticeable." Biscioni has no doubt that every change, every new thing that was added to the vessel in the Islands was a change for the worse.

Carlos Biscioni is particularly interested in sailing ships and in traditional navigation under sail. In his 'Yahoo' profile he describes himself as "an afflicted reader of anything to do with naval and nautical history." His passion and organising skills led him to found and direct ATNA and to occupy himself with preserving the legend of historic sailors like Vito Dumas and spreading the exploits of sailors of today like Hormiga Negra.

He arrived at the *Feuerland* story through a contact with Roberto Litvachkes, when he was researching on the internet the shipwreck of the German transatlantic liner *Monte Cervantes,* which sank in the Beagle Channel in 1930.

Through reading the book *El Tesoro del Monte Cervantes* by Enrique Inda, Biscioni heard about a small wooden vessel which participated in the rescue of the big cruise liner's passengers and later sank, and thought that it could have been Plüschow's *Feuerland*, because of its dimensions and the year. Biscioni and Litvachkes started exchanging information about this incident, and finally concluded that the *Feuerland* had not sunk in 1930, but that she continued doing service in the Islands.

The psychologist and the kinesiologist are now friends and share their nautical discoveries from that time on, but each one follows 'his' subject and approaches Plüschow's world from the direction of the enthusiasms that first caused them to be interested in the multi-faceted German explorer.

The dreams that each one reveals about making a scale model illustrate their differences graphically.

Roberto wants to construct a model of the *Silberkondor*, Plüschow's seaplane, with which he performed his main accomplishments; the thing that got him into the Patagonian history books and which gained him the loyalty of his followers. The plane would be the central object in a possible museum dedicated to Plüschow's memory.

Carlos, in contrast, has been working for some time on his plan to construct a scale model of the *Feuerland*. His original idea was that it would represent the boat as it was when it left Büsum in 1927. There is a model in the Büsum Maritime Museum, but Carlos Biscioni is sure that a much better one could be made in Argentina. However this was up to when he came into contact with Horacio González Llanos, during his investigation of the ship's life in its *Penélope* phase.

As soon as Biscioni heard about the participation of Plüschow's ship in the 'Malvinas War', his patriotic side began to push him towards this other story of the vessel. He was excited that the boat had been a small piece of an event that he had always thought of as important in the history of Argentina. Should he now concentrate on the *Feuerland* or on the *Penélope?*

Through González Llanos, he got in touch with Luna, Rivero, Ni Coló and me early in 2006. He asked if we would tell him what we remembered about the boat; not our memories of the war or of one another, but just what we remembered about the boat.

A little while later he wrote to us proposing that we might wish to participate in his plan for a new model. This would not be the *Feuerland* of 1927, but the *Penélope* of 1982. The proposal wasn't to represent the boat in its original phase, but to 'freeze' the schooner for all time in that war-time autumn when we seven sailed in her.

But I said 'schooner'! One of the major surprises in my interviews with Carlos Biscioni is the discovery that in spite of the fact that Plüschow and others call her such, *Penélope* is not a schooner.

"A schooner has two masts of equal length," Carlos explains to me. "This is like confusing a dog with a giraffe. They are different animals." The *Feuerland* has two masts of different heights, the tall one in the centre and the other in the stern. Because of this she is a 'ketch'."

"A ketch" I exclaim, "How ugly 'ketch' sounds. What happens if I keep on using the word 'schooner?'"

But there's no chance, I am talking with a lover of precision, although in his capacity as a teacher Carlos Biscioni shows patience with a layman such as I am. He takes a deep breath and explains:

"Everything has its name and in sailing it's not only about precision, it's also about poetry. It's beautiful when you understand the small differences in sails, sizes, movements and manoeuvres," he enthuses. "There were old sailors' songs composed so that sailors would not forget all the complicated steps. They are precise and beautiful songs which are at the same time both practical and poetical."

This is the moment when I believe I understand that one of the things that move the multi-faceted president of the Argentine nautical enthusiasts is the poetry of precision. What attracts him is the mixture of work well done and romantic tradition which the adventurous mariners of yesteryear had, just like Plüschow.

"It's about trying to understand nature. Today with GPS, all the electronics, and the machines which do everything, the captain is disconnected from the medium which contains him: the water," he says. It's been a couple of hours since the consulting room emptied. We remain, he and I, seated on the sofa between the navigation lights.

"If you want to arrive in Colonia from Buenos Aires in fifteen minutes, that's not sailing; for that you take an aeroplane. However when you are under sail," he continues, "you adore the wind, because that is your motor. You take care with the sails, because they put you in harmony with the wind. The tide and the stars put you in communion with something that existed a long time before you. This is what my grandfather explained to me; he said that sailing this way is like an undulating music, like the music of Wagner, which seems to be always the same and never is. The same happens with the water, with the sea and with the sails. Do you understand me?"

I understand that my questions about the boat in which I sailed in the Islands are taking me much further than I had expected.

* * *

So, without his schooner (or ketch?) *Feuerland*, Plüschow, Dreblow and Neubert set out on the last part of the voyage in March 1929, moving north to the areas which surround the lakes Viedma, Argentino and San Martin. These were the zones where the explorer had written "unexplored" on the map when he presented his project to Ullstein.

At the point in his book when he is about to tell of his historic flight over the Torres del Paine, Plüschow takes a jump back in time and recalls the conversation he had with Richard Lauezzari three years before.

"– And what lies beyond these mountains, Lauezzari? – I ask my friend from the Pampas.

"– Nobody knows. Nobody ever went there and nobody will go there. Those mountains are invincible. No doubt there's nothing there but ice, snow and glaciers. Who knows there might even be prehistoric beings or animals there!

"– And why has no one flown there till now? – I ask.

"– Flying! Crazy idea! Flying here! It's impossible. You can't fly here; nobody has ever tried it, or even thought about it. It would be madness!"

In the film, Plüschow and his retinue approach Paine on horseback. In the black and white of the old copy the gigantic finger of the mountain towers like a terrible warning. Even the clouds which pass by its flanks seem ominous. Timid guanacos can be seen in the far distance.

The caption which follows the vision of the colossus says: "We shake hands on it. Today that giant back there will be ours."

The following scene shows Plüschow and Dreblow shaking hands vigorously and getting into the seaplane. The *Tsingtau D-1313* gains height and arrives at Paine, flies round it and reveals for the first time the secret valleys, mountains and glaciers which its shoulders guard. The camera shows a choppy sea of ice and rock.

"The giant has been dominated" exclaims the following caption, and the *Silberkondor* poses smoothly on a lake's mirror.

The film ends with a farewell to "beautiful and wild Patagonia" and with a "See you next year!" which, given the circumstances of Plüschow's return to a Germany suffering a terrible economic, political and social crisis, was more an expression of his wishes than a certainty.

Images continue of snowy massifs, guanacos, waterfalls, woods and peaks, until there only remains the final imposing and metaphorical sight of two condors soaring in the heights.

The ending of the book is different. Plüschow asks Dreblow to stay on the ground and makes the last flight alone. In the heights he ponders the need always to go further, confronting dangers, nature and 'Fate.'

GUNTHER PLÜSCHOW and his copilot Ernst Dreblow are preparing themselves for a flight over unexplored territory in Tierra del Fuego and Patagonia. Source: Gerhard H. Ehlers, Odenthal, Germany.

On the voyage back home on a liner, the explorer is surprised to hear "suddenly, a prolonged and lugubrious cry, like the howl of a wild animal, coming through the dark night. Another howl ... another ... and another. How sinister this sounds in my ears."

It is three indians, two men and a woman, frozen with cold and covered in rags who climb on board. Their sharpened-stone hair cuts remind him of the features and coiffeur of the Botocudos. "Under the pale light of an electric lamp I now see these poor beings, in former times lords and masters of these immense labyrinths of land and channels, shivering with cold and hunger. Some people on board come bringing them bags of stale bread and other leftovers, while others give them needles, thread, socks and an old shawl."

One of the indians goes down to their canoe and returns with a lyre. "They begin to stamp and to jump, performing a grotesque and wild dance. Never in my life have I seen such a primitive dance as the one they are performing and never have I felt as oppressed and sad as now, in the face of this miserable spectacle. In contrast, the people around me laugh."

I have to confess that this glimpse of Gunther Plüschow's capacity to feel moved by the terrible plight of these human beings awakens some sympathy in me.

We will never know how Plüschow saw himself, or how he would have been if he had still been alive when the atrocious period of the Nazis arrived. Sometimes there are cracks through which we can glimpse answers, for example the repetition of certain structures in his way of relating fragments from his own life and the selection of those fragments. Plüschow wrote three books and the three share a very similar structure, owing much to Homer's *Odyssey*.

The accounts of the escape from Tsingtau, of his 'voyage' to Patagonia in the *Parma* and his adventure in the schooner and the seaplane are odysseys to distant lands where the hero meets dangers, has contact with different cultures and learns new things, before finally a time arrives when he feels the desire to return home, to his family and his native land. The three end at the moment of his return to his own particular Ithaca.

The fact that his ship should have been renamed *Penélope* without any intervention on his part, is one of the most striking of the many coincidences of this story.

"And now I see two little blonde heads with blue and joyful eyes", the author writes in the last paragraph of *Over Tierra del Fuego*. "Now I see little white hands waving and calling me to them across the immense ocean; it is the good Smutie and at her side, little Guntolf, my son."

* * *

Installed once more in the family apartment at Number 3 Heilbronnerstrasse, in a building in the east part of Berlin, Plüschow dedicated himself during the months following his return to editing his film and writing his book.

Around him, Germany was beginning the tragic decade of the 1930s. Plunged into depression and collective frustration, closed nationalism and anti-Semitism grew and a small group of radicals gained strength, led by an embittered Austrian-born First World War corporal, Adolf Hitler. One of the pillars of Hitler's Nazi creed was that the 1914-1918 war had not been lost because of the incompetence and criminal belligerence of the politicians and the military, but because of treason on the part of enemies within.

In 1925, Paul von Hindenburg had been appointed as the second president of the Weimar Republic (which had replaced the monarchy when the Kaiser fled after the defeat). Hindenburg had defeated the Russians in an important battle at the beginning of the war and was considered a military hero. He also supported the argument that the German army had not been defeated, but had been "hit from behind" by the enemy's fifth columnists.

According to contemporary reports, the showings of *Silberkondor über Feuerland* met with resounding success in the Berlin cinemas. Before each function Plüschow introduced his voyage and told the public, as if in passing, that he was getting money and support together to continue with his explorations. The film showed images of immense virgin territories and the ingenious German conquering the heights; it also was narrated with a good rhythm, an attractive structure and humour.

The skill as a cameraman of Kurt Neubert, *Garibaldi*, can be appreciated in the combination of shots of the ship from surprising angles, the use of different fields of focus for the principal scenes and the quality of the images of the sea, the mountains and the towers of ice. Close-ups and captions are used to present the action from different points of view.

The most surprising and amusing part for me occurs at the point where the *Feuerland* leaves Lisbon to undertake its long Atlantic crossing. The camera takes a close-up of the dog *Schnauf*, looking at the coast with apparent sadness and the scene-separating caption reads: "How nice it would be to be on land!" as if these were the dog's thoughts.

His film and book were a success in Berlin, but Plüschow wanted to return to South America with his material translated into Spanish so that he could share it with those who had helped him and also because he thought that the first beneficiaries of his Patagonian explorations had to be the Argentines and Chileans.

No one knows how he met Armand Guerra, the man that translated *Silberkondor über Feuerland* and later turned the film's captions into Spanish. The best conjecture is that it had to do with the circles of documentary film enthusiasts, for whom at this time Berlin was like the world's capital.

Guerra, a Spaniard who had been living in Berlin for the previous nine years, made films about 'social realism' and translated scripts for the Spanish-German production company, Filmfono. But the man was much more than that. For two decades he had been a risk-taking and persecuted anarchist leader, who had produced revolutionary propaganda in at least seven countries.

At first sight it seems impossible in 1929 to imagine a friendship between the military Prussian nationalist, Gunther Plüschow, admirer of Hindenburg and all he represented, and this anarchistic Spanish typographer. His friendship is perhaps another sign of hope with regard to Plüschow's future, had he not died in 1931.

In the introduction to the Spanish version of *Silberkondor über Feuerland* Guerra describes the "discreet and cheerful mezzanine" where "the intrepid captain Gunther Plüschow lives and immerses himself in continuous and intense work."

"A man of small stature, robust, although not fat, with two blue eyes that seem replete with the reflections of the sea and glaciers and with a high, but at the same time energetic and familiar voice, came out to meet me." Behind Plüschow there entered the room, "a tall svelte woman with a pleasant smile and eyes that were equally blue, but with a different shine: the captain's wife, the 'Smutie' onboard."

Guerra says that Plüschow charged him with the making of "a literary adaptation, a free but exact version of my German text, but a faithful portrait of all that I have seen on my voyages and an exact expression of all that my soul has experienced."

The translator comments that "a wish of the excellent captain Plüschow has the effect of a peremptory order." So Guerra distances himself from his cinematographic world and the creation of film scripts and immerses himself in the book. "With the frankness that characterises me I have to confess that few books have interested me as much as this one about the adventurous expedition to the almost unknown Tierra del Fuego" he says, adding that to be better prepared he had seen the expedition's film three times.

"The first time I saw the spectacle," Guerra relates, "it left a deep impression on me. As I was leaving I met Captain Plüschow again in the theatre's foyer. I could do no less than express to him my admiration for the heroism of which he and the others had shown such proof in crossing the ocean aboard that nut shell called *Feuerland* and nicknamed *'Holzpantine'*" (German for 'clog').

To Guerra's surprise, Plüschow told him that the supposed perils of the sea did not have much importance for him, but that the flights in the seaplane were much more 'problematic.' Guerra then comments: "The intrepid Plüschow appears to have lost the memory of all that he has suffered and the mortal danger that he ran at every step."

These words appear to come from a translator by trade, whose life scurries across the city between books and linguistic problems. However the life of Armand Guerra is at least as adventurous and fascinating as Plüschow's own, with the difference that in the convulsive times in which they were both called to live, Guerra opted to use his art as a tool in the political struggle. His revolutionary work causes his name still to resound among the heroes of Spanish anarchism in the fight against Franco.

Guerra was born in Liria, near Valencia, on January 4th 1886, thirty four days before Plüschow. According to the biographical article which his comrade Eric Jarry dedicated to him, this peasants' son worked as a typographer from the age of thirteen. In his youth he travelled through France, England, Italy, Egypt, Romania and Greece, always participating in revolutionary activities and writing in anarchist magazines. In 1913, he moved to Paris and worked in film. When he joined the collective social film project 'Cinema of the People,' he adopted the pseudonym 'Armand Guerra' for the first time.

From 1929 to 1931 he lived in Berlin. In the German capital he was a film director, author and script translator. Guerra spoke seven languages well.

This was the time during which Guerra abandoned his work in militant cinema and confined himself to the translation of Gunther Plüschow's book. "A fraternal friendship blossomed between us both from the time of our first interview, perhaps because of the affinity of our ideas and also because Plüschow was a great Hispanophile, and very enthusiastic about the people and language of Iberia," Guerra writes.

"During the next two months, the time that my adaptation of his fine book took, our friendship grew stronger to such an extent that on the eve of undertaking his new voyage to the virgin mountains of Patagonia, he asked me to accompany him." Guerra was wrapped up in obligations in Berlin.

In 1934, with the Nazis already in power in Germany, the anarchist film maker moved to Madrid, where the beginning of the civil war found him in the middle of another fiction film with a social background, *Carne de Fieras* (Wild Animals' Meat). From then on he participated actively on the Republican side, giving speeches throughout the whole country at the request of the anarchists' union CNT, making film documentaries under the title of *Estampas guerreras* (Warlike Images) and writing a book of memoirs, *A través de la metralla* (Under Fire) in which he tells of his experiences fighting against Franco's forces.

Armand Guerra managed to escape to France in February 1939, just before the fall of the Republic. A month later he was struck down by an aneurysm. He died in the street. "He was a tired traveller, who disappeared almost without baggage" says Eric Jarry.

Anticipating the advance of the Nazis into France, his widow burned his books, his papers and his films. It was believed up to 1992 that none of his films had been saved, but that year a copy of *Carne de fieras* surfaced at the Zaragoza film library.

Among the little that remains of Armand Guerra's work stands out this collaboration with Gunther Plüschow, which doesn't appear in any of the reviews of his life that I met in anarchist magazines and web pages. His work and relationship with such a non-anarchistic personality do not seem to fit in the linear account of the militant revolutionary's life.

The territory common to both men can be perceived on every page of *Over Tierra del Fuego.* The passion of each of them for adventure, danger, the epic search for what is always just beyond, and their idealism, are all jointly presented to us and revealed in Plüschow's text and Armand Guerra's translation.

* * *

If Plüschow had had problems getting funds and support together in 1927, things were even worse on his return. Even Ullstein was not disposed to finance a new voyage and a new documentary about the same zone.

However, instead of being discouraged, Plüschow remained firm in his intention and embarked for Buenos Aires on July 17th 1930 with a limited budget. It was moreover a time of convulsive changes in Argentina. A coup d'état was under way against the constitutional president Hipólito Yrigoyen, which seven weeks later would begin the half century of dictatorships, coups and counter-coups which would devastate Argentina.

Roberto Litvachkes tells us in his book that despite the difficult political climate prevailing, Plüschow succeeded in showing his film in the University of Buenos Aires and in the German Club. He travelled to Chile by train and arrived in November at Puerto Natales, where the terrible sight of his *Silberkondor,* which had been abandoned in a shed and gnawed by rats, awaited him.

When he began his flights with Dreblow again, Plüschow realised that the damage caused by a year's neglect and rodents was more serious than he had expected, but decided to go ahead anyway. In his book, Litvachkes writes: "Plüschow was aware that the Chilean authorities would want to inspect his plane to see if it complied with the requisite safety specifications and before that could happen, he moved into Argentine territory, where he set up a new camp."

His flights were becoming increasingly risky. "In the letters that he sent to Isot, he appears like a man who was overwhelmed and almost desperate, but I don't think he wanted to die," says Gerhard Ehlers. "He wanted to live to enjoy his triumph, but he felt abandoned by almost everyone. Ullstein wasn't sponsoring him now, he hadn't received the support he was expecting as a result of all the letters he had written and he felt that the North Americans and the French were hard on his heels. He was sending anxious letters to Heinkel asking for spares for his plane, but continued flying without them."

There's no unanimity among students of his career as to what Plüschow was searching for on this new journey. The reels of film containing the recorded images of these flights are lost. Menaced by storm clouds and all his worries and anxieties, on January 25th 1931, Plüschow took off from his last base near Lake Argentino.

In the middle of Plüschow and Dreblow's flight "a furious storm forced them to make an unplanned landing on a lake no more than 300 metres wide, surrounded by walls of rock ascending in height to 800 metres," Roberto Litvachkes tells us. "He couldn't avoid hitting one of the floats against a rock, which makes a split of a considerable size." The two men worked hard for three days to repair the float so they could leave their rocky prison. Plüschow noted in his diary that was prepared to face an aviator's death, but asked 'Fate' that it should not be in this remote place.

On January 28th the *Silberkondor* lifted off on its last flight. A few minutes later it spiralled down into Lake Argentino. Dreblow was hurled into the water and some spectators were able to get him to the beach, but he died a few hours later. Plüschow became tangled up in his parachute and plummeted onto the rocks, dying instantly.

Night falls through the window of Gerhard Ehlers' house in the middle of Germany. We have spent the whole day going over Gunther Plüschow's life. Gerhard is standing in the middle of the basement room, with Isot's book in his hand opened at the last page. "The great flight lifts into eternity" he reads, translating the German into English. "That afternoon the world receives the message by telegram: Plüschow has died." Ehlers gently closes the book and sits down in silence on the wooden swivel chair.

Night is also approaching in the Hipopótamo cafeteria in Buenos Aires. Roberto Litvachkes says, "I don't find it easy to explain the end and this last period of Plüschow's life, because there are still things I don't know, especially about his voyage to Germany, where I understand that he really didn't receive the support he was expecting."

Roberto continues talking about Plüschow's flights, his problems and the lack of understanding that he encountered. He tells me of his discovery of the 'macabre' collection of photos of his corpse which he found in Ushuaia.

He says that in Ullstein's archives they showed him a paper where someone requests that the photos are not shown to Isot. "It's a very sad ending," he laments, "but for me the important thing is that his story lives on in people's affections and that it lives on in Patagonia in the stories. It lives on in simple things, like in a family that preserves a metal plaque of him as if it were a holy relic, or the guide from El Calafate who burst into tears when he discovered a bit of steel from the plane's exhaust pipe..."

A few days after the news of Plüschow's death, a funeral elegy appeared in the Berlin press: "With the death of Gunther Plüschow, scientific documentary cine-photography loses one of its most enthusiastic collaborators. His magnificent film made during his voyage of exploration to Tierra del Fuego, which has received clamorous success, not only in Germany, but also in nearly all the countries of Europe and recently also in South America, is a document full of emotion and indescribable beauty."

The article is signed by Armand Guerra and ends like this: "The press throughout Chile and Argentina is dedicating whole columns to the gallant German airman, who, risking his life in support of both great South American countries, brought hitherto unknown natural beauties without number to the screen and would have brought other new and valuable documents to cinematography, if a tragic death had not surprised the generous hero. Rest in peace, dear friend. The whole world will honour your work."

CHAPTER 3

The dream of the history-loving sailor

Could it be the same boat? Is such a coincidence possible?

The young merchant marine officer Bernd Buchner had just come onto the bridge of the cruise ship *World Discoverer* to begin his watch, when the surprise left him paralysed. Anchored some 150 metres away towards the shore an old red and white painted wooden ketch was swaying in the gentle waves.

It was March 2002 and the cruise ship had just arrived in the harbour at West Point, its first stop in the Islands.

Immediately Buchner asked the previous officer on watch if he could hang on for a few minutes more and ran to his bunk, coming back on the bridge very shortly and holding in his hand a book published in 1929 that he had brought to read on the voyage. The book was *Silberkondor über Feuerland* by Gunther Plüschow.

On the book's cover was a photographic montage that showed the seaplane flying over an idyllic landscape in Tierra del Fuego (*Feuerland* in German). The title is an obvious play on words though, because the ketch *Feuerland* is also seen passing through the waters of a Fuegian channel surrounded by snowy mountains.

Buchner turned the pages of his book and looked at the vessel anchored in the harbour and with every fresh comparison became more convinced that this was the same boat. On his first stop in the Falklands, and without even looking for it, he had come across the historic ketch that had caught his attention so much when he was doing research before his first season sailing through Patagonia, the Southern Islands and Antarctica.

"Later, when I knew what they were using the boat for in those months, I understood that it was logical that it should be in West Point, but just then I thought it was an incredible coincidence," Buchner tells me in Hamburg a day after the *Feuerland's* arrival in Germany.

Thus begins the first of our long conversations in which he tells me how little by little he came to take the "crazy decision" to buy the boat and take it back to the very port where it was launched almost eighty years before. While we are eating in an open air restaurant above the Ovelgönne maritime museum, with a privileged view of the white and dismasted *Feuerland*, Bernd explains to me that this first sighting was a very frustrating experience for him.

"I looked at the boat through binoculars and the colour and the shape of the wheelhouse were clearly different, but the convex shape of the hull, so characteristic of the *Feuerland,* was the same". By radio, Bernd asked his friend Clemens Pütz, a German marine biologist and penguin specialist who was the cruise's scientific leader, if he could try to talk to the boat's owner and find out if it really was in fact Plüschow's historic ketch.

Pütz, who had gone ashore with the tourists, confirmed this and supplied some more facts that Buchner was unaware of: that the owner was one Michael Clarke and that the boat's name had been changed and she was now the *Penélope.*

'Unfortunately the stop at West Point only lasted from seven in the morning till eleven and my watch didn't finish till noon" says Bernd. Besides, it was his first season as an officer and he couldn't change his watch without warning just because he had spotted an old wooden boat which was surely the same as one he had seen in a book. He could only ask his friend Clemens if he would make a note of the owner's email address. Unfortunately this was the last voyage of the 2002 season and his next chance to approach the *Penélope* would be in the following season, nine months later.

The second and last stop during this voyage to the Islands was in Stanley and was also a short one. Piqued by curiosity, Buchner headed for the Government Archives, where Jane Cameron received him. "She gave me a file with stories and extracts relating to the *Penélope.* It was the first that I compiled about the ship's history in the Islands." There, amongst other documents, was Gerald Roberts' story, the text that accompanied the stamp issue, and a document in youthful handwriting that surprised the German merchant mariner. "It was the only history which dealt with the whole life of the *Penelope* and this girl had written it for a school competition," he told me with amazement.

In their after dinner chats on the *World Discoverer,* Bernd Buchner had talked to Clemens Pütz about his dream of buying some little classic boat to restore. He was thinking about something smaller that he might find in Germany.

"So why don't you buy this one?" the biologist suggested.

"I took it as a joke. We were 8,000 miles from home and I didn't know what state the boat was in or even if the owner wanted to sell it. I also didn't know what I would do with a boat of that type." But this mad idea began to work on its own account inside the sailor's head.

* * *

Bernd Buchner was born in Nuremberg at the heart of Germany's map and of its identity, a long way from the sea. His father was an accountant in a commercial centre and his mother a dental technician. "We lived quite well but not well enough to travel the world. We spent our summers in Stockholm where my uncle lived."

The uncle had a boat and it was in that Scandinavian port that the young Bernd began to dream of the sea. At night he avidly read stories of adventurers and explorers, especially Joseph Conrad's maritime novels and the epic C.S.Forrester series about Captain Hornblower, an English hero of the naval battles against Napoleon.

In 1994, with his future still undecided, the order arrived to report for military service.

In his year as a naval conscript he became part of the crew of a frigate which was charged with guaranteeing the effectiveness of the NATO blockade of Serbia. On land they were committing the worst massacres of the war in the former Yugoslavia, but danger remained far away from Buchner's ship. Stationed at the entrance to the Adriatic they made contact by radio with vessels entering and leaving and checked that they were not carrying prohibited cargos.

"The truth is that we didn't have a bad time," Bernd confesses. "We had long weekends on land, sometimes five or six days. I was twenty-two, we were sailing in the Mediterranean and every now and then enjoying ourselves in ports."

"My military service was somewhat different," I tell him.

When he got back to Nuremberg, Bernd began to study to be a history teacher. He liked history very much, but the open air, action and the sea attracted him more. A friend had a sail boat and all his free time was spent on board. "I remember the first time I put my sleeping bag in the cabin and saw the port hole. I immediately felt at home and I had never before set foot on that boat."

Bernd didn't give up thinking about his future. History attracted him very much, but was he going to spend all his life giving classes? Was that what he really wanted to do?

In 1997 he decided to change his orientation radically and signed up at the Polytechnic University to turn himself into an officer in the Merchant Navy. His first practical experience was on a cargo ship which left Amsterdam to go round the Mediterranean, crossed the Atlantic to Montevideo, Buenos Aires and Puerto Madryn, crossed it again to go to Senegal and Angola and then from Africa went to Brazil and the United States.

Soon Bernd saw the possibility of combining the freedom of the sea with his two juvenile passions: the exploration of distant polar lands and the living history of old ships. He began to ask for his practical studies to be on reconstructed old vessels and on scientific expeditions to the world's ends.

That was the time when he began to read about explorers who reconstructed vessels from sailing's romantic eras and would then set out in them to live headlong adventures, scorning the dependency on technology and the coldness of present-day vessels. He followed with special attention the epic exploits of Arved Fuchs, "a source of inspiration for me."

When I go into Fuchs's web page I understand a lot more about his attraction and also a little more about what fascinates and inspires Buchner in his own searches.

Fuchs, who appears smiling, wrapped up in a polar suit and with a frozen beard, talks about terrible storms, crystal clear skies, the exploration of remote regions and triumph over the elements aboard the cutter *Dagmar Aaen*, an old Danish fishing boat, powered by sail and built in 1931. The *Dagmar Aaen* is 18 metres long and made of wood, with a red hull and white upper parts. In the photos she is seen sailing between the ice floes of Greenland, completing the round the world voyage that Roald Amundsen could not make, or following the steps of Ernest Shackleton's tragic journey of 1916.

From 1991 Fuchs sailed 150,000 nautical miles in the vessel and accomplished other feats on foot, like getting to the South Pole with the famous climber Reinhold Messner without using motorised vehicles or animals, but "just with skis and the aid of the wind."

Romanticism and the love of adventure are not enough to do all these voyages. Because of this the adventurer's site has links to three sponsoring companies.

"He sailed all the passages around the North Pole, using an old boat for his expeditions just to show that it was possible," says Bernd with admiration. "I never saw him in person and he still doesn't know I exist, but I read a lot about him, I follow him, I saw the ship and I felt the importance of what he is doing."

Bernd doesn't like talking about heroes or idols but the idea of following in the footsteps of the great explorers of the past like James Cook in Polynesia fills him with the same ambition that others have for making millions, acquiring political power or winning a great literary prize.

Bernd Buchner's second voyage as part of his practical training was on the *Polarstern* (Polar Star), Germany's only Arctic and Antarctic scientific survey vessel. "It was very difficult to get them to take me as a student, but I insisted so much that they accepted me and later they asked me to return." He reached Antarctica for the first time on this ship and what he wanted to do with his life suddenly became clear.

Once he graduated, he got his first job on the *World Discoverer*, a cruise ship specialising in voyages to the most pristine destinations to see amazing landscapes and to get close to wildlife with the guidance of experts. Instead of casinos and shows at night, this cruise ship offers slide shows by scientists like Clemens Pütz as its entertainment.

Bernd had to board the ship in Ushuaia in December 2001 and to prepare for the voyage he set out to read about the new lands he was about to discover.

He began, as so often happens, at home. "In the attic, left over from my childhood, there was a collection of magazines about voyages, planes and ships. Skimming through the pages, for the first time I came across a short article about Gunther Plüschow. Although I had never heard of him, the article said that he had flown a seaplane over Patagonia, so I put it in the folder I was getting together."

A week later Bernd bumped into the same name again. In *Mare*, a delightful magazine about sailing, which features carefully written texts with surprising and poetic photos, there was a brief résumé of Plüschow's book, *Silberkondor über Feuerland.* A new edition had been published under the direction of Hans-Georg Prager, an expert on the aviator's life and works.

In a few days when he bumped into it for a third time, Bernd began to get the distinct impression that this name was following him.

A German television journalist had made a successful documentary about Patagonia. As a by-product of this programme he published a book in which he talked about Plüschow and his flights over Tierra del Fuego. Bernd remembers that the book mentioned in passing that "the explorer's boat was still working and was being used in the Falkland Islands for the transportation of sheep."

As the *World Discoverer* made two stops in the archipelago, the young officer thought that there was a remote possibility that it might be in Stanley, or that someone there might be able to give him an idea as to its whereabouts.

In the middle of his preparations for spending four months at the bottom of the map, Bernd went to his favourite book shop to ask for the book that Prager had just brought out. "It was sold out, but a few days later they rang me to say that they had found the original 1929 edition. 'But that must surely be very expensive, isn't it?' I asked. 'No' they replied, 'it actually works out to be two euros less than the other one.'"

And that is how, on that March morning at West Point, Bernd Buchner was already intrigued by Plüschow's adventures and had in his cabin the elegant first edition of his book with the black and white photos which show the *Feuerland* sailing across the Atlantic and between the gigantic ice floes at the end of the world, the *Silberkondor* flying over the Cordillera, the amusing poses of the ship's crew with the dog *Schnauf* and the look of concentration on the faces of Plüschow and his aeronautical mechanic, Ernst Dreblow, as they study the map.

* * *

Buchner had only had time to skim through the pages of Plüschow's book on this voyage. That was not just because he had a lot of new things to learn about his job in his first season of employment nor because he never tired of observing the landscapes of Patagonia, the Islands, South Georgia and Antarctica.

In February 2002, on the cruise ship's previous voyage he had begun a romance with a passenger, who today is his girlfriend and partner in this adventure and now is sitting at his side dipping her spoon into Bernd's icecream. It is already night and the three of us are sitting in front of Hamburg's lake which is full of swans, holiday makers and illuminated arches celebrating the recent end of the 2006 World Cup.

Carola Fiedler is about Bernd's age, but was born in the now disappeared East Germany. This meant, amongst other things, that she could not study marine biology as she had wanted. "It was a course open to very few and they selected those who had correct ideas and good contacts." Her dream of marine biology began with the television programmes of the intrepid Captain Jacques Cousteau, with his boat *Calypso,* his thin smile and his customary red watchcap.

Carola dreamed about being Cousteau but studied as an engineer in biotechnology, a field which she works in today for a multinational that sells high precision instruments.

As soon as she could, she saved to be able to sail, at least as a passenger.

Her first cruise was in the Baltic. "I had to share a cabin with a lady of 80 and the things she told me during the voyage had a big influence on me," Carola recalls. The old lady recommended that she should travel to the places of her dreams while she was still young and not work like crazy to save to travel later. In the summer of 2002 she decided to break the 'piggy bank' and blow her savings to go on a cruise with the *World Discoverer.*

"The majority of the passengers were old and she was the only woman the same age as the officers," says Bernd. "She came up onto the bridge a lot to do the ice watch." She appeared most of all when Bernd was there.

"We talked about ships a lot," Carola recalls. "He told me that he wanted to buy an old sailing boat. I was looking for a book about a couple living at the end of the world, which they had told me was in the ship's library."

The book was *Under the Spell of South Georgia* by Tim and Pauline Carr, the legendary couple who had a museum and a hundred-year old boat in Grytviken.

"But," Bernd interjects, "I had taken the book from the library and it was in my cabin."

"So, that's how you managed to get her into your cabin!" I blurt out. They both laugh.

At the end of February Carola returned to Germany and Bernd began the cruise ship's following voyage, during which he would see *Penélope* for the first time. In one of the frequent emails that he wrote from the ports the ship went to, Bernd began to tell the strange story of Plüschow's historic ketch, but Carola had already heard of the explorer. "I had the book at home," says Carola. "It belonged to my grandmother who remembered the admiration there was for Plüschow in the twenties."

With his contract hardly completed, Bernd rang the bell of Carola's house and since then they have been together.

Back in Germany, Bernd began to look for information about Plüschow and the *Feuerland*. He discovered the source used by the television journalist who said that the boat was still sailing in the Islands. It was an article published in the German Maritime Museum's magazine in 1977, written by a veterinarian specialising in

BERND BUCHNER and Carola Fiedler in winter garb in front of the *Feuerland* in Büsum.

marine fauna. Amongst his scientific findings, he mentioned that he had done his survey on the *Penélope* and that the basic facts of the boat's original identity could be found on a small metal plaque nailed to the mast, which read: "Feuerland, Büsum, 1927."

Bit by bit, Bernd Buchner was making contact with various groups of Plüschow fans and preservers of his memory, with whom he was piecing together the puzzle of the passionate life of the sailor and aviator. He bought Plüschow's two other books: *The Adventures of the Tsingtau Aviator* and *Under Sail in Wonderland*, also in cheap early editions.

From Wurzberg where he was living Bernd wrote an email to Michael Clarke. They saw each other again at West Point in December. Carola Fiedler travelled on this second voyage, not as a passenger but as Bernd's companion and the officer made sure that this time he would not be on watch when the ship arrived at West Point.

Michael jumped into the cruise ship's rubber boat with Bernd from the landing ramp in front of Roddy and Lily Napier's house, while Carola took a photo of them for posterity. The three of them then climbed onto the *Penélope.*

"I had conflicting feelings from the beginning," says Bernd. "As soon as I got aboard I felt the historic impact of being on Plüschow's boat, but at the same time as a sailor I saw that she was old and in poor shape. It was obvious that I would have to do a lot of work before I could sail her back to Germany and even more before she could get back to looking as she had when she left Büsum.

At this first meeting; Bernd had still not talked to Michael about his intentions. He was wondering about the next step to take when Michael told them that he had to go to Stanley to see the dentist and asked if they could take him on the *World Discoverer.*

In the cruise ship's luxurious dining room Bernd was able to sound out the boat's owner. He asked him what he thought about doing with the *Penélope* in the future. "Michael recognised that it was getting old and difficult to maintain in good condition. I told him to think of me if he decided to sell it at any time."

Michael would tell me later that the problem that he put to Bernd when the latter explained his intentions wasn't that he didn't want to sell the *Penélope*, but that he hadn't been able to find anything similar to replace her with. "I needed a boat for the increased amount of activity based at West Point that I was engaged in. I had been to Chile to look at boats but saw nothing convincing."

Bernd remembers having said that if one was going to replace a good German boat capable of working in extreme conditions, the best thing would be to buy another German boat and that the best place to look would be in the North German ports. "I told him that I would start to look for boats of that size as soon as I got home and would keep him informed."

Bernd began his turn on watch at eight o'clock and while the cruise ship completed its circuit of the East Falklands, Carola remained in the dining room taking to the Islander until the ship arrived in Stanley.

A few weeks later Michael wrote to Bernd saying that he had to go to Britain in June 2004 to see his family. Bernd took advantage of this opportunity and invited him on a tour of the ports and shipyards of Germany.

"I was trying to get things going, but very carefully," Bernd explains to me. "I didn't want him to think that I was keen to take something from him. I could see very well the affection that Michael and Jeanette had for that boat and to me at that time it meant nothing more than a connection to Plüschow. For him that ketch was his life, his known environment and his source of income. During the last decade he had lived through many things with that boat."

The two men, the quiet Islander who had spent all his life in the enclosed world of the Islands and the talkative German who finds his home on the seas of the world formed an extraordinary pair during two feverish weeks. Bernd is sure they went to all the ports and fishing ports in the North of Germany, but no boat came up to Michael's expectations.

In the middle of the voyage they called in to Büsum.

"I want to show you something," Bernd told Michael and took him to the maritime museum. On the second floor the museum guards one of its main treasures in a large glass case: the 10:1 scale model of the *Feuerland* that Karl-Heinz Schmidt made in his spare time aboard a cargo ship between 1931 and 1932. It impressed on Michael how important his ketch was in this neat and prosperous German port.

The museum, which is situated in front of a basin full of boats that could be *Penélope's* second cousins, shares a building with a fish processing plant. Because of this, while the visitor is looking at the nets, hooks anchors and other equipment connected with Büsum's fishing tradition, a strong smell of fish permeates the atmosphere and seems to be there to complete the experience.

Bernd and Michael are standing in front of the glass where the shiny model, restored by Kurt Winter in 2004, raises its main mast more than two metres from the floor. At first sight it does not seem like the same vessel. Almost everything – the wheelhouse, the entrance to the hold, the little house in the bow down through which the cabin is reached, the dark natural wood colour of the deck and the white paint everywhere – is changed.

Almost the only thing recognisable is the basic shape of the hull and the position of the masts. It looks like an idealised vision of a boat that never was like that. However Bernd explained to Michael that this is in effect how the *Feuerland* was in 1927 and how it would be again in a few years once the transformation he has dreamed about has been completed.

THE MODEL of Gunther Plüschow's *Feuerland* at the Büsum museum.

Michael looked at the model with interest, but couldn't help thinking that he liked his *Penélope* better, tarnished and stained by history as it was, but still the schooner that in 2001 celebrated its birthday with a cake which matched the brilliant red of its Falkland Islands colour.

CHAPTER 4

The long road home

When they left Büsum's maritime museum after looking at the *Feuerland* model, Bernd Buchner and Michael Clarke were worried men. After two weeks of visiting moorings and shipyards in the torrid summer of 2004 still no boat had appeared to have all the features that the Islander was looking for.

Almost at the end of their trip, in the little port of Petkum near Emden in Lower Saxony, Michael became enthusiastic about a solid steel-hulled cutter about two metres shorter than the *Penélope*. By a curious coincidence this boat was called *Condor* and Bernd didn't fail to impress on Michael the connection with name of Plüschow's seaplane.

"We had to decide rapidly because the owner had other plans and wasn't entirely settled on selling her," says Buchner. The deal was done, but in order that the vessel should be in condition to sail to the Islands – repeating Plüschow's epic voyage in a way – there was at least a month's work to do on her.

Michael went to England to attend to a family matter and when he returned to Emden again, Jeanette was with him and ready to work hard to help him prepare the boat which hadn't been sailed for a long time. When the time came to paint it, almost without thinking they chose red and white, the colours of the ketch that was waiting for them 8,000 miles away.

The refurbishment took two months then at five o'clock in the evening of September 5th, 2004, they left Petkum to sail across half the world with a minimal crew of three: Clarke, Buchner and an uncle of Bernd's who had no sailing experience but a lot of spirit and a great longing for adventure.

During the whole voyage the three stood watch in turns. "The worst, the night watch, fell to Michael," Bernd tells me.

Before heading south, they went north to Heligoland, where fuel is much cheaper. Having taken on enough to get across the

Atlantic they made stops at Santa Cruz in Tenerife, Cape Verde, San Salvador de Bahía and Río de Janeiro.

Bernd Buchner took advantage of his short periods of leisure to finally finish reading *Silberkondor über Feuerland*, which with so much else going on he had never managed to do. While the vessel was moving along with the Trade Winds, Bernd went down to the cabin to steep himself in the incidents of a similar voyage, through the same waters, 77 years previously.

However, both Michael and Bernd agree that the voyage didn't have the same festive elements or stop-and-start-again rhythm that can be seen in Plüschow's documentary. "We used the motor the whole time, trying to get there as quickly as possible," says Bernd. "We hardly spent any time in port. In Bahía for example, I dealt with the immigration procedures while Michael fixed a problem with the motor. As soon as we were ready, we left."

'No visits to the Botocudos then?"

'None at all!" smiles Bernd. "Anyway, as you know, it would be difficult to visit them nowadays."

Bernd disembarked in Río de Janeiro. He had run out of leave time between cruises. The uncle continued the voyage – nobody had got off yet – and a friend of Michael's who had flown from Port Stanley to help with the last leg of the journey was integrated into the group.

"I thought that they might give me problems in Argentina with the papers, so we decided to go directly to Stanley from Río without any stops," says Michael. The three of them put their foot on the accelerator and in a week – from Sunday 17th to Sunday 24th of September – they had travelled half the length of South America and arrived in the Islands' capital where a group of enthusiasts was waiting for them.

The next week an article in the *Penguin News* celebrated the epic journey of the Falkland Islands shepherd who had dared to cross the ocean in a boat only 15 metres long.

The *Penélope* was also waiting for them in Stanley. Now and for a further year Michael Clarke would have two red boats to occupy himself with. Michael asked his cousin Derek if he would help him to get both boats to West Point and they sailed on November 20th, Michael piloting the *Condor* and Derek at the wheel of the *Penélope*.

"I was her captain for a day and only that one time, but I loved the experience," Derek had told me in the plane from West Point with Doctor Barry Elsby. "My thing is flying, but I can appreciate the passion of these guys for the sea, the wind and the salty water in your face."

Among the photos of the ketch that Jeanette has on her computer's hard disc is one which shows the two boats, the *Condor* behind the *Penélope*, anchored in the bay at West Point. With the yellowing hills in the background they look like two brothers, both dressed by the same hand, waiting for the time to leave.

Almost a year passed before Bernd Buchner could travel to look for the boat he had bought. He had decided to take it to Stanley to repair and paint it there, where he could get spare parts and labour. He knew there was a lot of work to be done to put it in a condition to make the long voyage back to Germany.

The German remembers the last sail from West Point to Stanley as being like a journey back in time. Without modern instruments, without satellite or radar or echo sounder, he felt like Columbus.

It is because of this perhaps that in the course of an interview he surprised me by making a comparison with the Admiral's caravelles. "Did you know that the *Feuerland* is the same size as the *Pinta*? If you think of it like that the boat suddenly doesn't seem so small."

When they were arriving in Stanley harbour, they met the *Hanseatic*, another of those luxurious scientific cruise ships that take passengers to the southern lands. He knew that his friend Clemens Pütz was on board and talked to him by radio. Clemens was on the ship's bridge.

"In case you don't know where I am, Clemens," Bernd told him, "just look down!" The scientist laughed with pleasure and congratulated him on his purchase.

* * *

At the end of 2005 a select group of Bernd and Carola's friends received a strange joint email.

It began with a heading that fans of polar explorers are bound to recognise: "Men wanted for hazardous journey. Small wages, bitter cold, long months of complete darkness, constant danger, safe return doubtful. Honour and recognition in case of success. Signed Ernest Shackleton."

As all these friends knew, this is the ad that Shackleton used to recruit his *Endurance* expedition team in 1916, from which those chosen only just escaped with their lives after suffering great hardships.

This summons was to join the crew of the *Feuerland* which was due to leave after four months being repaired in the Islands. Bernd was hoping to leave by March 2006 at the latest. His objective was that after a voyage of two months, the sailors would arrive back in Germany in time for the football World Cup.

He still didn't know who would respond to his call but was already organising people as befits a captain. He proposed that the six volunteers picked should be divided into three pairs to share the six daily watches of four hours each. The first pair would take the watch from midnight to four in the morning and then the mid-day to four in the afternoon one.

At the end of the message, Carola and Bernd commented: "The *Feuerland* is an old lady, not a luxury yacht. Life on board will be simple, and sometimes cold and damp. We are going to get wet. We will use the motor for a large part of the voyage. It is going to be a unique adventure and because of this the inconveniences on board can be accepted."

After referring to his limited budget he informed them that whoever was appointed would have to pay the cost of their own air ticket to Mount Pleasant and finished with the sailors' traditional greeting, "Ahoy!"

They attracted five volunteers, including Carola's brother Jens Fiedler. To record the whole operation and to make a documentary about the ketch's return to Germany, a cameraman and his assistant were added to the crew.

You can buy this team's first product in the museum in Büsum. The DVD includes the complete version of *Silberkondor über Feuerland* and a silent documentary directed by Roland Topel which begins with the work done on the *Penélope* in Stanley and ends with the *Feuerland*'s arrival in Ovelgönne.

In the DVD's first scene Bernd and Michael can be seen working on the boat which is mounted on a platform at the side of the Canache in Stanley. In another scene we see how Michael brings planks of wood to repair a hole in the hull. Michael and Roland Botsch, one of Buchner's volunteers, nail the wood on. The historic process of painting the boat white once more, with a red line almost at the flotation mark and black down below, is well documented.

"That was the moment when you could begin to call her *Feuerland* again," says the new captain. In one picture Bernd is using a scapula to scrape off a layer of red, below which is a green layer and below that a black one. Recovering the past means taking off layer after layer and then painting coat after coat of the new, but original, colour by hand.

As Michael kept his rubber Zodiac to use with the *Condor*, Bernd bought another for the *Feuerland* and named it *Calypso* in homage to his girlfriend's idol, Jacques Cousteau.

When the boat was finally ready to leave, Bernd invited to a 'farewell party' some of the locals with whom he had come into contact during his voyages and the long restoration period.

The guests received a fax with a drawing of the boat sailing under four sails, as it did in Plüschow's time and as it appears on the stamp. "The crew of the *Penelope* wishes to thank you for the help you gave us during these last four weeks," the fax said. "Please join us at the Falkland Islands Company jetty this Monday April 3rd at 6 pm to toast together the ship's long history."

Among the guests were Ian Bury, the owner of the platform on which they mounted the ship to repair her, Jane Cameron and her friend Debbie Summers, the author of the first comprehensive tourist guide to the Islands and in charge of cruise ship operations for the agency, Sulivan Shipping.

"I met Bernd on his first voyage," says Summers. "When he told me about his plan to buy the *Penelope* I thought he was mad, but he was very tenacious and effective. I was very pleased to be invited to the farewell party, though that afternoon the wind was so strong that it nearly blew us into the water."

Bernd's intention was to set up a grill on the jetty and prepare a barbecue that the guests could eat on deck. "But that afternoon we had one of the worst storms ever recorded in Stanley," Jane tells me. "We all had to go down into the hold and the cabin part. Rain drops were coming in through the roof. Debbie and I looked at each other as if to say, "Are they really thinking about sailing to Germany in this?"

"I went back to thinking that Bernd was mad," laughs Debbie.

Bernd asked Jane to take a photo of him with the two guests who had the most stories to tell about the *Penélope* and the most intense relationship with her: Michael Clarke and Finlay Ferguson.

“The three of us were standing at the side of the base of the mast, like three generations of captains of this vessel,” Bernd says. Finlay, with a beer in his hand, looks pensive and perhaps a little sad in the photo. Michael looks stern and somewhat uncomfortable. The only one who seems joyful is Bernd.

Beer and sandwiches became the hasty menu for the party.

“Bernd opened up his laptop and began to show photos from the boat's past,” Finlay Ferguson remembers. “Among the first was one with Paul Christiansen and Joe Schmitt on New Island. Suddenly I jumped with surprise, ‘But that's my dad!’ It was a photo I had never seen before of a party on board the *Penelope* 75 years ago and my father was there. Now here we were looking at the photo in the same place and at another party: the last one for the *Penelope*.”

“I thanked them for coming on an afternoon of such bad weather,” Bernd tells me, “and I told them that I understood that

THE THREE LAST skippers at the *Penelope* farewell party: Ferguson, Clarke and Buchner in front of the Trafalgar painting. Photo courtesy of Bernd Buchner.

they might feel sad because the boat was going so far away. I tried to get them to understand that the boat was in good hands and that I would honour its history and its legacy, which, of course, included their own."

John Smith, the author of *Condemned at Stanley* and painter of the picture of the *Penélope* in the seventies, had expressed the same idea. He had said it to me almost in the same terms that one might talk about a child adopted by a couple who will give it what it needs. "Of course it hurts when a boat goes that was a presence in the Islands for 78 years, but surely the fate that awaited her here was to be abandoned down at the Canache with the *Weddell* and so many others. This is an opportunity for her to keep on living and, who knows, perhaps to return one day."

On April 6th John Fowler published in Mercopress (a news agency that deals particularly with the South Atlantic) a complete and thoughtful article about the departure of the boat, which he described as "part of the history of Tierra del Fuego, Patagonia and the Falklands."

"The Auxiliary Ketch *Penelope*, for over seventy years a familiar sight around the Falkland Islands", writes Fowler, "has spent the last weeks in Stanley being re-painted and repaired before embarking on the third stage of a remarkable life story, encompassing a German war hero and explorer, the pioneering days of Tierra del Fuego and much of the Falkland Islands recent history."

The former teacher reviews the essential points of Plüschow's life and voyages and dwells on the boat's time in the Islands.

"From her arrival in the Falklands in 1929, this sturdy little vessel, *Penelope*, has taken part in many different episodes of the Islands history. She has known many skippers and crewmen, some of whom have been in their own way every bit as colourful as Plüschow. She has shifted sheep and horses to and from islands, carried evacuees from the Argentine invasion and taken whole settlement populations on picnics in the summer. Her foc'sle was where the writer first saw a boiled penguin egg and where many a young islander has sat wide-eyed around the stove listening to the salty tales of old hands, while the roaring forties screeched through the rigging outside."

John Fowler quotes Bernd as expressing a wish that may also be one of his own; "that news of his journey and of *Feuerland/Penelope's* new lease of life will inspire people, who may have any stories, memorabilia or photographs connected to this gallant little ship to show them to the museum in Stanley so that its history in the Islands can be better documented."

The ship, however, did not leave the day after the party as its owner had planned.

Because of the weather the *Penélope* remained a further week in Stanley after its formal farewell. "We would be walking in the streets and people would say, 'Are you still here?'," Bernd recalls. Finally they set sail on Sunday the 9th.

When he learned their departure time, Finlay Ferguson drove alone in his Land Rover to the top of a hill from where he could look out over the entrance to the inner harbour. Standing on the bonnet, with his blue cap on his head, he was the last to bid farewell to the *Penélope* on her homeward voyage.

* * *

Bernd's original idea had been to pass by West Point so that Roddy Napier could say goodbye to the ketch, however the lost time caused him to head straight for the Patagonian coast. The DVD made by the team that travelled with him show enormous waves sweeping over the deck and Bernd at the wheel looking serious.

"We set off heading for Puerto Deseado, but we had waves of more than three metres from the West," Bernd explains to me. "If we sailed northwards she rolled like a pig. This is horrible for us, but doesn't affect the boat much; swaying from side to side is like rocking a cradle. But if we went directly for the coast, the waves were coming straight onto the bow, lifting up the keel then slamming it down with some force."

This movement was absolutely unbearable for the crew and Bernd wasn't sure either if the boat could stand it, so he decided to touch land further north at Comodoro Rivadavia, to keep the waves hitting the boat amidships.

In Comodoro Rivadavia, "no one was expecting us and the immigration authorities didn't know what to do with us," Bernd says.

However the world of the friends of Argentina's nautical tradition already had in hand the job of documenting this historic event. A sailing instructor friend of Carlos Biscioni arrived to take photos of the vessel in her first continental port.

Buchner's team was also doing its work. Roland Topel's documentary shows the crew members strolling peacefully through the streets of Comodoro, but away from the cameras Bernd was trying to speed up the immigration process. They took up their journey again at ten o'clock on the night of April 14th, heading for Puerto Madryn, where they arrived two days later after a somewhat calmer voyage than the crossing from the Islands.

"The journalists were waiting for us in Madryn," Bernd remembers. They published an interview with him in *El Chubut,* highlighting the ship's 'Plüschow period.' Even if just in passing, it was the return of a pioneer of Patagonian exploration. It was the first time that *Penélope* had crossed over to the continent since the thirties.

It was Monday April 17th, with the boat already moored at the Almirante Storni jetty in Puerto Madryn, when Horacio González Llanos sent a group email to those former members of the boat's crew with whom he had kept in contact, telling us that the *Penélope* was in Madryn, that its last port in Argentina would be Mar del Plata and that he was organising a trip in his car to see the 'schooner' there the following Saturday.

I opened my emails on the 21st and saw the first photos of the 'schooner'. They had been taken by another of Carlos Biscioni's nautical enthusiast friends in Puerto Madryn. Carlos generously distributed them among his cyber friends, among whom were the ex-crew members of the *Penélop*e during the war: González Llanos, Rivero and me.

That night I enlarged the photos on the computer in my house in Barcelona and studied them with surprise and mixed feelings. Many things about the boat were different from how I remembered them: the uniform white colour, the disappearance of the bow entrance, the German flag, the changed name on the stern – *Feuerland* instead of *Penélope* – and the port where the vessel was registered – Büsum instead of Stanley –. But the little square wheelhouse was the same, with the same door and the two steps and the little square windows. Also the same was the hull's convex shape.

The foreground of one of the photos showed the words painted on the stern. You could still make out the Falkland Islands names (*Penélope* and Stanley) because they had been carved in the wood. The new names were painted in black on white, but amplifying the image showed the traces of the old words: underneath the 'F' of *Feuerland* the capital was closed by the 'P' of *Penélope.* In the same manner the 'U' was crossed in the wood by the old incision of the 'N'.

This photo carried a comment from Biscioni: "You can't rub out its history."

In that same email of the 21st April Carlos Biscioni gave us the great news that at last the *Penélope* was heading for Buenos Aires. Carlos shared his joy at the news and at being able to add a lot of information, photos and stories for his book about the boat. He sent us messages almost every day. Now the important date was approaching: the 27th of April, the day of the ketch's arrival in the River Plate.

What was the *Penélope* doing in Argentina? Who were these men who were bringing her? Who was this German who had bought the boat?

Completely unaware of the questions which were flooding my head since the boat's reappearance, Bernd Buchner was becoming more and more convinced that his project of sailing to Germany was a pipe dream. The almost eighty-year old boat just wasn't in shape for such a voyage. In his email to his colleagues he had described an optimistic route with stops in Montevideo, Río de Janeiro, Recife, French Guyana, Barbados, three ports in the USA and finally Bremerhaven, close to where he had left with the *Condor*. In the end they didn't even make Montevideo.

In Topel's documentary the ketch can be seen entering Puerto Madryn in a glorious sunset and leaving Mar del Plata in the mysterious light of dawn. Meanwhile Bernd Buchner had his fingers crossed that they would get to Buenos Aires without any problems. He didn't know anyone there and didn't even have a clear idea of where he could moor the ketch. He had to get it back to Germany, but how?

"We had a lot of luck on the leg from Puerto Madryn to Mar del Plata because a strong stern wind grabbed us," says Bernd. "We were surfing over the waves at high speed, but if they had blown from any other quarter it could have been the boat's last voyage. I still had the idea of going from Mar del Plata to Uruguay and continuing the voyage from there, but after an inspection of the boat I realised that with luck we might just reach Buenos Aires."

Buchner was seeking help from all his contacts of whom the most effective turned out to be Hans-Georg Prager, the sailing empresario and Plüschow expert responsible for the modern German edition of *Silberkondor über Feuerland.* At Prager's urging a director of the Buenos Aires German Club promised help and on the 25th April 2006, the *Feuerland* began its last voyage in American waters.

On Thursday April 28th at six in the evening the *Feuerland* or the *Penélope* or both at the same time, entered the North Basin of the port of Buenos Aires. For the thousands of army ex-combatants it was as if the fox hole they had occupied in the Islands was sailing towards their city.

Biscioni and González Llanos didn't know how long the boat would be in Buenos Aires and hurried to organise the historic visit which would unite those who kept alive the memory of Plüschow and his deeds – Roberto Litvachkes and Erico Obernaus, the leader of the German community – and the representatives of the boat's story during the war in the Malvinas – González Llanos, Luna, Ni Coló, Rivero and the very active creator of the Apostadero Naval's web site, Daniel Gionco. Carlos Biscioni was the only one who knew the story of these two worlds.

That night from Thursday to Friday, Carlos could not sleep. He was overwhelmed by the possibility of seeing Plüschow's boat and the boat of the Malvinas sailors, and the excitement that the old crew members communicated to him, made him realise how inportant it was for Eduardo, Guillermo, Horacio and 'Uncle' Luna to see their 1982 'schooner' again.

There were only a few hours to go before they could all see the object of so many dreams and so many nightmares.

* * *

I could not sleep that night either. I was working in Barcelona and don't know what I would have given to be in Buenos Aires. I paced my office, went up to the university's cafeteria for my umpteenth coffee and tried to put my ideas in order. Finally I called my sister Carola and asked her if she would go, in part to 'represent' me, but also to take photos so that I could feel I was there. I knew as well that she had lived the war very intensely and that it would mean something to her to meet with the 'schooner.' Carola was immediately enthusiastic.

When she arrived at the YPF café on the corner of Córdoba and Madero, the guests and their families were seated at a large table and all talking at once. Horacio introduced her to everybody. Daniel Gionco suggested that before they went to see the boat he would take a photo of them all in the café to serve as a souvenir of the meeting. The five crew members: Luna, Rivero, González Llanos and Ni Coló grouped themselves in front of a cheerily coloured wall and Carola took my place as well.

Roberto Litvachkes gave her a copy of his book about Plüschow written in five languages, and Luna and Rivero's wives told her that their husbands had told them about all the dangers we had faced together and that they felt they already knew me.

"A lot of coffee and a lot of chat, but what I wanted was to see the boat," Ni Coló said.

They left the café. "All the ex-combatants were excited but also very friendly towards us," says Litvachkes. "The day was very fine; maybe there were a few clouds here and there, but I remember it as fine. We entered the naval area but González Llanos showed them his identity card and they directed us, crossing over to a big wall and from there to the boat."

"We walk along the jetty and there we see it," Guillermo goes on. "I recognised it almost immediately. We all wanted to go on board but the water was very low and the boat so far down that it was impossible. I thought about jumping for a moment but my legs started to tremble."

Luna's wife Susana was surprised by the size of the *Penélope*. "But it really is a nut shell!" she commented to Rivero's wife, Stella Maris, not knowing that Rivero had thought the same thing twenty four years ago. They all looked at the ketch with excitement but at the same time the strange feeling of finding themselves at the point of arriving at the place they had dreamed about so much, only to find that the gates were locked.

Looking at the object of their dreams from the jetty was the only thing permitted that day.

On deck below, Bernd Buchner was alarmed. In the middle of his tribulations and serious problems with the port authorities who were ordering him to leave when he had nowhere to go and as well as having no certainty at all about how to continue the voyage to Germany, suddenly twenty unknown people had appeared. Some of them were in tears and others were shouting joyfully.

"I remember poor Buchner and the look of panic on his face," says Litvachkes.

"I didn't know who these people were," Bernd remembers. "I was anxious, tired and preoccupied. I had a brief impulse to say to them, 'It's very nice of you to have come, but this really isn't a good moment for me.' They had no idea of the problems that were facing me, but logically were just very excited that the boat had got there somehow or other."

Finally Bernd was able to climb onto the jetty to talk to the visitors. He had had contact with Carlos Biscioni and Roberto Litvachkes although he had never met them. All the rest were unkown to him and all he knew about his boat's participation in the war had come from Finlay Ferguson's comments and Megan Middleton's scholarly work.

The experience was both therapeutic and frustrating at the same time for Guillermo Ni Coló. "We went with a vague possibility of being able to see it again and maybe get on board. I thought it was the last time that we would see it."

Guillermo was happy that he had been able to take with him María Inés, who had spend the hard days of the war waiting for his letters, with his three children. "I asked them to come with me and told María Inés that in this way she could also close a part of her history a little. I had told her about the *Penélope* many times and now she could see it and know what it was like." María Inés was very struck by the boats's size and poor condition. "I couldn't understand how they could sail through those waters in that."

Carlos Biscioni, who wasn't diving in his own memories concentrated more on the German owner whom he met that morning. "I had seen various shots of him in the photos that my friends had sent me. In all of them he looked serious, gloomy and worried." Biscioni compares him with the relaxed manner and jovial assurance that Gunther Plüschow exhibits in the 1929 documentary. "Even in the middle of storms he didn't lose his good spirits, but then he had a new boat with everything just so."

From his point of view he could see both the internal thought processes of the veterans and the German's anxieties. "With the problems they had with the boat, it was only his seriousness and skill that got them to Buenos Aires."

Bernd was also worried because the only person he was actually expecting, Prager's friend Thomas Leonhardt, had not arrived.

Finally the representative of the German Club did arrive and he, together with Obernaus, Litvachkes and Biscioni promised to help him move the boat to another anchorage where it could stay while Buchner completed the formalities – which in the end took nearly two months – to be able to load the ketch onto a cargo ship bound for Hamburg.

On the Sunday I spoke for a long time with Carola who was stunned to discover so many unknown stories and to have been able to chat with the men with whom I had spent those crucial war time days. My email inbox began to fill up with messages and photos from González Llanos, Ni Coló, Biscioni and Daniel Gionco, who was punctually informing the members of the Apostadero about the *Penélope's* historic visit. My screen filled with pictures of the "schooner" in Buenos Aires.

That weekend Bernd was able to moor his boat in the traditional Argentine Yacht Club, which is the same place where the *Feuerland* was moored during its outward journey in 1928. Immediately Biscioni and González Llanos began to negotiate a 'boarding' of the vessel with Buchner. Bernd offered them more by inviting them to go sailing on the River Plate with him on Wednesday the 17th.

I was following this news at a distance, feeding my anxiety with the emails that were coming and going. Biscioni took Buchner to visit the maritine museum at Tigre. González Llanos was preparing the meeting for the sailing trip. Gionco was telling the Plüschow story to the Naval Base members and invited those veterans who remembered the *Penélope's* nocturnal patrols in those far off days in Stanley harbour, to become reacquainted with the vessel at the Yacht Club.

One of those nights, June 4th, the telephone in my house in Barcelona rang at two in the morning. It was the excellent but distracted *Clarín* journalist Gabriel Giubellino, who had forgotten the time difference and wanted to interview me about the role of press agencies in present day journalism. His boss, Miguel Wiñazki, who also directs the Journalism Masters Degree Course that the newspaper runs at the University of San Andrés, had suggested he should call me as a supposed expert in those matters.

"It's two in the morning," I told him, dead with sleep. I was so sleepy that I didn't have the strength to be annoyed.

"Oh well" he answered, "So when can I call you? I have to finish this piece for tomorrow."

We talked again the following night, after which he had to return to something "totally unconnected" which he had to do in the afternoon.

The next afternoon Gabriel sent me an email which began, "I can't believe such a coincidence". The other article he had to write was about the *Feuerland*. "I went on board that battered little boat this afternoon, and last night I saw Plüschow's film with my five-year old son. It makes you cry. I don't know if you have seen it, but it's exciting; a really cracking documentary."

Gabriel wrote two articles for *Clarín* about the boat, combining in each Plüschow's voyages and the boat's participation in the war. The first, which was published on June 6th begins in a powerful and graphic manner: "Anchored in the Argentine Yacht Club, the *Feuerland* lowers the tone amongst so much fine shipping. Battered, without sails and with deteriorated paint work, only its rounded shapes give it a pleasant touch, as if it might be smiling. It's difficult to believe that this ketch has just arrived from the Malvinas where it survived for 77 years."

After reviewing Plüschow's story and mentioning the boat's participation in the war, Gabriel finishes with another accurate description: "With its tractor steering wheel and Land Rover horn the *Feuerland* resembles those reconditioned wrecks seen in the provinces, but it is a good boat and valued by its captain, a Class of 1971 Merchant Navy officer, who works taking tourists to Antarctica and the Malvinas. Bernd knows its history and was able to buy it. It is made of oak and is noble and lively."

The article concludes with an erudite plea to Neptune to allow the spirited sailor and his boat to return to these shores again some day.

* * *

May 17th dawned clear and autumnal. Carola, who had been invited on the sail, had been suffering a severe stomach ache since the day before and my father wanted to go in her – and my – place. He met up with Horacio, Eduardo, Guillermo, 'Uncle' Luna, Carlos Biscioni and Roberto Litvachkes at the entrance to the Yacht Club.

Carlos had brought along a photographer to record the historic occasion and amongst other guests, with all the glory of Argentine sailing achievement: Hernan Álvarez Forn, the legendary 'Black Ant' sailor in seven seas and Antarctic adventurer. In fact, 'Ant' was the only one that Bernd Buchner knew, because they had met in the White Continent the previous year. Also present, of course, was Gabriel Giubellino with his photographer.

They all got on the club's boat and were on board in a few minutes. "We were getting nearer and my palpitations were increasing," Guillermo told me. "I went on board and began to touch everything. When I went up into the wheelhouse, my legs buckled. With all the jumbled memories I began to cry unconsolably."

That's how Bernd Buchner found him. "I entered the wheelhouse and there was one of your comrades, clinging to the wheel and crying. I was beginning to understand what this boat meant to a group which I had no idea about."

Everybody could take turns at the wheel. Guillermo wanted to stay in the wheelhouse looking out through the porthole as he had done so many times in May 1982, but his excitement didn't let him repeat this, "Everything was just too much to cope with and all the rest showed us so much respect."

Eduardo Rivero told my dad about the night of the bombardment and took him to see the places in the boat where everything had happened. "First he showed me where the bathroom was, and afterwards the wheelhouse windows that were broken," my old man told me on the phone. "The worst was when he showed me the place on the deck, on the left, at the side of the fuel drum, where he found you stretched out and covered in glass."

The photos of that morning's sailing on the River Plate show glimmering flashes of an experience that was memorable for everybody: Eduardo at the wheel, Guillermo kissing the wood, Luna posing calmly with the river and the icebreaker *Almirante Irízar* in the background, Roberto Litvachkes with his Einsteinian hair blowing in the wind, Enrique Herrscher smiling at the camera with the wheelhouse and the red and white life buoy behind him, González Llanos at the side of the main mast.

To try to participate a little bit in the trip from a distance, I studied the photos, which also showed me in some of their details the individual 'eye' or interest of each photographer.

Gonzáles Llanos, for example, had shot portraits of his former subordinates, each one seated at the table in the forward cabin. He had also posed with them, arms around each other, on deck and had also focused on the Argentine flag which flew from the stern mast. Biscioni had taken photographs of everybody present, many of which would appear in the ATNA web page. He had also shown details which were interesting from a nautical point of view, like the ship's wheel and the painted name which still allowed the carved name underneath to be visible. My dad had made a photographic survey of each section to be able to send me a general idea of how the boat looked and Daniel Gionco, who had documented the first visit in the North Basin, took different angles of the whole boat.

The next day *Clarín* carried Giubellino's article under the title "*Emotional reunion on the historic ketch Feuerland.*"

The article begins like this: "When Malvinas veteran Guillermo Ni Coló sat down on the mast lying on the deck of the ketch *Feuerland*, his eyes clouded over and when he went up into its wheelhouse he doubled over and burst out crying. His tears contained sad memories of a war. With three other sailors who served on her in 1982, yesterday he returned to sail this historic vessel again before it returns to the German port where it was built in 1927."

After once again telling Plüschow's story and recommending Litvachkes' book, the journalist returns to the veterans' excursion. "It is a gift from God. I didn't believe that any ex-combatant would be able to return to tread the ground where he was in the war," said the former Able Seaman, Eduardo Rivero."

According to Giubellino, 'Uncle' Luna was studying the mast as if inspecting it. What was he looking for? "A fragment of the shrapnel that hit us when a shell exploded above us in Fox Bay. It must be there in the veneered part of the wood."

To end his piece the journalist chooses a dry and evocative sentence from Ni Coló: "We slept with our boots on," and the corollary, "Yesterday we left the fear behind. With the clear profile of the city seen from the river in front of us, there was joy; joy at being able to tell about it and joy at being able to live it."

* * *

Time and money were running out for Bernd Buchner and the negotiations over putting the boat in a cargo ship and transporting it to Germany were dragging on. "If I had had a lot of money I could have imposed conditions, but as it was, I was dependent on what they could offer me. These cargo ships carry containers, very rarely a vessel and when they do they are usually very expensive racing yachts. Where were they going to put the *Feuerland*? How were they going to raise and lower her?

The first time I called Bernd by phone, I dialled a German cell phone number and he answered me from Martín Garcia Island. While waiting for an answer from the Hamburg Sud shipping company he had gone to visit this wooded refuge which still shelters the ruins of the non-commisioned officers' school where Oscar Luna studied at the end of the fifties. In the middle of the River Plate the reception is excellent and Bernd's voice sounds as if we were in the same city.

I was wanting to organise my trip to Hamburg, but he was still not sure when the boat would be arriving.

Finally, on June 18th, the seventy-nine year old *Feuerland* lived a new experience when it was hoisted up and put inside a much bigger ship. By another of the many coincidences in this story, the cargo vessel in which Plüschow's boat travelled is called *Monte Cervantes,* the same as the German liner which sunk in the Beagle Channel in 1930. For a time both Litvachkes and Biscioni were of the opinion that the ketch had taken part in her rescue.

The Hamburg Sud people and Bernd's crew had placed some solid bands underneath the ketch's hull and the crane of the *Monte Cervantes* plucked her out of the water. It was then that Bernd Buchner learned that far from the thirty tons that he thought his boat would weigh, in fact she weighed nearer fifty. "It is a lot for a boat of that size, but has to do with the hardness, thickness and reinforcement of the hull," he explains.

Buchner's film cameraman who couldn't remain for the almost two months enforced stay in Buenos Aires, came back for this operation. Because of this the images in the DVD that the Büsum museum distributes pause after the arrival in the Argentine capital and start again when the boat is being lifted up and into *Monte Cervantes.* There you can see how they place the ketch on a wooden platform between containers. They had taken down the masts in May and put them along the deck.

Among so many contretemps the least was that Bernd could not return to Germany in time for the start of the World Cup which his compatriots were staging there. But he remembers perfectly that the day in which the cargo ship arrived with his boat in its hold the German team played its last game, the deserved struggle for third place against Portugal. Like many German fans he didn't think much of his team's chances, so the 3-1 victory, which gave them the 'consolation prize' was all the sweeter.

The following day was the final, when the French star Zinedine Zidane head butted the Italian defender Marco Materazzi and afterwards Italy won inelegantly on penalties. That morning Bernd arrived very early at the port of Hamburg's Terminal 8 for the lowering of his *Feuerland*. Once again two straps embraced her hull and the ship's crane lifted the little vessel into the air and lowered her gently into European water, bring to an end a voyage lasting 79 years.

On Wednesday July 12th, Bernd and three members of his crew boarded the white ketch and sailed down the wide River Elbe towards the Ovelgönne old boat museum. In an extravagance

THE *FEUERLAND* at the Ovelgönne jetty the day it 'came back home'.

of production Roland Topel and his assistant were filming them from another boat.

The recording shows the arrival into the small basin, the mooring manoeuvres and Bernd coming out of the wheelhouse door. It finishes with a shot taken from the communicating bridge between the dock and the jetty. From above, the ketch is seen relaxing at home at last.

At its side, approaching with tranquil elegance, Christian Bauer comes into view rowing his wooden skiff. He is wearing a straw hat and roomy bermudas. At his side, a bearded man with a blue cap and a light blue shirt is taking photographs of the ketch.

You cannot tell from the documentary that at this moment I am remembering a distant night and a war lost in the fog of history.

EPILOGUE

Memory is a schooner in the fog

"Are you still having nightmares?" Guillermo Ni Coló asks me.

The question leaves me disorientated. It is me who's interviewing him. He is telling me that the day after the Fox Bay bombardment he didn't want to go near the water source, because sailor Turano's body was there, covered by a blanket. He tells me that he hadn't wanted to see terrible things if it could be avoided. He hadn't wanted to be attacked by nightmares when he returned.

"And you?" he asks me suddenly. "Are you still having nightmares?"

We're sitting at our usual table in the Congress pizzeria, the usual place for the annual meetings of the members of the Apostadero Naval Malvinas, called by the indefatigable Daniel Gionco and also the place where I meet Ni Coló, who works just a block away in the National Congress.

A few days have gone by since the barbecue at his house in Saladillo and I am in full pursuit of my old comrades' stories when Guillermo brings me back to my own post-war experience and the submerged memory of my nightmares.

"For years I didn't dream about the Islands," I say, "but now that I am occupied day and night with the *Penélope* story I sometimes dream that I am sailing, but they aren't horrible nightmares like I had for two years after I returned. Those have gone now."

"We are tackling some succulent milanesas and in between one mouthful and the next I remember the most frequent nightmares I had in 1982 and 1983. In one they come to take me to go to war and drive me once again to the Edificio Libertad where there are a lot of other ex-combatants. They make us line up. Suddenly I look at myself and discover that where my chest and stomach should be there is a huge hole, as big as a football. I'm driven to despair by this hole, but nobody else seems alarmed. In some versions everybody has these holes and in others only me. I can put my hand in the hole and pass it right through my body.

I remember how I was surprised some years later when a monument in homage to the Malvinas veterans was mounted in front of the Army main headquarters in Buenos Aires. You can still see it today from the street in Paseo Colon. It's a statue of an unknown soldier in fighting attitude with his helmet and rifle, who has a whole through his body, just like in my dream. Every time I pass by there I remember the feeling I had when I returned from the war: the feeling of being empty, incomplete and furious.

The other recurrent dream I had was that I come back from the war minus my left leg. All my comrades, likewise, are missing an arm or a leg. An officer makes us go to the warehouse where the sweet potatoes cans were in Stanley to look for whatever extremity we are lacking. We all go in and the place is piled up to the roof with arms and legs. I have a mark like a large freckle on my left knee and I am seated on this mountain of limbs grabbing hold of legs and then discarding them because they do not have this mark. Suddenly I see the officer with whom I went on the hospital ship to get cigarettes leaving the warehouse, and notice that he's carrying my leg. The feeling of anguish when I wake up is even worse than that from the other nightmare.

"I tried to school myself not to have nightmares," Guillermo tells me, "and I don't have them. What I would like is to go back into the past and see how it really was. I'd like to close my eyes and have them show me a kind of film where I see myself and the things that happened to me filmed in the Malvinas: what I did, how I walked, how I ran; I'd like to see all of that."

But after a pause he acknowledges that, yes, he does sometimes have nightmares: "Very sad dreams," he says. "I dream that they come to my house to get me to go to the Malvinas and I say goodbye to my children knowing that I am not coming back and that farewell is terrible."

Guillermo tells me that he thinks more about the Islands since he left the armed forces. He became well-known as an ex-combatant in 2004 when he published his book, *64 Days Dead*. "From the time of the book being launched, they've been calling me from colleges in different cities and I go everywhere presenting the book and talking about that all the time. Before that it didn't happen to me."

I ask him what it is that people want to know; what questions he gets asked when he goes to introduce his book.

"When they announce that a veteran is going to present a book, a lot of young people go who were not even born, or were very young and they want to know what happened. They are curious to know about the Malvinas war. My book only talks about a small part, but people want to know more. They ask me about everything, absolutely everything. And then I understand that something is missing, that people still need to be told so many things..."

I already know some isolated facts about Guillermo. Now he explains to me that after the war he decided he would not renew his contract in 1983, the year in which it was due to end.

"I knew that it would be very difficult to be the ideal military person I dreamed of being. My ambition was to do something important; to the maximum, but for a member of the armed forces, the maximum is war. I didn't meet it at the end of my career but at the beginning. That experience of war came to me very early on," he tells me.

We finished lunch a little while back and are now drinking coffee. Guillermo keeps on stirring and stirring the sugar in his cup with his spoon and then tells me:

"I can't go to war. I can't kill anybody and you know it. I would go to fight to defend my life and my country, if everybody went and there was no other solution..."

I ask him what he thinks now that he, like me, has a son, who in a few years will be the age we were when we went to the Malvinas.

"I would not want a repetition of those things and to have to say goodbye to a son of mine going to war ... no, no ... I have inculcated in him the value of defending one's country, sure, but not like we did it, no."

We stay silent for a while.

He starts up again. "When I left the Navy I didn't know what to do. I bought the *Clarín* newspaper, turned to the classifieds, sat down next to the Obelisco and began to look at job offers. I said to myself, "Really I don't know how to do anything!"

Guillermo had thought that his studies to be a non-commissioned officer would be the equivalent of completing his secondary education, but on leaving he discovered that he would have to study for a further three years to graduate.

"So without a secondary certificate, without work experience and only with this qualification … it seemed very difficult. I joined the Congress as a junior and they sent me to the photocopier; to the photocopier and to the public counter. I thought, 'I don't want to spend my life photocopying'"

Living in Saladillo and travelling each day to the capital to work and later to study, Ni Coló completed his secondary education and later, after many days of work and many nights of study, qualified as a lawyer.

Guillermo looks at his watch. He has to return to the Congress. He is working as a legal advisor in the Radical Civic Union (UCR) building in the Labour Affairs Committee. I go with him. We enter the building's annexe, across Rivadavia Avenue from the impressive Legislative Palace. In the office of the UCR deputy for whom he is an advisor, the secretaries greet him cheerfully and with deference.

Before saying goodbye, Guillermo tells me about his experience as legal advisor on a committee closely related to his former life: the Defence Committee.

On the first day in 2002 we all met together and the legal advisors were introducing themselves. There were a lot of lawyers and a lot of military and when I introduced myself I said that I was an ex-combatant of the Malvinas war. I was the only one." When they formed the sub-committees they decided unanimously to give him the Malvinas one. Using his position, he says, he struggled to bring forward "a law which would guarantee that the state would concern itself with the veterans."

The situation of the majority of ex-combatants causes him pain. During the past 24 years, more soldiers have committed suicide than were killed in combat. Due, in the most part, to the lack of support of the Argentine authorities and society for its veterans, and a direct psychological consequence of the war, this tragedy is unacceptable in Ni Coló's view.

The last project that Guillermo presented has to do with one of his dreams, that of allowing ex-combatants the opportunity to return to the Islands.

"To go and see what it is all about … there are lots of people asking that the Argentine state should coordinate voyages of veterans to the Islands, accompanied by psychologists from the Ministry of Health and that – if this is finally done – a register should be made of those that want to go, recording where each one served, so that these voyages can be organised."

He looks directly at me as he tells me his final dream: "I would like to go with you guys, my comrades, to talk about all that we lived through."

* * *

I am drinking *mate* and eating biscuits in Eduardo Rivero's flat. Eduardo's mother, who is in Buenos Aires for medical treatment, made the biscuits. In previous interviews he has already told me clearly and with pleasure the details of his arrival in the Malvinas, his days on the *Buen Suceso,* the night of shrapnel on the *Penélope* and the slow voyage back to Stanley. Now he is going to tell me about his post war experience, the hardest of the seven of us.

From the very moment that he fell onto the schooner's motor in the middle of the bombardment, Eduardo knew that he had a serious back problem. "When I arrived in Mendoza I was on leave for thirty days then I returned to my previous ship, the destroyer *Domecq Garcia.* In November I changed to the patrol boat *Murature,* but the pain was getting worse and worse.

The able seaman often had to go to the Naval Hospital. The pains in his back made working difficult and hardly allowed him to sleep. "I remember being with a traumatologist, an old gentleman who asked me to walk and then said, 'You have flat feet' and I said, 'Excuse me, but if I had flat feet they wouldn't have taken me into the Navy and wouldn't have sent me to the Malvinas,' and I asked for another doctor." The new doctor diagnosed a herniated disc and the displacement of the fourth and fifth vertebrae.

The years passed and the pain did not go away. Everything became complicated after the day he fainted. "I was at home with Stella Maris and I was in the bathroom with a tap running. I bend down to regulate it and when I start to straighten up after bending down I faint with the pain in my spine. Stella takes me to the Naval Hospital."

"When did this happen?" I ask.

"June 18th, 1989," says Stella Maris, who, when it comes to for tragedies, has the memory of an elephant. She has just come in from work and enters into the conversation with some recollections which it seems have never emerged before.

"It was horrible," resumes Eduardo, screwing up his face as if it was happening again. "It was as if they had ripped out my heart and crushed it. I was fifteen days in the Naval Hospital unable to walk. They gave me injections for the spine pain and then they got me up and gave me a plaster corset from the chest down to the groin. I looked like a tortoise. Thirty-five days went by like that and then they cut it off, but it was still hurting. They cut it off every night and had it back on again during the day.

Rivero's physical pain began to complicate his mental problems. "I suffered a psychological slump and they took me in for thirty days because of psychosis problems related to the war." Meanwhile he continued to change postings from ship to ship, now as Leading Seaman, but the pains and the setbacks continued until he went into the operating theatre on the 19th December 1991.

"The operation on my spine was scheduled for eight in the morning and at quarter to eight my wife tells me she is pregnant with our son Cristian. They are lifting me onto the stretcher and she tells me, 'you've got to come out, you've got to come out'," says Eduardo.

He came out from the operation at four in the afternoon. At first he could not move, but little by little he was beginning to walk hanging onto the trolley on which they brought his food.

We spent the Christmas of '91 in the hospital," says Stella Maris.

Eduardo Rivero spent the next ten years pretty down. He never became an NCO and left the Navy in 1994 as Leading Seaman. Convalescence seemed eternal to him and it took him several years before he obtained his present work, as a civilian contracted security guard for the Circle of Officers of the Sea, right in the centre of the capital. There he works twelve hour shifts, "two days on, two days off." Today he has to start at 6pm and will finish tomorrow at first light.

"We've had a lot of problems in these years," he says, passing me the *mate*. "My wife had thyroid problems, then cancer. She was operated on twice and they burned it. On learning that his mother had cancer, my son developed epilepsy. I think it was all a consequence of Malvinas."

"You relate everything with..."

"Yes, everything comes from nerves, everything."

"So the war affected them and you and..."

"...all my family. In 2000 my son was eight and when he learned that his mother had cancer he went to look up 'cancer' on the Internet at school." Eduardo looks at Stella Maris asking for help with the date; "My love, when did they tell you, in 2000...?"

"On the 25th of September 2000," she says, every syllable loaded with bitterness.

Now I ask her directly, "And, when did Cristian develop epilepsy?"

"The 28th of September" Stella Maris tells me, "a Thursday."

* * *

Among many other consequences, this long search I am involved in is impregnating my skin with the smell of the sea and the languid lullaby of ships. I am walking the streets of Buenos Aires caught between the *Penélope's* sailors and those nostalgic for the *Feuerland,* when I come to a halt in front of the windows of the Buenos Aires Photo Club. There is an exhibition of students' photographs of nautical subjects. From outside I can see about forty photographs, mostly in black and white. I don't know what I am looking for, but I go in.

I walk the length of the long wall where the photos hang. Details stand out like the roughness of wood, the smooth or spiky surface of the sea, rivers with trees shading their banks. I go deeper into the world of these photographs and get the feeling that this is where I have been these last months. There are ships, boats, yachts, launches, mooring ropes, cables, tillers, men working in the innards and depths of old rusty vessels, old sailors, young fruit sellers, passengers, many cloudy skies, evenings, stranded or half-submerged hulks and there are also those aground on beaches with seagulls circling above their condemned hulls.

Water is always expressive. I go from one side of the wall to the other and I cannot stop looking at the photos. I realise that ships excite me and the perspective of these photographers that stopped them at a given moment to freeze them in time for ever.

Today I am going to visit 'Uncle' Luna.

Oscar Luna is working in charge of the boilers in the office building of the National Atomic Energy Committee (CNEA) in Libertador Avenue. Like Eduardo Rivero, Luna was working in a public building with links to the Navy, but he is contracted to a private company. In his case the company is in charge of the maintenance of the buildings elevators and boilers. He comes to look for me at the main door of the building, wearing a blue overall and still walking with a sailor's easy steady pace.

We go to the top floor cafeteria where I had been on other occasions to swap war memories with him. We sit at a table in front of a large window. The terrible white columns of the ESMA facade rise up the other side of the street.

Sometimes details stick in the memory more than other more relevant things. Luna tells me that when he got back from the Islands they were all summoned "to do the paperwork" at the same time. "I don't know why they did that. There were a lot of us and they kept us waiting the whole morning."

He doesn't remember any nightmares, but, okay, he does sleep with a green cap on. "There I slept with my boots on like the rest of you and my overalls, but I didn't wear a cap. I don't know why I put the hat on. Also I live near the El Palomar airport. When the planes went over, I used to get down on the floor of the room instinctively."

Luna came out of the Navy a year after the war ended like Guillermo Ni Coló. "I left as a Chief Petty Officer. I knew that I wasn't going to rise any higher," he tells me. "And from then I started to work. It's another life, as if you've been a prisoner and then they let you go. And when you leave, what are you going to do? What could I do, me? Security. So I went as a security guard with a company that transports money, to work on the lorries."

Later he began as a boiler man, using his mechanical knowledge. He worked for several years in the boilers of a paper mill. Luna says that he does not like talking about the war with his work colleagues.

"In the paper mill there were two guys who had been conscripts in the army. They told everyone that they had been at the front, that they had fought. They were violent. We were eating once and they were throwing plastic things and glasses at the walls." 'Uncle' Luna went on eating in silence.

"Twice I presented job applications and when they heard I had been in Malvinas they didn't give me the job." He assures me, "now I don't mention it so they can't discriminate against me."

Two days before leaving Buenos Aires I go back to the CNEA. Luna invited me for lunch, but not in the top floor cafeteria with the big window. He has a surprise for me, down with him in the boiler room. His four workmates, all wearing the company's blue overall, are seated at the table with soup plates and spoons ready to enjoy the food.

And not for nothing; 'Uncle' Luna has just cooked a tremendous stew with lentils, chorizo, potato and red peppers.

When I began this investigation I thought that there were some things that were never going to happen again, and yet here I was once more eating one of Luna's stews, while he tells stories about his voyages around the world with the frigate *Libertad* and the youngest of his companions opens his eyes wide at so much voyaging and so much world.

The *Clarín* article in which Gabriel Giubellino tells of the ex-combatants' sailing excursion hangs on the wall. The photo shows Ni Coló, Luna, Rivero, and González Llanos on the schooner's deck. "Former Malvinas soldiers sail in the boat they used in the war" the article says.

"I didn't know that Luna had been in the war," says one of his work mates, Nicolai Popov, an enormous Ukrainian of 52, with white hair and moustache like snow in sunlight.

While we eat, Popov tells us about the 43-degrees-below-freezing cold of Siberia, about his years in the Red Army and about his father who fought against the Germans in the Second World War and ended up in a German concentration camp. "The countryside here is very different," Popov says.

"People are gentler, more relaxed. I never saw Luna nervous, for example. Always calm." Between mouthfuls of exquisite stew, the Ukrainian keeps on telling us about a distant world.

"It's hard there" he explains. "Much war. Better here."

'Uncle' Luna listens to his companion, takes a swig of Coca-Cola, then grabs my arm and asked me if I enjoyed the meal. I tell him, "of course," so he lifts up my plate and goes slowly to the pot to serve me another portion of lentil stew.

* * *

Before returning to Spain, I still have one voyage to make: a re-encounter, a return; it will be the last one to complete the circle.

My father, who at 76 continues to hold seminars and to give classes in business administration and system theory for both national and foreign universities, has to go to teach in Trelew during my last weekend and asks me to go with him. We fly one Friday at dawn and by mid-morning are crossing the bare Patagonian hills towards our destination at Puerto Madryn.

The last time I had been in Puerto Madryn was when we arrived on the *Norland* on June 21st 1982. That day we had done the reverse journey from Madryn to Trelew in the Navy's bus.

Now, from the last hill, the city appears much bigger, with areas of identical houses in the suburbs. On the way we realise that this is the first journey that we have ever made together, just my dad and me. Usually the four of us travelled as a family and in more recent times we have made some flights to Argentina or to Spain with my two parents, my wife and my son. I don't feel that it is too late. I am going to show my dad the exact place where I returned from the war.

OSCAR LUNA (second from the left) and his mates of the maintenance team at the National Atomic Energy Comission (CNEA) in Buenos Aires. At his side, the Ukranian worker Nicolai Popov.

Our first stop is in the office of the Business Administration professor who invited my father to give some classes at the San Juan Bosco National University of Patagonia. Ricardo Barrera knows a lot about the history of this part of Patagonia. Seated at his desk in front of neat rows of books about business he tells me how the inhabitants of Puerto Madryn experienced the return of the troops from the Islands.

"The day of the arribal of the largest ship, the *Canberra*, we weren't ready to receive 4,000 hungry soldiers," Barrera says. "They put them in a wool shed that is now the municipal bingo hall. The neighbours like us got organised to give them something to eat, some taste of home, as best we could in those circumstances."

The Barrera family took four soldiers home. They had to promise to return them to their barracks at night. "We gave them a stewpot full of milk with Nesquik. It disappeared immediately. We just couldn't fill them. It was a terrible thing."

Ricardo was struck by the fact that they didn't talk about the war. "They only commented about things on the ship. Later we had to take them back. It upset me that they were put in that shed. It was very cold." The following morning Ricardo Barrera saw General Mario Benjamín Menéndez eating a copious breakfast in the Hotel Playa, where he was staying. "The hotel was three blocks away from where the boys were crushed into the wool shed" the professor adds.

His use of the word 'crushed' surprises and upsets me and brings with it a lot of memories.

Ricardo takes us to meet one of the people who know most about the ins and outs of life in Puerto Madryn. The veteran journalist Pepe Castro is a complete institution in the city. Flitting around his office in the LU17 radio station, Pepe also remembers the arrival of the ex-combatants. "People went out to receive them with affection. A lot of the boys came to the radio station to talk on the phone to their families," he says.

As for a lot of people in Patagonia, the war in the Islands was much closer and more worrying for Pepe Castro than for those who were following the news on television in Buenos Aires. "I went to the capital and people were eating along the Costanera and carrying on having fun as if nothing was happening." The journalist invites us for coffee and continues linking togethers memories, most of them related to the lack of foresight and the inefficiency of the military commanders during the war.

Pepe Castro recalls that on the 29th of May 1982, the Battalion Commander of the zone invited journalists for the celebration of Army Day. Early that morning, Castro had already received General Galtieri's speech from the official news agency Telam. At eleven, when they went to the military headquarters, an officer approached the journalist and explained that due to communication problems they still had not received the General's speech. 'Do you happen to have a copy?' Castro had to go back to his office and bring the agency's cable so that the Commander could read his chief's speech.

"And we were a unit in the battle zone, a nexus in the line between Buenos Aires and the Islands!" Castro exclaims.

After drinking the obligatory hot chocolate and toasting the success of the war, the journalists were taken into the military unit's Situation Room. "I swear I am not lying", he says, "but the map of the Islands that they had pinned to the wall with drawing pins was from the kids' magazine *Billiken*. How were they going to win a war like that?"

At mid-day Ricardo Barrera takes us to the old Aluar jetty. Now it is much longer and closed to the public. I explain to the NCOs of the Coast Guard why I am there and they let me enter. I walk down the cement jetty which extends into the sea. A cargo ship stretches along at the end. The rusty skeletons of the fishing boats that the Coast Guard has been decommissioning for decades lie on the beach.

I recognise it. This is the place. The bare hills file off into the distance behind the Aluar sheds. A long platform brings the aluminium to the ships. Now and again the fins of playful dolphins break the surface of the sea. The winter sun brings a timid gleam to the foam and the wind strokes my cheek. I am in the place where I arrived almost a quarter of a century ago.

My dad is waiting for me by the car. I just want to hug him and to tell him that in some way that I can't explain, my return from the Islands is over and that I feel at this moment that I am bringing to a close the journey that my mum, my sister, he and I began that night when we said goodbye at the front door, the night in which my father drove me to the naval headquarters, the night when I climbed the Edificio Libertad's interminable stairs to begin our long journey to the war.

* * *

I am once more in the place where I began the quest, the voyage, the return. It is Friday December 6th, 2006, the last day of my journey. I am standing in the entrance of Hamburg's central train station, eager to meet the old ketch *Penélope* and her owners again. I look at my watch; it is ten o'clock as we agreed. Surely Germans won't arrive late.

I see them at last; they are at the other entrance, waving their arms. Bernd Buchner looks younger, with a thick turtle neck sweater, short hair and cropped beard. Carola is smiling at his side. They are still on honeymoon after two months when Bernd was away working on a cruise ship on the Great Lakes, between Canada and the United States.

We get in the car and set off for Büsum. The *Feuerland* is waiting there under the red and white lighthouse, which is the best known image of the port. On the way Bernd tells me about his boat's last voyage.

On August 11th, almost a month after its arrival in Hamburg, Bernd Buchner and his crew began the final leg of the long road back to where the boat was launched in 1927. However this part of the journey still had more problems in store; at the last moment an important piece of the starter motor broke and the boat had to be towed.

On August 12th, which was the date arranged from the start, a crowd was waiting on the Büsum jetty for the prodigal's return. Among those present were the military attachés from the Argentine and Chilean embassies and the majority of the city's old repositories of memories, like Kurt Winter, who was a child when the boat left. There were also Plüschow experts and admirers like Hans-Georg Prager and Gerhard Ehlers.

Onto the *Feuerland,* which was bedecked with colourful flags like on its first voyage, stepped Guntolf Plüschow, the explorer's son – who had come from Canada for the occasion – and Olaf Christiansen, the son of the First Officer. That was a night of dinners and parties in Büsum.

We leave the *autobahn* and drive between Büsum's charming chalets. With Bernd and Carola I enter the workshop of Reimer Landberg, with whom they are negotiating the difficult and costly work which will take the *Penélope* back in time. They discuss dates, pointing with their fingers at the calendar on the wall.

Afterwards we cross the street. Bernd shows me the dry dock facing the sea where the schooner will be installed for repair. Now another somewhat bigger boat is in there with its ribs exposed to the air. A welder with mask and blow torch is working there with great concentration.

Bernd Buchner has a dilemma. He has to find a way to get the money that he needs to reconstruct the boat without losing control of the project.

It is much more expensive working with traditional tools and reproducing curves and tackle which no longer exist than modernising a boat to "leave it like new".

Each conversation with Landberg leaves him more convinced of the cost of "leaving it like old" but he doesn't give up. The state authorities connected with maritime heritage are the ones that could help most, but Bernd knows that in exchange they would wish the schooner to become public property. He wants to continue being the owner of his precious *Feuerland.*

ME AT THE PUERTO MADRYN jetty, where the old pier stood: the place where the *Vorland* left me on my return from war. Photo by Enrique Herrscher.

ME SITTING at the wheel of the *Feuerland* seconds before coming ashore for the last time, in Büsum on December 2006 (photo by Bernd Buchner).

We walk along the pavement towards the boat. Through the leaden drizzle I now see my 'schooner' weighed down by the weight of so many stories. The masts are covered in black plastic and the wheel house is secured with a padlock. A notice in German advises that the historic vessel can not be visited until its restoration is complete.

We go down to the hold, to the bunks and the gas stove. On the wall is a picture which I didn't notice when I visited the boat five months back. It's a reproduction of a painting of the battle of Trafalgar. Bernd shows me how the boat has changed with time and what he wants to do to return it to its original state. He goes from one corner to another drawing up plans: here he wants to take out the Chilean planks and return the robust German oak. Down below he dreams of reinstalling Plüschow's cabin as it appears in the original plans. Up above he is thinking of fitting a traditional wooden wheel. The bridge is going to be solid and shiny as in the old days.

Now we go. Bernd turns off all the lights. As my vision fades so do the smells become more prominent: the reek of concentrated damp, of petrol, of wet wood, of rope: a mixture of marine odors that I recognise from years ago. These are the smells of back then.

I sit at the wheel for the last time. Carola takes photos of me. We join Bernd in the wheelhouse doorway. With Bernd following, Carola jumps from the lintel onto the plastic surface of the mast that lies on the deck; from there to the boat's gunwale and finally to land.

There's only me left. I jump from the boat, but slip and fall on the wet stones of the quay.

Now I am finally on the other side.

SOURCES AND
Bibliography

This is a non-fiction work, for which the author has done everything possible to check the authenticity and accuracy of the information he presents. Sources, except when otherwise indicated in the text, come from interviews and conversation with the author. For the most part, the interviews were recorded, to ensure that what appears between inverted comas reflects faithfully the ideas and views of the people to whom these words are attributed.

All the Argentines who speak in the first and third parts express themselves in Spanish. In the case of the Falkland Islanders the language used was English. I have tried to be as faithful as possible to the content and intention of what was said in my translations of the dialogues. In the third part, the interviews with Bernd Buchner, Carola Fiedler and Gerhard Ehlers were conducted in English. Ingrid Gaa and Martin Virtel spoke to me in Spanish.

Regarding the manner of referring to Islands' topography, the names Malvinas and Falkland Islands are used according in the context of the people speaking or being spoken about. Where this context is neutral, the archipielago is referred to as 'the Islands.'

Names of places within the islands are given for the most part in their local version. As to the capital, Puerto Argentino is only used to signify those weeks when it was under the control of the Argentine forces, and when the story is being told from the point of view of members of those forces at that time.

The sources of all articles quoted in the book are given in the text. The articles originally written in Spanish were translated by John Fowler.

Before giving the complete bibliography, I would like to list three web pages which were of particular use and to whose authors I am particularly grateful.

The Apostadero Naval Malvinas page (www.aposmalvinas.com.ar), creating and maintained with precission and enthusiasm by the engineer Daniel Gionco, former conscript who served as a member of the Apostadero; the official page of the Association of the Friends of the Argentine Nautical Tradition (www.atna.com.ar), whose principal author is its president, the great organizer and lover of all things nautical Carlos Biscioni; and the Expedition Feuerland page (www.expeditionsschiff-feuerland.de) which now has very interesting material, albeit only in German. It contains valuable information about the ship and its return to German, which comes principally from Bernd Buchner and Carola Fiedler.

Which respect to the books employed, I divide them in two groups: those I mention explicitly in the text, and those which were of great use, although they don't appear to be mentioned. They are obviously only a small part of the more than 200 books I consulted about the war, about Malvinas/Falklands history, about Gunther Plüschow and his times, and the historical context of each part in order to write this book.

Books used in the First Part

64 días muerto, by Guillermo Ni Coló (Editorial Dunken, Buenos Aires, 2004). Ni Coló's testimony, his valuable perspective, his excellent memory and capacity for description were all of great use to me as, I am sure, to all those interested in the Falklands War from the Argentine point of view.

Poker de ases en Malvinas (Instituto de Publicaciones Navales, Buenos Aires, 2004) and *Civiles por Malvinas* (Editorial Cruz del Sur, Buenos Aires, 1995), by Jorge Muñoz. Precise accounts of the events of the Falklands War, primarily about the four "auxiliary" vessels : *Forrest, Monsunen, Yehuín* and *Penélope,* but also about the different groups of civilians who were involved, including amongst others, merchant sailors, doctors, journalists and Catholic priests.

Sea Harrier Over the Falklands, by Commander 'Sharkey' Ward (Cassell, London, 2000). I lifted the brief account of the attack on Fox Bay from this book, but the whole work is an impressive, clear and detached view by a military professional.

Falkland Islanders at War, by Graham Bound (Leo Cooper, London, 2002). This exhaustive investigation by the Falkland Islands journalist, who founded the weekly newspaper Penguin News, was of the greatest use to me in understanding the experience of the Islanders themselves during the war. I quote fragments of this book in the first two parts.

Malvinas: Diario del regreso (Iluminados por el fuego), by Edgardo Esteban with the collaboration of Gustavo Romero Borri (Editorial Sudamericana, Buenos Aires, 1999). The war memories of Esteban, together in later editions with an account of his visit to the Islands in 1999, contains facts, reflections and interesting narrative strategies which led to the creation of the film *Iluminados por el Fuego,* which has won many awards.

Although not mentioned in the book, these works were particularly useful to me

Falklands by Rodolfo H. Terragno (Ediciones de la Flor, Buenos Aires, 2002).

Historia y futuro de las Malvinas, by Rodolfo H. Terragno (Librería Histórica, Buenos Aires, 2006).

Las guerras por Malvinas, by Federico G. Lorenz (Edhasa, Buenos Aires, 2006).

¿Por qué Malvinas?, by Rosana Guber (Fondo de Cultura Económicas, Buenos Aires, 2001).

De chicos a veteranos, by Rosana Guber (Editorial Antropofagia, Buenos Aires, 2004).

Tierra de nadie. Los mitos sobre Malvinas, by Ignacio Montes de Oca (Editorial Sudamericana, Buenos Aires, 2006).

Los chicos de la guerra, by Daniel Kon (Editorial Galerna, Buenos Aires, 1982).

Partes de guerra, by Graciela Speranza and Fernando Cittadini (Numa Ediciones, Buenos Aires, 1997).

Malvinas, la guerra inconclusa, by Carlos Busser (Ediciones Fernández Reguera, Buenos Aires, 1987).

Malvinas a sangre y fuego, by Nicolás Kasanzew (A supplement of the magazine Siete Días, Buenos Aires, 1982).

Pequeñas guerras británicas en América Latina, by Andrew Graham-Yooll (Editorial de Belgrano, Buenos Aires, 1998) or *Small Wars You May Have Missed* (Junction Books, London, 1983).

Task Force (1985) and *The Fight for the 'Malvinas'* (1989), by Martin Middlebrook (Both published by Penguin, London).

La guerra austral, by Manfred Schönfeld (Desafíos Editores, Buenos Aires, 1982).

Las Malvinas: de la guerra 'sucia' a la guerra 'limpia', by León Rozichner (Centro Editor de América Latina, Buenos Aires, 1985).

Books used in the Second Part

Falkland Islanders at War, by Graham Bound (Leo Cooper, London, 2002).

From the Falklands to Patagonia, by Michael Mainwaring (Allison & Busby, London, 1983).

The History of the Falkland Islands, by Mary Cawkell (Anthony Nelson, Shropshire, 2001).

Falkland People, by Angela Wigglesworth (Peter Owen, London, 1992).

A Visitor's Guide to the Falkland Islands, by Debbie Summers (Falkland Conservation, London, 2001).

74 Days (Quetzal, Hampshire, 1984), *Those Were The Days* (Falkland Islands Trust, Bluntisham, 1989) and *Condemned at Stanley* (Picton Publishing, Chippenham, 1985), by John Smith.

The Penelope, by Megan Middleton: a resumée in the Falkland Islands Journal 2001, of the work which won her the 2000 Alastair Cameron Prize.

These texts, amongst others, were also useful to me in giving context, although their use is not necessarily obvious in the book.

El último confín de la Tierra, or *The Uttermost Part of the Earth,* by E. Lucas Bridges (Editorial Sudamericana, Buenos Aires, 2000), (Dover Publications, 1988).

Toda la historia de las Malvinas, by E. M. S. Danero (Tor, Buenos Aires, 1964).

Corrals and Gauchos, by Joan Spruce (Peregrine Publishing, Bangor, 1992).

The Falkland Islands I Knew, by Howell Evans (Anthony Nelson, Shropshire, 2001).

Forward into Hell, by Vincent Bramley (John Blake Publ., 2006).

The Gurkhas, by John Parker (Headline, London, 1999).

Going to the Wars, by Max Hastings (Pan Books, London, 2000).

Task Force, by Martin Middlebrook (Penguin, London, 1985).

The fight for the 'Malvinas', by Martin Middlebrook (Penguin, London, 1989).

Nuestras Malvinas, by Juan Carlos Moreno (Comisión Nacional de Cultura, Buenos Aires, 1938).

Books used in the Third Part

Gunther Plüschow, a Life Full of Dreams, Adventures and Challenges for an Impossible Love: the Patagonia, by Roberto Litvachkes (Serie del Sur, Buenos Aires, 2006). Litvachkes takes us through Plüschow's life in four languages (Spanish, English, German and Portuguese) and gives us the necessary context to enable us to enjoy the historic film *Silberkondor über Feuerland,* which accompanies his book.

Sobre la Tierra del Fuego, by Gunther Plüschow, translated by Armand Guerra (Simurg, Buenos Aires, 2005); *Silberkondor über Feuerland* (Ullsteinverlag, Berlin, 1929).

Las aventuras del aviador de Tsingtau, by Gunther Plüschow, translated into Spanish by Ilona Selmeczi, with a prologue Roberto Litvachkes (Serie del Sur, 2006); *Die Abenteuer des Fliegers von Tsingtau* (Ullsteinverlag, Berlin, 1916); *My escape from Donington Hall: preceded by an account of the siege of Kiao-Chow in 1915* (Nabu Press, 2010).

Segelfahrt ins Wunderland, by Gunther Plüschow (Deutscher Verlag, Berlín, 1926) – only in German.

Gunther Plüschow, by Isot Plüschow (Deutscher Verlag, Berlín, 1935) – only in German.

These other books gave me a fuller picture of the characters, their world and time, and of the experience of the sea and sailing:

De Tsing-Tao a las Falklands. El último crucero del almirante Von Spee, by Hans Pochhammer (Joaquín Gil, Barcelona, 1931).

El tesoro del Monte Cervantes, by Enrique S. Inda (Marymar, Buenos Aires, 1999).

Historical Magallanes, by Osvaldo Wegmann (Impresos Vanig, Punta Arenas, sin fecha).

Un siglo de noticias, by Juan M. Miranda (Editorial Atelí, Punta Arenas, 2000).

Pequeña historia fueguina, by Armando Braun Menéndez (Editorial Francisco de Aguirre, Santiago, 1971).

Pequeña historia magallánica, by Armando Braun Menéndez (Editorial Francisco de Aguirre, Santiago, 1969).

Crónica de las tierras del sur del Canal Beagle, by Mateo Martinic Beros (Editorial Francisco de Aguirre, Buenos Aires, 1973).

Patagonia azul y blanca, by Clemente Dumrauf (Ediciones Continente, Buenos Aires, 2004).

El náufrago de las estrellas, by Eduardo Belgrano Rawson (Editorial Sudamericana, Buenos Aires).

Mar de fondo, by José Luis Sanpedro (Debolsillo, Barcelona, 2004).

A Book of Sea Journeys, compilation by Ludovic Kennedy (Collins, London, 1981).

Pini, my love, this book is for you and would not have existed without you.

José Pablo, my precious and rebellious adolescent, this began when you were four and started asking me about my war. I hope I was able to answer your incisive youthful questions somehow. Don't ever give up asking questions and questioning everything.

To my mother, Sonia, the person who most felt my absence during the war and whom I love more than I can express: It's over, Mum! We're on the other side now!

This book and my search has a lot to do with my father, Enrique. You're on every page, papá. Without your example, your teaching and your love I wouldn't have been able to do this or many other things.

I owe a gigantic 'thank you' to my sister Carola, and also to my brother in law Juanjo, my nephew Ivan, my niece Lara, my cousins Paula and Daniela and my aunt Carmen. I miss you all very much. Thanks a lot to my Costa Rican family in law, especially doña Marta and don Félix.

Throughout the investigation for this book I received many moving examples of openness, appreciation and honesty from the protagonists of the various parts of this story. I hope I have been able to do justice to their confidence and to the time that they gave up for me.

In first place I want to thank from my heart my ship mates from the *Penélope*: Eduardo Rivero, Guillermo Ni Coló, Oscar Luna, Horacio González Llanos, Daniel Peralta and Carlos Contreras. Meeting them again was one of the richest experiences of this voyage.

In Buenos Aires, Roberto Litvachkes and Carlos Biscioni helped me and honoured me with their knowledge and their work. I thank Carlos and Hernán Biasotti and Hernán Masoni for an unforgettable day of nautical immersion.

I'm very thankful to Daniel Gionco, the soul of the Apostadero, who from a distance keeps together so many ex-combatants. Osvaldo Niella, Jorge Muñoz, Francisco Pacheco and Nick Tozer all gave me valuable information.

In the Falklands, I want to thank first of all captain Finlay Ferguson, a man and a sailor for all seasons. I hope I've been able to reflect faithfully the excitement I felt for meeting him again. Michael and Jeannette Clarke honoured me with their unforgettable hospitality and their invaluable help. I'm all also grateful to Roddy and Lilian Napier of West Point and to the two stupendous Figas pilots Tom Chater and Derek Clarke. I learned a lot during my chat with Dr. Barry Elsby.

Elsewhere I have recorded my debt and deep gratitude to Jane Cameron, a wonderful human being who was essential to my search for historical information. I also want to express my gratitude to Fraser and Helen Wallace, the owners of 10 John Street, to Debbie Summers, George Betts, John Smith, to Richard, Jenny and Adam Cockwell, to Megan Middleton, Tony Smith and Celia Stewart.

In the 'German part', Bernd Buchner and Carola Fiedler were generous and patient with my questions and requests. Martin Virtel and his family took me up and helped me understand Hamburg. Martin was for me a nexus of great value between Germany and Argentina.

Gerhard Ehlers and Ingrid Gaa were very hospitable. They opened their archives and shared their own paths of discovery of Plüschow for me, and they helped me to understand and appreciate the country from which my father fled in 1936.

My friend and colleague Sebastian Schoepp translated the Expedition Feuerland's web page for me, and my aunt, the journalist and translator Marion Kaufmann, carried out the heavy task of summarising and translating passages from Plüschow's *Segelfahrt ins Wunderland* for me. I feel honoured to be her colleague and friend.

I'm grateful for the support and advice of my colleagues at the Master in Journalism bcny at il3-University of Barcelona, especially my friend Juan Pedro Chuet-Missé, and my students for the last 12 years. Their questions, dreams, doubts and their own projects were an inspiration and a permanent journalistic challenge to me. Thanks also to my ex student and friend Eugenio

Fernández, who researched for me the life and works of Armand Guerra in Barcelona and Paris.

My best friend, Jerry Brignone, has been a soulmate, a debate 'sparring' partner and an inspiration since before I was sent to the war, and especially in my years trying to get my voice and my anger out as a writer.

At my Spanish language publisher, Tusquets, I want to thank Mariano Roca, Paula Lucantis and all the team in Buenos Aires, and the late Antonio López de Lamadrid, Beatriz de Moura and all the team in Barcelona. I am particularly grateful to my editor, great writer and old friend Sergio Olguín. His drive, his clarity, his sharp scisors and his eye to detect the excesses of sentimentality which sometimes I'm prone to saved me from ridicule and helped me more than he can imagine during the months of writing the text in Spanish.

This English language project was born from the vision and tenacity of the brave Fueguino editor Federico Gargiulo. His phone call from Ushuaia started this version moving, and our meetings in Buenos Aires put me to work with the same passion that inhabited me in 2006 and 2007. His idea of placing photos along the way, for example, makes it, I think, a different book, with a new layer of meaning.

Finally, this reincarnation of *Los viajes del Penélope* is the direct result of an event for which I cannot thank life enough: the appearance – or reappearance – of John Fowler. First through long and emotive e-mails, then through reading his translation and finally working with him for almost a fortnight in Barcelona, I have come to understand, enjoy, discover and appreciate many things about the Falklands, about him and about the value of friendship. This is now your book as much as mine, John.

Este edición de 1000 ejemplares se terminó de imprimir en noviembre de 2010
en Grella Artes Gráficas, Cochabamba 4001 - Capital Federal.